GLOBAL TRENDS IN DIGITAL TECHNOLOGIES

DIGITAL POLICIES AND REGULATIONS

DR. MANMOHAN CHATURVEDI

This book is dedicated to my parents and series of teachers who shaped
my personality and bestowed abilities to express myself coherently

Contents

Preface

My technology journey goes back to 1972, when I graduated as engineer with specialisation in electronics. About 35 years of managing technology for the Indian Air Force and exposure to Opto-Electronics and Optical Communication during MTech. at IIT Delhi in 1983 , had left me in awe at the pace at which technology, particularly in Information and Communication domain, was evolving.

Post retirement, my association with research (a PhD from IIT Delhi in Information Security in 2013) and teaching assignments, technical consultancy in IIT Delhi post 2013, have further reinforced my belief that only constant in Digital Technology is a fast paced change .

Digital systems seem to envelope us from all sides. We find ourselves in the midst of a digital revolution that is reshaping every aspect of our world. From the way we communicate and work to how we learn, shop, and even think, digital technologies have become an integral part of our daily lives. This transformation is not confined to any single country or region; it is a global phenomenon that is redefining the very fabric of our societies and economies.

Above impressions have prompted me to attempt compilation of this book on '**Global trends in Digital Technologies - Digital Policies and Regulations**' .

This book covers diverse digital technologies, related issue of future of work in a digital world, resultant digital policies and regulations. The concluding chapter has pragmatic suggestions for a manager to navigate successfully the evolving digital landscape.

In compiling this book, I have extensively used internet resources and AI tools to help me organize the text on various facets of emerging Digital Technologies. Thus an attempt is made to ensure that the Common Body of Knowledge (CBK) on emerging global trends in Digital Technologies is mostly covered. My experience and insights helped me to validate and improve the contents further.

The sections on Glossary and Bibliography, at the end of book, may help the reader to have an idea of related issues and if possible, to dive deeper using the chapter wise references.

I hope this book may serve as a resource for all professionals whether **managers or practitioners of Technology** to refresh their understanding about this important Digital world that has engulfed all aspects of our life and is sure to shape the future of humanity in more than one way.

Dr. Manmohan Chaturvedi

Acknowledgements

I would like to acknowledge constant encouragement and guidance of my PhD supervisor Prof. M.P. Gupta, MODI FOUNDATION CHAIR PROFESSOR, of Department of Management Studies at Indian Institute of Technology Delhi.

His inspiration has spurred me on to contibute my bit to the academic pursuits

About The Author

Air Commodore Manmohan Chaturvedi is a retired officer from Indian Air Force. He graduated from Delhi College of Engineering (1972), completed post-graduation (1985) and PhD (2013), both from IIT Delhi. He has about 35 years of experience in managing technology and human resource for Indian Air Force. An alumnus of National Defense College, New Delhi, he has held various appointments dealing with policies and strategic issues besides commanding a Base Repair Depot.

Dr Chaturvedi was a project consultant at IIT Delhi till 31 March 22, on a Government of India project for designing serious games for teaching Cybersecurity concepts. Prior to this, he was a consultant at CISO cybersecurity Pvt Ltd Gurgaon.

He was a Professor and Associate Dean in School of Engineering and Technology, Ansal (now Sushant) University,till 30 May 14.

He has published journal papers and presented many conference papers at prestigious institutions nationally and internationally. He was invited, as a part of a project funded by European Commission on 'Building International Cooperation in Trustworthy ICT', as a member of International Advisory group in seminars on Cyber Security at Brussels, Lisbon, Malaga and Vilnius.

He has worked as a consultant on a government of India project at IIT Delhi, to formalize the criteria for government website evaluation and ranking.

As a Cyber Security expert, he participated in the International Committee of the Red Cross (ICRC) expert meeting on "THE POTENTIAL HUMAN COST OF CYBER OPERATIONS" in Nov 2018 at Geneva.

He is a guest faculty at IIT Delhi, and has taught 'International Telecommunication Management' course to MBA/MTech students for nine successive years (from 2015 to 2024). Earlier he taught two courses on 'Operations analyses' to Indian Navy officers at IIT Delhi in 2011 and 2015.

He is a Fellow of Institute of Electronics & Telecommunication Engineers and Senior Member of IEEE. His publications can be viewed at link below:

https://scholar.google.com/citations?user=AqzkRw8AAAAJ&hl=en

CHAPTER ONE

Introduction to Global Trends in Digital Technologies

The Global Digital Landscape

In the early decades of the 21st century, we find ourselves in the midst of a digital revolution that is reshaping every aspect of our world.

The purpose of this book is to explore the current trends in global digital technologies, their impacts, and the future they are shaping. As we embark on this journey, it is crucial to understand that the digital landscape is not a monolith. It is a complex, multifaceted ecosystem that varies significantly across different parts of the world, influenced by factors such as economic development, cultural norms, regulatory environments, and technological infrastructure.

Defining Digital Technologies in a Global Context

Before delving into trends, it's essential to establish what we mean by "digital technologies" in a global context. At its core, digital technology refers to electronic tools, systems, devices, and resources that generate, store, or process data. This includes:

1. Hardware: The physical components of digital systems, ranging from smartphones and computers to sensors and wearable devices.

2. Software: The programs and applications that run on hardware, including operating systems, mobile apps, and enterprise software.

3. Networks: The infrastructure that allows digital devices to communicate, including the internet, cellular networks, and satellite systems.

4. Data: The information generated, collected, and processed by digital systems, including big data and analytics.

5. Emerging Technologies: Cutting-edge innovations such as artificial intelligence, blockchain, virtual and augmented reality, and quantum computing.

In a global context, the definition of digital technologies must also consider:

- Varying levels of technological adoption and infrastructure across different countries and regions
- The role of digital technologies in economic development and social change
- Cultural differences in the use and perception of digital technologies
- The impact of digital technologies on global challenges such as climate change, healthcare, and education

The Current State of Global Digital Technologies

As of 2024, the global digital landscape is characterized by rapid innovation, increasing connectivity, and growing concerns about privacy, security, and the societal impacts of technology.

Connectivity and Access

The internet, the backbone of the digital world, has seen tremendous growth in global access. According to the International Telecommunication Union (ITU), as of 2023, approximately 66% of the world's population uses the internet. However, this figure masks significant regional disparities. While internet penetration in North America and Europe exceeds 90%, in Africa it stands at around 40%.

Mobile technology has been a key driver of digital access, particularly in developing countries. The GSMA reports that by 2025, 72% of the world's population will have a mobile internet subscription. 5G networks are being rapidly deployed in developed countries, promising faster speeds and lower latency, while many developing nations are still working on expanding 4G coverage.

Artificial Intelligence and Machine Learning

Artificial Intelligence (AI) and Machine Learning (ML) have moved from the realm of science fiction to become practical tools used across industries. From personalized recommendations in e-commerce to predictive maintenance in manufacturing, AI is transforming business processes and decision-making.

The global AI market is expected to grow at a CAGR of 37.3% from 2023 to 2030, according to Grand View Research. However, concerns about bias in AI algorithms, the ethical use of AI, and its impact on employment are growing alongside its adoption.

Cloud Computing and Edge Computing

Cloud computing has become the foundation of many digital services, offering scalable, on-demand computing resources. The global cloud computing market is projected to reach $1,554.94 billion by 2030, growing at a CAGR of 15.7% from 2022 to 2030 (Allied Market Research).

Simultaneously, edge computing is gaining traction, bringing computation and data storage closer to the location where it is needed. This is particularly important for IoT applications and in scenarios where low latency is crucial.

Internet of Things (IoT)

The IoT continues to expand, with billions of connected devices generating vast amounts of data. From smart homes to industrial IoT applications, these interconnected devices are creating new possibilities for automation, efficiency, and data-driven decision making.

Statista predicts that by 2025, there will be 75 billion IoT connected devices in use worldwide. This proliferation of connected devices is raising concerns about privacy and security, as each device potentially represents a point of vulnerability in networks.

Blockchain and Cryptocurrencies

Blockchain technology, initially developed for cryptocurrencies like Bitcoin, is finding applications beyond finance. From supply chain management to voting systems, blockchain's potential for creating transparent, tamper-resistant records is being explored in various sectors.

The cryptocurrency market, while volatile, has gained mainstream attention. Central banks around the world are exploring the possibility of issuing their own digital currencies (CBDCs), which could significantly impact global financial systems.

Virtual and Augmented Reality

Virtual Reality (VR) and Augmented Reality (AR) technologies are evolving beyond gaming and entertainment. They are finding applications in education, healthcare, manufacturing, and retail. The global AR and VR market is expected to reach $454.73 billion by 2030, growing at a CAGR of

40.7% (Allied Market Research).

Quantum Computing

While still in its early stages, quantum computing has the potential to revolutionize fields such as cryptography, drug discovery, and complex system modeling. Major tech companies and governments are investing heavily in quantum research, with the expectation that it could solve problems that are intractable for classical computers.

Global Digital Divides and Inclusion

Despite the rapid advancement of digital technologies, significant disparities exist in access and usage, both between and within countries. These digital divides are multifaceted, encompassing:

1. Access Divide: Differences in the availability of digital infrastructure and devices.

2. Usage Divide: Variations in the ability to effectively use digital technologies.

3. Outcome Divide: Disparities in the benefits derived from digital technology use.

Addressing these divides is crucial for ensuring that the benefits of digital technologies are equitably distributed. Initiatives such as the UN's Sustainable Development Goals (SDGs) recognize the importance of digital inclusion, with SDG 9.c aiming to "significantly increase access to information and communications technology and strive to provide universal and affordable access to the Internet in least developed countries by 2020."

Digital Economy and Transformation

Digital technologies are reshaping economic structures globally. The digital economy, encompassing e-commerce, digital services, and the gig economy, is growing rapidly. According to the World Bank, the digital economy is equivalent to 15.5% of global GDP, growing two and a half times faster than global GDP over the past 15 years.

Digital transformation is occurring across industries, from manufacturing (Industry 4.0) to agriculture (precision farming) and healthcare (telemedicine). This transformation is creating new business models, changing labor markets, and altering global value chains.

However, the pace and nature of this transformation vary significantly across the globe. While some countries are at the forefront of adopting advanced digital technologies, others are still working on basic digital infrastructure. This disparity has implications for global competitiveness and economic development.

Challenges and Concerns

The rapid advancement of digital technologies brings with it a host of challenges and concerns:

1. Privacy and Data Protection: As more of our lives move online, concerns about data privacy and protection have intensified. Regulations like the EU's General Data Protection Regulation (GDPR) are setting new standards for data protection, but challenges remain in balancing innovation with privacy rights.

2. Cybersecurity: The increasing digitization of critical infrastructure and the proliferation of connected devices have expanded the attack surface for cybercriminals. Cybersecurity has become a major concern for governments, businesses, and individuals alike.

3. Digital Ethics: The use of AI in decision-making processes, the spread of misinformation on social media, and the addictive design of digital platforms have raised important ethical questions about the development and deployment of digital technologies.

4. Environmental Impact: While digital technologies offer solutions for environmental monitoring and energy efficiency, the growing energy consumption of data centers and the electronic waste generated by frequent device upgrades are significant environmental concerns.

5. Job Displacement: The automation potential of AI and robotics has raised concerns about job displacement, particularly in routine and repetitive tasks. While new jobs are being created in the digital economy, there's a growing need for reskilling and upskilling of the workforce.

6. Digital Sovereignty: Countries are increasingly concerned about their digital sovereignty, leading to debates about data localization, tech nationalism, and the need for domestic digital capabilities.

Looking Ahead: Future Trends

As we look to the future, several trends are likely to shape the global digital landscape:

1. Increased AI Integration: AI is expected to become more pervasive, with advancements in natural language processing, computer vision, and predictive analytics.

2. 5G and Beyond: While 5G is still being rolled out, research into 6G has already begun, promising even faster speeds and lower latency.

3. Quantum Supremacy: Practical applications of quantum computing could emerge, potentially revolutionizing fields such as cryptography and drug discovery.

4. Extended Reality: The lines between physical and digital realities may blur further with advancements in AR and VR technologies.

5. Green Tech: There will likely be a greater focus on sustainable digital technologies to address environmental concerns.

6. Decentralized Web: Blockchain and related technologies could lead to more decentralized internet architectures.

7. Human Augmentation: Technologies that enhance human cognitive and physical capabilities may become more prevalent.

Conclusion

The global digital landscape is complex, rapidly evolving, and profoundly impactful. As we navigate this digital age, it's crucial to understand not just the technologies themselves, but their broader implications for society, economy, and the environment.

This book aims to provide a comprehensive overview of global digital technology trends, exploring their current state, impacts, and future trajectories. By examining these trends through a global lens, we hope to offer insights that will be valuable to policymakers, business leaders, researchers, and anyone interested in understanding and shaping our digital future.

As we embark on this exploration, we invite readers to approach these topics with a critical and open mind. The future of digital technologies is not predetermined; it will be shaped by the choices we make as societies and as a global community. By understanding these trends and their implications, we can work towards harnessing the power of digital technologies to create a more equitable, sustainable, and prosperous world for all.

CHAPTER TWO

CLOUD COMPUTING AND EDGE COMPUTING

1. Introduction

In the rapidly evolving landscape of information technology, two paradigms have emerged as transformative forces: cloud computing and edge computing. These technologies are reshaping how data is processed, stored, and delivered, fundamentally altering the architecture of modern computing systems and the way businesses operate in the digital age.

Cloud computing, which has been a dominant force for over a decade, centralizes computing resources in remote data centers, offering scalable and on-demand services to users worldwide. It has revolutionized how organizations manage their IT infrastructure, enabling unprecedented flexibility and cost-efficiency.

On the other hand, edge computing has risen as a response to the limitations of cloud computing, particularly in scenarios requiring low latency and real-time processing. By bringing computation and data storage closer to the sources of data generation, edge computing addresses the challenges posed by the exponential growth of Internet of Things (IoT) devices and the increasing demand for faster, more reliable services.

We explore the intricacies of both cloud and edge computing, delving into their definitions, architectures, benefits, and challenges. We will examine how these technologies compare, complement each other, and are being integrated to create hybrid solutions that leverage the strengths of both approaches.

Furthermore, we describe the wide-ranging applications of cloud and edge computing across various industries, from manufacturing and healthcare to smart cities and autonomous vehicles. This chapter will also touch upon emerging trends, security considerations, and the environmental impact of these technologies.

As we navigate through this chapter, it will become clear that cloud and edge computing are not mutually exclusive but rather complementary technologies that, when used in conjunction, have the potential to drive innovation, enhance efficiency, and unlock new possibilities in our increasingly connected world.

2. Cloud Computing

2.1 Definition and Concepts

Cloud computing is a model for enabling ubiquitous, convenient, on-demand network access to a shared pool of configurable computing resources (e.g., networks, servers, storage, applications, and services) that can be rapidly provisioned and released with minimal management effort or service provider interaction.

Key characteristics of cloud computing include:

1. On-demand self-service: Users can unilaterally provision computing capabilities as needed without requiring human interaction with each service provider.

2. Broad network access: Capabilities are available over the network and accessed through standard mechanisms that promote use by heterogeneous thin or thick client platforms.

3. Resource pooling: The provider's computing resources are pooled to serve multiple consumers using a multi-tenant model, with different physical and virtual resources dynamically assigned and reassigned according to consumer demand.

4. Rapid elasticity: Capabilities can be elastically provisioned and released, in some cases automatically, to scale rapidly outward and inward commensurate with demand.

5. Measured service: Cloud systems automatically control and optimize resource use by leveraging a metering capability at some level of abstraction appropriate to the type of service.

2.2 Types of Cloud Services

Cloud computing services are typically categorized into three main models:

1. Infrastructure as a Service (IaaS): Provides virtualized computing resources over the internet. IaaS offers fundamental compute, network, and storage resources to consumers on-demand, over the internet, and on a pay-as-you-go basis.

2. Platform as a Service (PaaS): Delivers a platform allowing customers to develop, run, and manage applications without the complexity of maintaining the underlying infrastructure.

3. Software as a Service (SaaS): Offers software applications over the internet, on-demand and typically on a subscription basis. SaaS eliminates the need for organizations to install and run applications on their own computers or infrastructure.

Additionally, there are several deployment models for cloud computing:

1. Public Cloud: Services are delivered over the public internet and shared across organizations.

2. Private Cloud: The cloud infrastructure is provisioned for exclusive use by a single organization.

3. Hybrid Cloud: A composition of two or more distinct cloud infrastructures (private, community, or public) that remain unique entities but are bound together by standardized or proprietary technology.

4. Multi-Cloud: The use of multiple cloud computing and storage services in a single heterogeneous architecture.

2.3 Benefits and Challenges

Benefits of cloud computing include:

1. Cost Efficiency: Reduces capital expenditure on hardware, software, and services.

2. Scalability: Easily scales up or down based on demand.

3. Flexibility: Enables access from anywhere with an internet connection.

4. Reliability: Offers data backup, disaster recovery, and business continuity.

5. Performance: Regularly upgraded to the latest generation of fast and efficient computing hardware.

Challenges of cloud computing include:

1. Security and Privacy: Concerns about data security and privacy in shared environments.

2. Downtime: Dependence on internet connectivity and service availability.

3. Limited Control: Less control over underlying computing infrastructure.

4. Vendor Lock-in: Difficulty in migrating from one cloud provider to another.

5. Compliance: Meeting regulatory and data residency requirements

3. Edge Computing

3.1 Definition and Concepts

Edge computing is a distributed computing paradigm that brings computation and data storage closer to the sources of data. This approach aims to improve response times and save bandwidth by processing data near the edge of the network, where it is generated, instead of relying on a central location that can be thousands of miles away.

Key concepts of edge computing include:

1. Decentralization: Moving computing resources from centralized data centers to the network edge.

2. Proximity: Placing computational power closer to data sources and end-users.

3. Low latency: Reducing the time it takes for data to travel between its source and processing location.

4. Bandwidth optimization: Reducing the amount of data that needs to be transmitted to central locations.

5. Context awareness: Leveraging local context to make more informed decisions.

3.2 Edge Computing Architecture

The edge computing architecture typically consists of the following components:

1. Edge devices: These are the data-generating devices such as IoT sensors, smartphones, or industrial equipment.

2. Edge nodes: Local processing units that can be anything from small single-board computers to more powerful edge servers.

3. Edge gateways: Devices that aggregate data from multiple edge devices and perform initial processing or filtering.

4. Edge data centers: Small-scale data centers located closer to the edge of the network, capable of more substantial processing and storage.

5. Cloud data centers: Traditional centralized facilities that handle long-term storage and complex analytics.

The architecture follows a hierarchical structure, with data flowing from edge devices through various levels of processing before reaching the cloud, if necessary.

3.3 Benefits and Use Cases

Benefits of edge computing include:

1. Reduced latency: By processing data closer to its source, edge computing significantly reduces response times.

2. Bandwidth conservation: Less data needs to be sent to the cloud, reducing network congestion and costs.

3. Enhanced privacy and security: Sensitive data can be processed locally, reducing exposure to potential breaches.

4. Improved reliability: Edge systems can continue to function even if the connection to the central cloud is lost.

5. Real-time processing: Enables applications that require immediate response, such as autonomous vehicles or industrial automation.

Use cases for edge computing:

1. Internet of Things (IoT): Edge computing is crucial for managing the vast amounts of data generated by IoT devices.

2. Autonomous vehicles: Real-time processing of sensor data is essential for safe operation.

3. Augmented and Virtual Reality: Low-latency processing is necessary for a seamless user experience.

4. Smart cities: Edge computing enables efficient management of urban infrastructure and services.

5. Healthcare: Enables real-time monitoring and rapid response in critical care situations.

6. Manufacturing: Supports real-time monitoring and control of industrial processes.

7. Content Delivery Networks (CDNs): Improves content delivery speed by caching at the network edge.

Challenges of edge computing:

1. Resource constraints: Edge devices often have limited processing power and storage capacity.

2. Security: Distributed nature of edge computing creates new security challenges.

3. Management complexity: Coordinating a large number of distributed edge nodes can be challenging.

4. Standardization: Lack of uniform standards can lead to interoperability issues.

5. Cost: Initial investment in edge infrastructure can be significant.

4. Comparison of Cloud and Edge Computing

While cloud and edge computing are often seen as competing paradigms, they are in fact complementary approaches that address different aspects of modern computing needs. Here's a detailed comparison:

4.1 Data Processing Location

- Cloud: Centralized data centers, often geographically distant from data sources.
- Edge: Distributed, closer to data sources and end-users.

4.2 Latency

- Cloud: Higher latency due to data traveling longer distances.
- Edge: Lower latency, enabling real-time applications.

4.3 Bandwidth Usage

- Cloud: Requires significant bandwidth to transmit data to and from central locations.
- Edge: Reduces bandwidth usage by processing data locally.

4.4 Scalability

- Cloud: Highly scalable, can easily accommodate growing resource needs.
- Edge: Scalability is more complex and may require additional hardware at multiple locations.

4.5 Computing Power

- Cloud: Access to vast computing resources for complex tasks.
- Edge: Limited computing power, but sufficient for many local processing needs.

4.6 Storage Capacity

- Cloud: Virtually unlimited storage capacity.
- Edge: Limited storage, often focusing on short-term data retention.

4.7 Reliability

- Cloud: Dependent on internet connectivity; potential for widespread outages.
- Edge: Can operate independently, more resilient to network issues.

4.8 Security and Privacy

- Cloud: Centralized security model, but potential for large-scale breaches.
- Edge: Distributed security model, potentially reducing the impact of breaches.

4.9 Cost Structure

- Cloud: Pay-as-you-go model, operational expenditure (OpEx).
- Edge: Often requires upfront investment, capital expenditure (CapEx).

4.10 Use Cases

- Cloud: Ideal for big data analytics, machine learning, and applications requiring vast computing resources.
- Edge: Suitable for real-time processing, IoT applications, and scenarios with limited connectivity.

5. Integration of Cloud and Edge Computing

The future of computing lies not in choosing between cloud and edge, but in effectively integrating both paradigms. This integration, often referred to as "fog computing" or "cloud-to-edge" architecture, aims to leverage the strengths of both approaches.

5.1 Hybrid Architecture

A hybrid cloud-edge architecture typically involves:

1. Edge devices and gateways for local processing and data collection.

2. Edge data centers for regional data aggregation and processing.

3. Central cloud infrastructure for long-term storage and complex analytics.

5.2 Data Flow in Hybrid Systems

1. Real-time data is processed at the edge for immediate action.

2. Relevant data is sent to edge data centers for short-term storage and analysis.

3. Aggregated data and complex workloads are sent to the cloud for in-depth analysis and long-term storage.

5.3 Benefits of Integration

1. Optimized Performance: Leveraging edge for low-latency needs and cloud for complex processing.

2. Improved Scalability: Edge handles local scaling, while cloud manages global scaling.

3. Enhanced Reliability: Edge provides resilience against network issues, while cloud ensures data durability.

4. Cost Efficiency: Balancing local processing with cloud resources to optimize costs.

5. Comprehensive Data Insights: Combining real-time edge analytics with cloud-based big data analysis.

5.4 Challenges in Integration

1. Complexity: Managing distributed systems across edge and cloud requires sophisticated orchestration.

2. Data Consistency: Ensuring data remains consistent across edge and cloud environments.

3. Security: Implementing cohesive security measures across diverse environments.

4. Standardization: Lack of universal standards for cloud-edge integration.

6. Industry Applications

The integration of cloud and edge computing is transforming various industries. Here are some key applications across different sectors:

6.1 Manufacturing and Industrial IoT

- Real-time monitoring and control of production lines using edge devices.
- Predictive maintenance using edge analytics and cloud-based machine learning.
- Supply chain optimization through integrated edge-cloud systems.
- Quality control using edge-based computer vision and cloud-based analytics.

6.2 Healthcare and Life Sciences

- Remote patient monitoring using edge devices with cloud-based data aggregation.
- Real-time health data analysis for immediate intervention in critical care.
- Secure storage and analysis of patient records in the cloud.
- Edge-based processing for medical imaging devices, with cloud storage for long-term archiving.

6.3 Retail and Consumer Services

- In-store analytics using edge computing for real-time customer insights.
- Inventory management combining edge-based RFID systems with cloud-based supply chain management.
- Personalized shopping experiences using edge computing and cloud-based customer profiles.
- Smart checkout systems leveraging edge computing for speed and cloud for transaction processing.

6.4 Smart Cities and Urban Infrastructure

- Traffic management systems using edge computing for real-time control and cloud for long-term planning.
- Smart grid management with edge devices for local load balancing and cloud for overall optimization.
- Waste management optimization using edge-based sensors and cloud-based route planning.
- Public safety systems combining edge-based video analytics with cloud-based AI for threat detection.

6.5 Telecommunications and 5G Networks

- Network function virtualization (NFV) at the edge for improved service delivery.
- Content delivery networks (CDNs) using edge caching and cloud-based content management.

- 5G network slicing leveraging edge computing for low-latency applications.
- Mobile edge computing (MEC) for enhanced mobile services and applications.

6.6 Automotive and Transportation

- Autonomous vehicles using edge computing for real-time decision making and cloud for high-level navigation and fleet management.
- Connected car services combining edge-based sensors with cloud-based analytics for predictive maintenance and personalized services.
- Traffic flow optimization using edge devices for local coordination and cloud for city-wide planning.
- In-vehicle infotainment systems leveraging edge computing for responsiveness and cloud for content delivery.

6.7 Energy and Utilities

- Smart metering systems using edge computing for real-time monitoring and cloud for billing and analytics.
- Renewable energy management with edge computing for local grid stability and cloud for overall energy distribution.
- Oil and gas pipeline monitoring using edge sensors for immediate leak detection and cloud for long-term maintenance planning.
- Energy consumption optimization in buildings using edge-based building management systems and cloud-based analytics.

6.8 Agriculture and Environmental Monitoring

- Precision agriculture using edge devices for local condition monitoring and cloud for farm-wide optimization.
- Environmental monitoring systems combining edge-based sensors with cloud-based analytics for climate change studies.
- Livestock management using edge computing for individual animal monitoring and cloud for herd management.
- Forest fire detection systems using edge-based cameras and sensors with cloud-based AI for early warning.

7. Future Trends

As we look ahead, several trends are shaping the future of cloud and edge computing:

7.1 AI and Machine Learning at the Edge

- Increasing deployment of AI models on edge devices for real-time inference.
- Federated learning techniques allowing edge devices to contribute to

model training without sharing raw data.

7.2 5G and Beyond

- 5G networks enabling more powerful edge computing capabilities.
- 6G research focusing on even tighter integration of communication and computation.

7.3 Edge-Native Applications

- Development of applications specifically designed to leverage edge computing capabilities.
- New programming models and tools for distributed edge-cloud environments.

7.4 Serverless Computing at the Edge

- Extension of serverless computing paradigms to edge environments.
- Event-driven architectures spanning cloud and edge.

7.5 Quantum Computing Integration

- Exploration of quantum computing at the edge for specific use cases.
- Hybrid quantum-classical systems spanning edge and cloud.

8. Security Considerations

As cloud and edge computing become more prevalent, security concerns have grown increasingly complex. Here are key security considerations for integrated cloud-edge environments:

8.1 Data Protection

- Encryption: Implementing end-to-end encryption for data in transit and at rest.
- Data Minimization: Processing sensitive data at the edge to reduce exposure.
- Access Control: Implementing robust authentication and authorization mechanisms across the entire infrastructure.

8.2 Device Security

- Secure Boot: Ensuring the integrity of edge devices from startup.
- Regular Updates: Maintaining a rigorous patching schedule for all edge devices.
- Physical Security: Protecting edge devices from tampering and unauthorized physical access.

8.3 Network Security

- Segmentation: Isolating different parts of the network to contain potential breaches.
- Intrusion Detection: Implementing advanced intrusion detection and prevention systems.

- Secure Protocols: Using secure communication protocols between edge devices and the cloud.

8.4 Identity and Access Management

- Zero Trust Architecture: Adopting a "never trust, always verify" approach.
- Multi-Factor Authentication: Implementing strong authentication methods across the infrastructure.
- Principle of Least Privilege: Ensuring users and devices have only the minimum necessary permissions.

8.5 Compliance and Governance

- Data Residency: Ensuring data is stored and processed in compliance with local regulations.
- Audit Trails: Maintaining comprehensive logs for all activities across the edge-cloud ecosystem.
- Privacy by Design: Incorporating privacy considerations into the design of edge-cloud systems.

8.6 Threat Detection and Response

- AI-powered Security: Leveraging machine learning for advanced threat detection.
- Distributed Security Operations: Implementing security measures at both edge and cloud levels.
- Incident Response: Developing and regularly testing incident response plans for various scenarios.

9. Environmental Impact

The rise of cloud and edge computing has significant implications for energy consumption and environmental sustainability:

9.1 Energy Consumption

- Data Centers: Cloud computing has led to the proliferation of large data centers, which are significant energy consumers.
- Edge Devices: The increasing number of edge devices contributes to overall energy consumption.
- Cooling Requirements: Both cloud data centers and larger edge computing nodes require substantial cooling, impacting energy use.

9.2 Positive Impacts

- Efficiency Improvements: Cloud data centers often operate more efficiently than traditional on-premises servers.
- Resource Optimization: Cloud and edge computing enable better resource utilization, potentially reducing overall energy consumption.
- Smart Grid Management: Edge computing facilitates more efficient energy

distribution and use in power grids.

9.3 Negative Impacts

- E-Waste: The rapid turnover of edge devices and data center equipment contributes to electronic waste.
- Carbon Footprint: The energy consumption of data centers and edge devices contributes to carbon emissions.
- Resource Extraction: The production of computing hardware requires the extraction of rare earth minerals and other resources.

9.4 Sustainability Initiatives

- Renewable Energy: Many cloud providers are investing in renewable energy sources for their data centers.
- Energy-Efficient Hardware: Development of more energy-efficient processors and devices for edge computing.
- Circular Economy: Efforts to improve recycling and reuse of computing hardware.

9.5 Future Considerations

- Green Algorithms: Developing more energy-efficient algorithms for both cloud and edge computing.
- Sustainable Edge: Exploring solar-powered edge devices and other sustainable energy sources.
- Policy and Regulation: Potential for increased regulation around the environmental impact of digital infrastructure.

10. Conclusion

Cloud and edge computing represent complementary paradigms that are reshaping the digital landscape. While cloud computing offers vast scalability and computing power, edge computing brings processing closer to data sources, enabling real-time applications and reducing latency.

The integration of these technologies is driving innovation across industries, from manufacturing and healthcare to smart cities and autonomous vehicles. However, this integration also brings challenges, particularly in terms of security and environmental sustainability.

As we move forward, the key to success lies in striking the right balance between cloud and edge computing, leveraging the strengths of each approach to create more efficient, responsive, and sustainable computing ecosystems. The future will likely see even tighter integration of these technologies, along with advancements in areas such as AI, 5G, and potentially quantum computing.

Ultimately, the evolution of cloud and edge computing will continue to play a crucial role in shaping our increasingly connected and data-driven world, offering exciting possibilities for innovation while also presenting important challenges that must be addressed.

CHAPTER THREE

ARTIFICIAL INTELLIGENCE AND MACHINE LEARNING

1. Introduction to Artificial Intelligence (AI) and Machine Learning (ML)

1.1 Definitions and key concepts

Artificial Intelligence (AI) refers to the development of computer systems capable of performing tasks that typically require human intelligence. These tasks include visual perception, speech recognition, decision-making, and language translation. AI systems aim to mimic human cognitive functions, enabling machines to learn from experience, adjust to new inputs, and perform human-like tasks.

Machine Learning (ML), a subset of AI, focuses on the development of algorithms and statistical models that enable computer systems to improve their performance on a specific task through experience. Rather than following explicitly programmed instructions, ML systems learn from data, identifying patterns and making decisions with minimal human intervention.

Key concepts in AI and ML include:

- Algorithms: Step-by-step procedures or formulas for solving problems or performing tasks.

- Data: The information used to train and test AI and ML models.

- Model: A representation of a system or process, used to make predictions or decisions.

- Training: The process of teaching an AI or ML system to perform a task by exposing it to data.

- Inference: The process of using a trained model to make predictions or decisions on new, unseen data.

1.2 Brief history of AI and ML

The field of AI has its roots in the mid-20th century, with significant developments occurring over the past seven decades:

1950s: The term "Artificial Intelligence" is coined by John McCarthy. Alan Turing proposes the Turing Test as a measure of machine intelligence.

1960s: Development of early AI programs, including ELIZA, a natural language processing computer program.

1970s: The first AI winter occurs due to limitations in computing power and algorithmic approaches.

1980s: Expert systems gain popularity, and neural networks resurface with the introduction of backpropagation.

1990s: Machine learning begins to flourish with the development of new algorithms and increased computing power.

2000s: Big data and improved computing capabilities lead to significant advancements in AI and ML applications.

2010s: Deep learning achieves breakthrough results in various domains, including image and speech recognition.

2020s: Large language models and generative AI make significant strides, leading to applications like ChatGPT and DALL-E.

Throughout this history, AI and ML have evolved from theoretical concepts to practical tools that are now integral to many aspects of our daily lives, from smartphone assistants to recommendation systems and autonomous vehicles.

As we delve deeper into the world of AI and ML, we'll explore the fundamental concepts, techniques, and applications that have shaped this rapidly evolving field.

2. Fundamentals of Artificial Intelligence

2.1 Types of AI: Narrow AI vs. General AI

Artificial Intelligence can be categorized into two main types:

Narrow AI (or Weak AI):

Narrow AI refers to AI systems designed and trained for a specific task. These systems excel in their designated areas but lack the ability to transfer their intelligence to other domains. Examples include:

- Virtual assistants like Siri or Alexa
- Image recognition software

- Chess-playing programs
- Recommendation systems on streaming platforms

Narrow AI is currently the most common and practical form of AI in use today.

General AI (or Strong AI):

General AI refers to AI systems that possess the ability to understand, learn, and apply intelligence across a wide range of tasks, similar to human intelligence. Key characteristics include:
- Ability to reason, plan, and solve problems
- Abstract thinking and transfer learning
- Self-awareness and consciousness (A debateable attribute; Awareness and Consciouness as exhibited by humans does not appear to be possible)

While General AI remains largely theoretical, it is a major goal in AI research and development.

2.2 AI approaches: Rule-based systems, Expert systems, and Machine Learning

AI systems can be developed using various approaches:

Rule-based systems:

These systems use pre-defined rules to make decisions or solve problems. Characteristics include:
- Explicit if-then rules
- Deterministic outcomes
- Limited ability to handle unexpected scenarios

Example: A simple chatbot that responds based on keyword matching

Expert systems:

These are more advanced rule-based systems that aim to replicate the decision-making ability of a human expert. Features include:
- Knowledge base containing domain-specific information
- Inference engine to apply rules and make decisions
- Ability to explain reasoning

Example: Medical diagnosis systems

Machine Learning:

ML systems learn from data without being explicitly programmed. They can be categorized into three main types:

a) Supervised Learning:
- Learns from labeled data
- Predicts outcomes for new, unseen data
- Examples: Classification, regression

b) Unsupervised Learning:

- Learns from unlabeled data

- Discovers patterns and structures in data

- Examples: Clustering, dimensionality reduction

c) Reinforcement Learning:

- Learns through interaction with an environment

- Maximizes rewards based on actions taken

- Examples: Game playing AI, robotics

Each of these approaches has its strengths and weaknesses, and the choice of approach depends on the specific problem, available data, and desired outcomes.

3. Machine Learning: Core Concepts

3.1 What is Machine Learning?

Machine Learning is a subset of AI that focuses on the development of algorithms and statistical models that enable computer systems to improve their performance on a specific task through experience. Key aspects include:

- Data-driven approach: ML systems learn from examples rather than following explicit programming.

- Pattern recognition: ML algorithms identify patterns in data to make predictions or decisions.

- Iterative improvement: ML models typically improve their performance as they are exposed to more data.

3.2 Types of Machine Learning

a) Supervised Learning:

In supervised learning, the algorithm learns from labeled data, where both input features and corresponding output labels are provided. The goal is to learn a function that maps inputs to outputs. Examples include:

- Classification: Predicting a categorical label (e.g., spam detection in emails)

- Regression: Predicting a continuous value (e.g., house price prediction)

b) Unsupervised Learning:

Unsupervised learning algorithms work with unlabeled data, attempting to find inherent structures or patterns. Common applications include:

- Clustering: Grouping similar data points (e.g., customer segmentation)

- Dimensionality reduction: Reducing the number of features while preserving important information

c) Reinforcement Learning:

This type of learning involves an agent interacting with an environment, learning to take actions that maximize cumulative rewards. Applications include:

- Game playing AI (e.g., AlphaGo)
- Autonomous vehicles
- Robotics

3.3 Key ML algorithms and their applications

a) Linear Regression: Predicting continuous values based on linear relationships between variables.

Application: Predicting sales based on advertising spend.

b) Logistic Regression: Predicting binary outcomes.

Application: Credit risk assessment.

c) Decision Trees: Tree-like models for classification and regression.

Application: Customer churn prediction.

d) Random Forests: Ensemble of decision trees for improved accuracy and reduced overfitting.

Application: Fraud detection in financial transactions.

e) Support Vector Machines (SVM): Classifying data by finding the optimal hyperplane that separates different classes.

Application: Image classification.

f) K-Means Clustering: Grouping similar data points into clusters.

Application: Market segmentation.

g) Principal Component Analysis (PCA): Reducing dimensionality while preserving important information.

Application: Feature selection in high-dimensional datasets.

h) Neural Networks: Models inspired by biological neural networks, capable of learning complex patterns.

Application: Image and speech recognition.

These algorithms form the foundation of many ML applications and are often combined or modified to suit specific problem domains.

4. Deep Learning and Neural Networks

4.1 Introduction to Deep Learning

Deep Learning is a subset of Machine Learning that uses artificial neural networks with multiple layers (hence "deep") to progressively extract higher-level features from raw input. Key aspects of Deep Learning include:

- Ability to automatically learn feature representations
- Scalability with large amounts of data and computational power

- State-of-the-art performance in many complex tasks, such as image and speech recognition

4.2 Neural Networks: structure and function

Artificial Neural Networks (ANNs) are inspired by biological neural networks in the human brain. They consist of interconnected nodes (neurons) organized in layers:

- Input Layer: Receives the initial data
- Hidden Layer(s): Processes the information
- Output Layer: Produces the final result

Each neuron in the network:
- Receives inputs from the previous layer or the input data
- Applies a weighted sum to these inputs
- Passes the result through an activation function
- Sends the output to the next layer

The learning process in neural networks involves adjusting the weights and biases to minimize the difference between predicted and actual outputs. This is typically done using an algorithm called backpropagation, which calculates the gradient of the error with respect to the network's parameters.

4.3 Convolutional Neural Networks (CNNs) and Recurrent Neural Networks (RNNs)

CNNs:

Convolutional Neural Networks are specialized neural networks designed primarily for processing grid-like data, such as images. Key features include:
- Convolutional layers: Apply filters to detect local patterns
- Pooling layers: Reduce spatial dimensions and extract dominant features
- Fully connected layers: Combine features for final classification

Applications of CNNs:
- Image classification and object detection
- Facial recognition
- Medical image analysis

RNNs:

Recurrent Neural Networks are designed to work with sequential data by maintaining an internal state (memory). This makes them suitable for tasks involving time series or sequence data. Key features include:
- Ability to process sequences of varying length
- Shared parameters across different time steps
- Variants like LSTM (Long Short-Term Memory) and GRU (Gated

Recurrent Unit) to address the vanishing gradient problem

Applications of RNNs:

- Natural language processing tasks (e.g., language translation, sentiment analysis)
- Speech recognition
- Time series prediction (e.g., stock prices, weather forecasting)

5. AI and ML Applications

5.1 Natural Language Processing (NLP)

NLP focuses on the interaction between computers and human language. Key applications include:
- Machine translation
- Sentiment analysis
- Chatbots and virtual assistants
- Text summarization

5.2 Computer Vision

Computer Vision deals with how computers gain high-level understanding from digital images or videos. Applications include:
- Facial recognition systems
- Autonomous vehicles
- Medical image analysis
- Augmented reality

5.3 Robotics and Autonomous Systems

AI and ML play crucial roles in developing intelligent robots and autonomous systems:
- Industrial robots for manufacturing
- Autonomous drones for delivery and surveillance
- Self-driving cars
- Smart home systems

5.4 Healthcare and Medicine

AI and ML are revolutionizing healthcare through applications such as:
- Disease diagnosis and prognosis
- Drug discovery and development
- Personalized treatment plans
- Medical image analysis (e.g., detecting tumors in X-rays or MRIs)

5.5 Finance and Business

The financial sector has widely adopted AI and ML for various purposes:
- Algorithmic trading
- Fraud detection

- Credit scoring
- Customer service chatbots
- Predictive analytics for business intelligence

These applications demonstrate the wide-ranging impact of AI and ML across various industries and domains. As we continue to advance these technologies, we can expect to see even more innovative applications emerging.

6. Challenges and Limitations of AI and ML

6.1 Ethical considerations

As AI and ML systems become more prevalent in society, they raise important ethical questions:

- Privacy concerns: AI systems often require large amounts of data, which can include personal information.
- Accountability: Determining responsibility when AI systems make mistakes or cause harm.
- Job displacement: The potential for AI to automate tasks currently performed by humans.
- Autonomy and decision-making: Concerns about AI systems making important decisions without human oversight.
- Weaponization of AI: The potential use of AI in warfare and its implications.

6.2 Bias and fairness in AI systems

AI systems can inadvertently perpetuate or amplify existing biases:

- Data bias: If training data is not representative, it can lead to biased outcomes.
- Algorithmic bias: The design of algorithms can inadvertently favor certain groups over others.
- Historical bias: AI systems learning from historical data may perpetuate past discrimination.

Addressing bias requires:
- Diverse and representative training data
- Regular audits of AI systems for fairness
- Inclusive teams developing AI technologies

6.3 Explainability and interpretability

Many advanced AI systems, particularly deep learning models, operate as "black boxes," making it difficult to understand how they arrive at their decisions. This lack of transparency can be problematic in critical applications such as healthcare or criminal justice.

Challenges include:

- Developing techniques to make AI decision-making processes more transparent
- Balancing model complexity with interpretability
- Meeting regulatory requirements for explainable AI in certain industries

6.4 Data quality and quantity

The performance of ML models heavily depends on the quality and quantity of available data:

- Data scarcity: Some domains lack sufficient data for effective model training.
- Data quality issues: Noisy, incomplete, or inaccurate data can lead to poor model performance.
- Data privacy regulations: Restrictions on data collection and use can limit the development of AI systems.

6.5 Generalization and adaptability

AI systems often struggle to generalize beyond their training data or adapt to new situations:

- Overfitting: Models may perform well on training data but fail to generalize to new, unseen data.
- Domain adaptation: Difficulty in applying models trained in one domain to another related domain.
- Concept drift: Changes in the underlying data distribution over time can degrade model performance.

6.6 Computational resources and energy consumption

Training and deploying large AI models requires significant computational resources:

- Environmental impact: The energy consumption of large-scale AI systems raises sustainability concerns.
- Cost: High-performance hardware needed for AI can be expensive, limiting accessibility.
- Scalability: Challenges in scaling AI systems to handle increasing data volumes and complexity.

6.7 Security vulnerabilities

AI systems can be vulnerable to various attacks:

- Adversarial attacks: Subtle manipulations of input data to fool AI systems.
- Data poisoning: Introducing malicious data into training sets to compromise model performance.

- Model stealing: Attempts to replicate proprietary AI models through careful querying.

Addressing these challenges and limitations is crucial for the responsible development and deployment of AI and ML technologies. It requires ongoing research, collaboration between different disciplines, and proactive policy-making to ensure that AI benefits society while minimizing potential risks.

7. Future Trends in AI and ML

7.1 Emerging technologies

a) Federated Learning:
This approach allows training AI models on distributed datasets without centralizing the data, addressing privacy concerns and enabling collaboration across organizations.

b) Quantum Machine Learning:
Leveraging quantum computing to potentially solve complex ML problems faster than classical computers, particularly in areas like optimization and simulation.

c) AI-augmented creativity:
Advanced generative models for art, music, and writing, pushing the boundaries of AI in creative fields.

d) Neuromorphic Computing:
Hardware designed to mimic the structure and function of biological neural networks, potentially leading to more efficient AI systems.

e) AutoML and AI-assisted ML:
Automating the process of model selection and hyperparameter tuning, making ML more accessible to non-experts.

7.2 Potential societal impacts

a) Healthcare revolution:
- Personalized medicine based on genetic and lifestyle data
- AI-assisted drug discovery and development
- Early disease detection and prevention

b) Education transformation:
- Personalized learning experiences tailored to individual students
- AI tutors and adaptive learning platforms
- Automated grading and feedback systems

c) Climate change and sustainability:
- AI-optimized energy grids and smart cities
- Improved climate modeling and prediction

- AI-driven solutions for sustainable agriculture and resource management
    d) Transportation and mobility:
- Widespread adoption of autonomous vehicles
- AI-optimized traffic management systems
- Advanced route planning and logistics optimization
    e) Work and employment:
- Automation of routine tasks across various industries
- New job roles centered around AI development and management
- Potential for universal basic income as a response to job displacement
    f) Enhanced decision-making:
- AI-assisted policy-making and governance
- Improved risk assessment and predictive modeling in various fields
- AI systems augmenting human decision-making in complex scenarios
    g) Human-AI collaboration:
- Development of more intuitive and natural interfaces for human-AI interaction
- AI systems designed to complement human skills rather than replace them
- Ethical frameworks for AI as it becomes more integrated into daily life

8. Conclusion

8.1 Recap of key points
- AI and ML have evolved from theoretical concepts to practical tools impacting various aspects of our lives.
- The field encompasses a wide range of approaches, from rule-based systems to advanced neural networks.
- Applications span numerous domains, including healthcare, finance, transportation, and creative industries.
- Despite significant progress, AI and ML face challenges related to ethics, bias, explainability, and computational resources.

8.2 The future of AI and ML
As AI and ML continue to advance, we can expect:
- Increased integration of AI into everyday life and business processes
- Greater focus on responsible AI development, addressing ethical concerns and potential risks
- Continued breakthroughs in AI capabilities, potentially leading towards artificial general intelligence
- Interdisciplinary collaboration to tackle complex societal challenges using AI

The field of AI and ML is rapidly evolving, with new discoveries and applications emerging regularly. As these technologies become more powerful and pervasive, it's crucial to approach their development and deployment thoughtfully, considering both the immense potential benefits and the associated risks and challenges.

CHAPTER FOUR

INTERNET OF THINGS (IOT) AND INDUSTRIAL IOT

1. Introduction to IoT

The Internet of Things (IoT) refers to the vast network of interconnected devices that collect and exchange data via the internet. These devices, embedded with sensors, software, and other technologies, can range from simple household items to sophisticated industrial tools.

The concept of IoT has revolutionized how we interact with our environment, enabling seamless communication between devices and systems, and providing unprecedented levels of data collection and analysis. This interconnectedness allows for improved efficiency, enhanced decision-making, and the creation of new services and business models.

The IoT ecosystem encompasses a wide array of technologies, including wireless sensors, control systems, automation, and machine learning algorithms. As this network continues to grow, it's reshaping industries, transforming cities, and changing the way we live and work.

2. The Evolution of IoT

The term "Internet of Things" was coined by Kevin Ashton in 1999, but the concept of connected devices has roots dating back to the 1970s. Here's a brief timeline of IoT evolution:

1970s: Early ideas of connected devices emerge.

1990s: The term "Internet of Things" is conceived.

2000s: The concept gains traction as internet connectivity becomes more widespread.

2008-2009: The number of connected devices exceeds the world's population.

2010s: Rapid growth in IoT adoption across various sectors.

2020s: IoT becomes integral to smart cities, industries, and everyday life.

The growth of IoT has been driven by several factors, including:

- Advancements in sensor technology
- Increasing internet connectivity and speed
- Decreasing costs of computing power and data storage
- Development of cloud computing platforms
- Progress in data analytics and artificial intelligence

3. Key Components of IoT Systems

An IoT system typically consists of four main components:

a) Sensors/Devices: These are the physical objects embedded with sensors, software, and other technologies that collect and send data.

b) Connectivity: This includes the various methods of transmitting data, such as WiFi, Bluetooth, LPWAN, cellular, or satellite.

c) Data Processing: This involves cloud-based or edge computing systems that analyze and process the collected data.

d) User Interface: This is how processed data is made accessible to end-users, often through applications or web interfaces.

These components work together to create a functional IoT ecosystem. For example, a smart thermostat (device) uses WiFi (connectivity) to send temperature data to a cloud server (data processing), which then allows users to control their home temperature via a smartphone app (user interface).

4. IoT Applications in Everyday Life

IoT has permeated various aspects of our daily lives. Some common applications include:

a) Smart Homes: IoT enables home automation systems, including smart thermostats, lighting, security systems, and appliances.

b) Wearable Devices: Fitness trackers and smartwatches collect health data and provide personalized insights.

c) Smart Cities: IoT facilitates efficient urban management through smart traffic systems, waste management, and energy grids.

d) Connected Cars: Vehicles equipped with IoT technology offer enhanced navigation, predictive maintenance, and improved safety features.

e) Healthcare: IoT devices enable remote patient monitoring, medication management, and improved hospital operations.

f) Agriculture: Precision farming techniques use IoT sensors for crop monitoring, automated irrigation, and livestock management.

5. Introduction to Industrial IoT (IIoT)

Industrial IoT, or IIoT, refers to the use of IoT technologies in industrial settings. It involves interconnected sensors, instruments, and other devices networked together with industrial applications, including manufacturing and energy management.

IIoT aims to improve operational efficiency, reduce downtime, and enable new business models through data-driven insights. It's a key component of Industry 4.0, the fourth industrial revolution characterized by the integration of digital technologies in industrial processes.

6. IIoT vs. Traditional IoT

While IIoT and consumer IoT share many similarities, there are several key differences:

a) Scale and Complexity: IIoT systems often involve thousands of sensors and devices, operating in complex industrial environments.

b) Reliability and Durability: Industrial devices must withstand harsh conditions and operate continuously with minimal downtime.

c) Security Requirements: IIoT systems often handle sensitive data and control critical infrastructure, requiring more robust security measures.

d) Data Volume and Velocity: Industrial applications typically generate and process much larger volumes of data at higher speeds.

e) Integration with Legacy Systems: IIoT often needs to work alongside existing industrial control systems and machinery.

7. Key Technologies Enabling IIoT

Several technologies are crucial for the implementation of IIoT:

a) 5G Networks: High-speed, low-latency 5G connectivity enables real-time data transfer and control in industrial settings.

b) Edge Computing: Processing data closer to its source reduces latency and bandwidth usage, critical for many industrial applications.

c) Artificial Intelligence and Machine Learning: These technologies enable predictive maintenance, process optimization, and autonomous decision-making.

d) Digital Twin Technology: Creating digital replicas of physical assets allows for simulation, monitoring, and optimization of industrial processes.

e) Blockchain: This can enhance security and traceability in supply chain management and other industrial applications.

8. Applications of IIoT

IIoT has found applications across various industries:

a) Manufacturing: Predictive maintenance, quality control, and supply chain optimization.

b) Energy and Utilities: Smart grids, remote monitoring of oil and gas facilities, and efficient resource management.

c) Transportation and Logistics: Fleet management, asset tracking, and predictive maintenance for vehicles and infrastructure.

d) Healthcare: Equipment monitoring, inventory management, and facility optimization in hospitals.

e) Agriculture: Precision farming, livestock monitoring, and automated greenhouse management.

f) Mining: Safety monitoring, equipment tracking, and automated operations in hazardous environments.

9. Challenges and Considerations in IoT and IIoT

While IoT and IIoT offer numerous benefits, they also present several challenges:

a) Security and Privacy: The vast network of connected devices increases the attack surface for cybercriminals.

b) Interoperability: Ensuring different devices and systems can communicate effectively is an ongoing challenge.

c) Data Management: The sheer volume of data generated by IoT devices presents storage and processing challenges.

d) Scalability: As IoT networks grow, maintaining performance and reliability becomes more complex.

e) Power Management: Many IoT devices operate on battery power, necessitating efficient energy use.

f) Regulatory Compliance: IoT systems must adhere to various data protection and industry-specific regulations.

g) Skills Gap: There's a growing need for professionals with expertise in IoT technologies and data analysis.

10. Future Trends and Predictions

The future of IoT and IIoT is likely to be shaped by several emerging trends:

a) AI and Machine Learning Integration: Increased use of AI for autonomous decision-making and predictive analytics.

b) 5G and Beyond: The rollout of 5G and development of 6G will enable new IoT applications requiring high-speed, low-latency connectivity.

c) Edge Computing Growth: More data processing will occur at the edge to reduce latency and bandwidth usage.

d) Increased Focus on Security: Development of new security protocols and technologies specifically for IoT ecosystems.

e) Expansion of Digital Twin Technology: More industries will adopt digital twins for simulation and optimization.

f) IoT-as-a-Service: Growth of platform-based services to simplify IoT implementation for businesses.

g) Convergence with Other Technologies: IoT will increasingly intersect with blockchain, augmented reality, and quantum computing.

11. Conclusion

The Internet of Things and Industrial IoT are transforming how we interact with our environment and how industries operate. As these technologies continue to evolve, they promise to bring about unprecedented levels of connectivity, efficiency, and innovation.

However, realizing the full potential of IoT and IIoT will require addressing significant challenges, particularly in the areas of security, interoperability, and data management. As we move forward, it will be crucial to balance the tremendous opportunities these technologies offer with careful consideration of their implications for privacy, security, and society as a whole.

The future of IoT and IIoT is bright, with continued growth and innovation expected across various sectors. As these technologies become more deeply integrated into our daily lives and industrial processes, they will undoubtedly play a pivotal role in shaping our increasingly connected world.

5G AND BEYOND

1. Introduction

The advent of 5G (fifth-generation) mobile networks marks a significant milestone in the evolution of telecommunications technology. As the successor to 4G LTE, 5G promises to revolutionize not just how we communicate, but how we live, work, and interact with the world around us. With its promise of ultra-fast speeds, near-zero latency, and massive connectivity, 5G is set to enable a new era of digital transformation across industries and society at large.

However, the story doesn't end with 5G. As we stand on the cusp of this technological leap, researchers and industry leaders are already looking beyond, envisioning the next generation of wireless technology, tentatively called 6G. This forward-thinking approach reflects the rapid pace of technological advancement and the ever-growing demands of our increasingly connected world.

This comprehensive exploration will delve into the intricacies of 5G technology, its potential applications, and the challenges it faces. We will examine the current state of 5G deployment worldwide and its projected impact on various sectors of the economy. Furthermore, we will look beyond 5G, exploring the emerging concepts and technologies that could shape the future of wireless communications.

As we embark on this journey through the present and future of mobile networks, we will also consider the broader implications of these technologies. From economic and societal impacts to environmental considerations and regulatory challenges, the rollout of 5G and the development of future networks raise important questions that extend far beyond the realm of technology.

By the end of this exploration, readers will have a thorough understanding of 5G technology, its potential to transform our world, and a glimpse into the possibilities that lie beyond. As we stand at this technological crossroads, it's crucial to understand not just the capabilities of these new networks, but also their implications for our shared digital future.

2. Evolution of Mobile Networks

To fully appreciate the significance of 5G and beyond, it's essential to understand the evolution of mobile network technologies:

1G (1980s): Analog cellular networks, voice calls only
- First generation of wireless cellular technology
- Analog signals, poor voice quality, limited capacity

2G (1990s): Digital networks, introduction of text messaging
- Global System for Mobile Communications (GSM)
- Improved voice quality, text messaging (SMS), basic data services

3G (2000s): Mobile broadband
- First mobile data services
- Video calling, mobile internet access
- Enhanced data rates for GSM Evolution (EDGE)

4G (2010s): High-speed mobile broadband
- Long-Term Evolution (LTE) and LTE-Advanced
- Fast data speeds, improved quality of service
- Enabled streaming services, mobile gaming, and more

5G (2020s): Ultra-fast speeds, low latency, massive connectivity
- New Radio (NR) technology
- Millimeter wave (mmWave) spectrum
- Network slicing and virtualization

Each generation has brought significant improvements in speed, capacity, and functionality, paving the way for new applications and services. 5G represents a major leap forward, not just in terms of speed, but in its potential to enable transformative technologies and applications.

3. Understanding 5G Technology

3.1 Key Features of 5G

5G is characterized by three main capabilities:

a) Enhanced Mobile Broadband (eMBB):
- Peak data rates up to 20 Gbps
- User experienced data rates of 100 Mbps to 1 Gbps
- Support for high-quality video streaming, virtual reality, and augmented

reality

b) Ultra-Reliable Low-Latency Communication (URLLC):

- Latency as low as 1 millisecond
- Crucial for real-time applications like autonomous vehicles, remote surgery, and industrial automation

c) Massive Machine-Type Communications (mMTC):

- Support for up to 1 million connccted devices per square kilometer
- Enabling large-scale IoT deployments and smart city applications

3.2 5G Network Architecture

5G introduces a more flexible and scalable network architecture:

a) Radio Access Network (RAN):

- New Radio (NR) technology
- Massive MIMO (Multiple Input, Multiple Output) antennas
- Beamforming for improved signal quality and efficiency

b) Core Network:

- Software-defined networking (SDN)
- Network Function Virtualization (NFV)
- Network slicing for customized services

c) Edge Computing:

- Distributed computing resources closer to end-users
- Reduced latency and improved performance for time-sensitive applications

3.3 5G Spectrum

5G operates across a wide range of frequency bands:

a) Low-band (< 1 GHz):

- Wide coverage area, good building penetration
- Limited capacity and speed improvements over 4G

b) Mid-band (1-6 GHz):

- Balance of coverage and capacity
- Significant speed improvements over 4G

c) High-band (mmWave, > 24 GHz):

- Extremely high speeds and capacity
- Limited coverage and poor obstacle penetration

The use of higher frequency bands, particularly mmWave, is a key enabler of 5G's high-speed capabilities but also presents challenges in terms of coverage and signal propagation.

4. 5G Use Cases and Applications

The unique capabilities of 5G enable a wide range of applications across various industries:

4.1 Enhanced Mobile Broadband (eMBB)

a) Consumer Applications:
- 4K/8K video streaming
- Cloud gaming
- Virtual and Augmented Reality (VR/AR)
- 360-degree video

b) Business Applications:
- High-quality video conferencing
- Remote work and collaboration tools
- Large file transfers and cloud services

4.2 Ultra-Reliable Low-Latency Communication (URLLC)

a) Autonomous Vehicles:
- Vehicle-to-everything (V2X) communication
- Real-time traffic management
- Enhanced safety features

b) Industrial Automation:
- Remote control of machinery
- Real-time monitoring and analytics
- Precision manufacturing

c) Healthcare:
- Remote surgery
- Real-time patient monitoring
- Augmented reality-assisted procedures

4.3 Massive Machine-Type Communications (mMTC)

a) Smart Cities:
- Intelligent traffic management
- Smart utility metering
- Environmental monitoring

b) Agriculture:
- Precision farming
- Livestock monitoring
- Automated irrigation systems

c) Logistics and Supply Chain:
- Asset tracking
- Fleet management
- Warehouse automation

These use cases demonstrate the transformative potential of 5G across various sectors of the economy and society.

5. 5G Deployment and Global Adoption

The rollout of 5G networks is progressing rapidly around the world:

a) Global Deployment Status:

- Many countries have launched commercial 5G services
- Varying stages of deployment across regions

b) Regional Progress:

- South Korea, China, and the United States are leading in 5G adoption
- European countries are making steady progress
- Developing nations are in early stages of 5G planning and deployment

c) Deployment Strategies:

- Non-Standalone (NSA) 5G: Initial deployments leveraging existing 4G infrastructure
- Standalone (SA) 5G: Full 5G core network implementation

d) Challenges in Deployment:

- High infrastructure costs
- Spectrum allocation issues
- Technical challenges in dense urban environments

e) Industry Collaboration:

- Public-private partnerships for 5G development
- International standards organizations coordinating global efforts

The pace of 5G adoption varies significantly across regions, influenced by factors such as existing infrastructure, regulatory environments, and economic considerations.

6. Challenges in 5G Implementation

While 5G offers immense potential, its implementation faces several challenges:

a) Infrastructure Costs:

- High costs associated with network equipment and deployment
- Need for densification of cell sites, especially for mmWave

b) Spectrum Allocation:

- Limited availability of suitable spectrum in some regions
- Balancing between different spectrum bands for optimal coverage and capacity

c) Energy Consumption:

- Increased power requirements for 5G base stations
- Need for energy-efficient solutions to support sustainability goals

d) Security Concerns:
- Expanded attack surface due to increased number of connected devices
- Need for robust security measures to protect against cyber threats
  e) Health and Safety Concerns:
- Public concerns about potential health effects of 5G radiation
- Need for clear communication and adherence to safety standards
  f) Interoperability:
- Ensuring seamless integration with existing 4G networks
- Compatibility challenges between different vendors' equipment

7. Beyond 5G: Towards 6G and Future Networks

Even as 5G deployment is ongoing, research into the next generation of wireless technology is already underway.

7.1 Potential Features of 6G

While still in the conceptual stage, 6G is expected to offer:

a) Extremely High Data Rates:
- Theoretical speeds up to 1 Tbps
- Support for high-fidelity holographic communications
  b) Ultra-Low Latency:
- Latency reduced to microseconds
- Enabling true real-time applications
  c) Massive Connectivity:
- Supporting up to 10 million devices per square kilometer
- Enabling ubiquitous IoT and smart environments
  d) Artificial Intelligence Integration:
- AI-native network design
- Self-optimizing and self-healing networks
  e) Extended Reality (XR):
- Seamless integration of AR, VR, and Mixed Reality
- Immersive telepresence and holographic communications

7.2 Emerging Technologies for Beyond 5G

Several cutting-edge technologies are being explored for future networks:

a) Terahertz (THz) Communications:
- Utilizing frequencies above 100 GHz
- Enabling ultra-high-speed, short-range communications
  b) Visible Light Communication (VLC):
- Using light for data transmission
- Potential for high-speed, secure indoor communications

c) Quantum Communications:
- Leveraging quantum entanglement for secure communications
- Potential for unhackable networks
   d) Orbital Angular Momentum (OAM):
- Exploiting the orbital angular momentum of electromagnetic waves
- Potentially increasing spectral efficiency
   e) Cell-free Massive MIMO:
- Distributed antenna systems for improved coverage and capacity
- Blurring the lines between cells in traditional cellular networks

8. Societal and Economic Impact

The advent of 5G and beyond is expected to have far-reaching societal and economic implications:
   a) Economic Growth:
- Potential to add trillions of dollars to the global economy
- Creation of new industries and business models
   b) Job Market Transformation:
- Creation of new job categories in telecommunications and related fields
- Potential job displacement in some sectors due to automation
   c) Digital Divide:
- Potential to bridge the connectivity gap in underserved areas
- Risk of exacerbating inequality if not deployed equitably
   d) Education and Skill Development:
- Enhanced e-learning capabilities
- Need for workforce reskilling to adapt to new technologies
   e) Healthcare Transformation:
- Improved telemedicine and remote healthcare services
- Potential for personalized medicine and real-time health monitoring
   f) Smart Cities and Urban Planning:
- Efficient resource management and improved public services
- Enhanced quality of life through smart infrastructure

9. Environmental Considerations

The environmental impact of 5G and future networks is a topic of growing importance:
   a) Energy Efficiency:
- Potential for improved energy efficiency in various sectors through IoT and smart systems
- Concerns about increased energy consumption of 5G networks themselves

b) E-Waste:
- Increased device turnover as consumers upgrade to 5G-compatible devices
- Need for improved recycling and circular economy practices
c) Climate Change Mitigation:
- Potential for 5G to enable more efficient resource use and reduce emissions in various industries
- Importance of considering the carbon footprint of network infrastructure
d) Ecosystem Impact:
- Concerns about the potential effects of increased electromagnetic radiation on wildlife
- Need for further research and monitoring

10. Regulatory and Security Aspects

The deployment of 5G and development of future networks raise important regulatory and security considerations:

a) Spectrum Regulation:
- Need for harmonized spectrum allocation across regions
- Balancing between different uses (commercial, government, scientific)
b) Cybersecurity:
- Increased importance of network security due to critical applications
- Development of new security standards and protocols
c) Privacy Concerns:
- Managing data privacy in an increasingly connected world
- Balancing innovation with user privacy protection
d) International Cooperation:
- Need for global standards and interoperability
- Addressing geopolitical concerns around 5G infrastructure
e) Ethical Considerations:
- Ensuring responsible development and deployment of AI-enabled networks
- Addressing potential societal impacts of ubiquitous connectivity

11. Future Outlook and Conclusion

As we look towards the future of wireless communications, several key trends emerge:

- Continued evolution of 5G technology and widespread global adoption
- Increasing convergence of 5G with other technologies like AI, IoT, and edge computing
- Ongoing research and development towards 6G and beyond
- Growing focus on sustainable and energy-efficient network solutions

- Increasing importance of security and privacy in hyperconnected environments

The journey from 5G to 6G and beyond represents more than just an improvement in wireless technology. It signifies a fundamental shift in how we interact with the digital world, promising to blur the lines between physical and virtual realities. As these technologies continue to evolve, they will undoubtedly bring both tremendous opportunities and significant challenges.

The successful implementation and adoption of these advanced networks will require collaboration between governments, industry leaders, researchers, and the public. It will be crucial to address concerns around security, privacy, and environmental impact while harnessing the transformative potential of these technologies.

As we stand on the brink of this new era in telecommunications, one thing is clear: the future of wireless technology holds the promise of reshaping our world in ways we are only beginning to imagine. The journey beyond 5G is not just about faster speeds or more connections, but about creating a more connected, efficient, and innovative global society.

CHAPTER SIX

CYBERSECURITY IN THE DIGITAL AGE

1. Introduction

In the digital age, where our lives are increasingly intertwined with technology, cybersecurity has become a critical concern for individuals, businesses, and nations alike. As our dependence on digital systems grows, so does our vulnerability to cyber threats. From personal data breaches to large-scale attacks on critical infrastructure, the potential impacts of cybercrime are far-reaching and potentially devastating.

Cybersecurity refers to the practice of protecting systems, networks, and programs from digital attacks. It encompasses a wide range of technologies, processes, and practices designed to defend against, detect, and respond to cyber threats. In today's interconnected world, where data is often described as the new oil, ensuring the confidentiality, integrity, and availability of information has never been more crucial.

The landscape of cybersecurity is constantly evolving, driven by rapid technological advancements and the increasing sophistication of cyber criminals. As organizations embrace digital transformation, adopt cloud computing, and leverage the Internet of Things (IoT), they also expand their attack surface, creating new vulnerabilities that malicious actors can exploit.

This comprehensive exploration of cybersecurity in the digital age will delve into the history and evolution of cybersecurity, examine the current threat landscape, and discuss the various technologies and strategies employed to combat cyber threats. We will explore how cybersecurity impacts different sectors of the economy and society, and consider the crucial role that human factors play in maintaining digital security.

Furthermore, we will examine the regulatory frameworks that govern cybersecurity practices, discuss emerging trends in the field, and consider the challenges that cybersecurity professionals face. Finally, we will look towards the future, exploring how cybersecurity is likely to evolve in response to new technologies and threats.

As we navigate through this complex and critical topic, it becomes clear that cybersecurity is not just a technical issue, but a multifaceted challenge that touches on aspects of technology, human behavior, economics, and public policy. Understanding these various dimensions is crucial for anyone seeking to grasp the importance of cybersecurity in our increasingly digital world.

2. Evolution of Cybersecurity

The history of cybersecurity is closely tied to the development of computer technology:

1960s-1970s: Early Days
- Focus on physical security of computer systems
- Introduction of password protection
- Creation of the first computer worm (Creeper) and antivirus program (Reaper)

1980s: Emergence of Personal Computers
- Rise of computer viruses (Brain, Morris Worm)
- Development of antivirus software
- Establishment of first Computer Emergency Response Team (CERT)

1990s: Internet Era
- Proliferation of malware and hacking incidents
- Development of firewalls and intrusion detection systems
- Introduction of encryption technologies

2000s: Rise of Cybercrime
- Emergence of sophisticated malware (Stuxnet)
- Growth of organized cybercrime
- Development of comprehensive security suites

2010s-Present: Era of Advanced Persistent Threats (APTs)
- Nation-state cyber espionage and warfare
- Cloud security and mobile device management
- Artificial Intelligence and Machine Learning in cybersecurity

This evolution reflects the ongoing arms race between cybercriminals and security professionals, with each advance in attack techniques met by new defensive strategies.

3. The Current Cybersecurity Landscape

The modern cybersecurity landscape is characterized by:

a) Increased Attack Surface:
- Cloud computing and distributed systems
- Internet of Things (IoT) devices
- Mobile and remote working environments

b) Sophisticated Threat Actors:
- Nation-state sponsored groups
- Organized cybercrime syndicates
- Hacktivists and insider threats

c) Complex Attack Vectors:
- Advanced Persistent Threats (APTs)
- Ransomware and crypto-jacking
- Social engineering and phishing

d) Data Privacy Concerns:
- Growing awareness of data rights
- Stricter data protection regulations (e.g., GDPR, CCPA)

e) Skills Shortage:
- Global shortage of cybersecurity professionals
- Widening gap between attacker and defender capabilities

f) Emerging Technologies:
- AI and machine learning in both attack and defense
- Quantum computing threatening current encryption methods

This landscape requires a proactive and multi-layered approach to cybersecurity, combining technological solutions with human expertise and organizational processes.

4. Types of Cyber Threats

Understanding the various types of cyber threats is crucial for effective cybersecurity:

a) Malware:
- Viruses, worms, trojans, and spyware
- Ransomware encrypting data for ransom
- Fileless malware residing in system memory

b) Phishing and Social Engineering:
- Email phishing and spear-phishing
- Vishing (voice phishing) and smishing (SMS phishing)
- Pretexting and baiting

c) Man-in-the-Middle (MitM) Attacks:
- Session hijacking
- SSL stripping
- Wi-Fi eavesdropping
    d) Denial-of-Service (DoS) and Distributed Denial-of-Service (DDoS):
- Volumetric attacks
- Protocol attacks
- Application layer attacks
    e) SQL Injection and Cross-Site Scripting (XSS):
- Exploiting vulnerabilities in web applications
- Injecting malicious code into trusted websites
    f) Zero-Day Exploits:
- Attacks targeting previously unknown vulnerabilities
- Often used in advanced persistent threats
    g) Password Attacks:
- Brute force attacks
- Dictionary attacks
- Credential stuffing
    h) Insider Threats:
- Malicious insiders
- Negligent employees
- Compromised credentials

Understanding these threats allows organizations to develop targeted defenses and mitigation strategies.

5. Cybersecurity Technologies and Strategies

A comprehensive cybersecurity approach involves multiple layers of protection:

a) Network Security:
- Firewalls and Intrusion Detection/Prevention Systems (IDS/IPS)
- Virtual Private Networks (VPNs)
- Network segmentation and microsegmentation

b) Endpoint Security:
- Antivirus and anti-malware software
- Endpoint Detection and Response (EDR)
- Mobile Device Management (MDM)

c) Data Security:
- Encryption (at rest and in transit)
- Data Loss Prevention (DLP) tools

- Database Activity Monitoring (DAM)
   d) Identity and Access Management (IAM):
- Multi-factor authentication (MFA)
- Single Sign-On (SSO)
- Privileged Access Management (PAM)
   e) Cloud Security:
- Cloud Access Security Brokers (CASB)
- Cloud Workload Protection Platforms (CWPP)
- Secure Access Service Edge (SASE)
   f) Application Security:
- Web Application Firewalls (WAF)
- Runtime Application Self-Protection (RASP)
- Secure coding practices and DevSecOps
   g) Security Information and Event Management (SIEM):
- Log collection and analysis
- Real-time threat detection
- Incident response automation
   h) Artificial Intelligence and Machine Learning:
- Anomaly detection
- Predictive analytics
- Automated threat hunting

These technologies and strategies work together to create a robust defense against cyber threats, following the principle of defense in depth.

6. Cybersecurity in Various Sectors

Cybersecurity challenges and approaches vary across different sectors:
   a) Financial Services:
- Protection of sensitive financial data
- Compliance with regulations (e.g., PCI DSS)
- Defense against financial fraud and cyber heists
   b) Healthcare:
- Safeguarding patient data (HIPAA compliance)
- Securing medical devices and IoT in healthcare
- Protecting against ransomware targeting hospitals
   c) Government and Defense:
- Protecting critical infrastructure
- Countering nation-state cyber espionage
- Ensuring election security

d) Retail and E-commerce:
- Securing online transactions
- Protecting customer data
- Defending against card skimming and online fraud
    e) Manufacturing and Industrial Control Systems:
- Securing operational technology (OT) environments
- Protecting intellectual property
- Defending against industrial espionage
    f) Education:
- Protecting student data
- Securing research information
- Addressing challenges of BYOD in educational settings
    g) Telecommunications:
- Securing network infrastructure
- Protecting against DDoS attacks
- Ensuring privacy of communications
    Each sector faces unique challenges and requires tailored cybersecurity strategies to address its specific risks and regulatory requirements.

7. The Human Factor in Cybersecurity

While technological solutions are crucial, the human element remains a critical factor in cybersecurity:
    a) Security Awareness Training:
- Educating employees about cyber threats and best practices
- Regular phishing simulations and testing
- Cultivating a security-aware culture
    b) Social Engineering Prevention:
- Training to recognize and resist manipulation tactics
- Implementing verification procedures for sensitive requests
- Encouraging skepticism and caution
    c) Insider Threat Management:
- Background checks and continuous vetting
- Behavioral analytics to detect anomalous activities
- Access controls and principle of least privilege
    d) Cybersecurity Workforce Development:
- Addressing the global shortage of cybersecurity professionals
- Promoting diversity in the cybersecurity field
- Continuous learning and skill development programs

e) Human-Centric Security Design:
- Designing security measures that are user-friendly
- Balancing security with usability to prevent workarounds
- Involving end-users in security decision-making processes
f) Incident Response and Human Decision-Making:
- Training for effective incident response
- Developing decision-making frameworks for cyber crises
- Stress testing and scenario planning

8. Regulatory and Compliance Frameworks

Cybersecurity is increasingly governed by various regulations and standards:

a) General Data Protection Regulation (GDPR):
- EU regulation on data protection and privacy
- Impacts organizations worldwide dealing with EU citizens' data
b) California Consumer Privacy Act (CCPA):
- Similar to GDPR, focusing on California residents' data rights
- Potential model for other U.S. state privacy laws
c) Health Insurance Portability and Accountability Act (HIPAA):
- U.S. regulation for protecting medical information
- Applies to healthcare providers, insurers, and their business associates
d) Payment Card Industry Data Security Standard (PCI DSS):
- Security standard for organizations handling credit card data
- Mandated by major card brands
e) National Institute of Standards and Technology (NIST) Cybersecurity Framework:
- Voluntary framework for improving critical infrastructure cybersecurity
- Widely adopted beyond its original scope
f) ISO/IEC 27001:
- International standard for information security management systems
- Provides a systematic approach to managing sensitive company information
g) Sarbanes-Oxley Act (SOX):
- U.S. law requiring public companies to have proper internal control structures
- Includes IT controls related to financial reporting

Compliance with these regulations is not only a legal requirement but also a way to ensure a baseline level of security practices.

9. Emerging Trends in Cybersecurity

The field of cybersecurity is constantly evolving. Some key emerging trends include:

a) Zero Trust Security:
- Assumes no trust by default, even within the network perimeter
- Continuous verification of every user, device, and transaction

b) AI and Machine Learning in Cybersecurity:
- Automated threat detection and response
- Predictive analytics for proactive defense
- AI-powered attacks and defenses

c) Cloud-Native Security:
- Security tools and practices designed for cloud environments
- Shift from perimeter-based to identity-based security

d) DevSecOps:
- Integration of security practices throughout the software development lifecycle
- Automated security testing and continuous monitoring

e) Extended Detection and Response (XDR):
- Unified security incident detection and response across multiple security layers
- Integration of endpoint, network, and cloud security

f) Quantum Cryptography:
- Leveraging quantum mechanics for unbreakable encryption
- Preparing for post-quantum cryptography to counter quantum computing threats

g) Cyber Insurance:
- Growing market for insurance against cyber incidents
- Influencing cybersecurity practices through policy requirements

h) Privacy-Enhancing Technologies (PETs):
- Homomorphic encryption allowing computation on encrypted data
- Federated learning for collaborative AI without sharing raw data

10. Challenges in Cybersecurity

Despite advancements, several challenges persist in the cybersecurity field:

a) Complexity of Systems:
- Increasing interconnectivity and interdependence of systems
- Difficulty in securing legacy systems alongside modern technologies

b) Speed of Threat Evolution:
- Rapid development of new attack techniques

- Challenge of keeping defenses up-to-date
    c) Skills Shortage:
- Global shortage of qualified cybersecurity professionals
- Difficulty in retaining talent due to high demand
    d) Balancing Security and Usability:
- Ensuring security measures don't impede productivity
- Making security intuitive and user-friendly
    e) Supply Chain Security:
- Vulnerabilities introduced through third-party vendors and suppliers
- Difficulty in ensuring security across complex supply chains
    f) IoT Security:
- Securing billions of connected devices with limited computing power
- Lack of standardization in IoT security
    g) Cloud Security Challenges:
- Shared responsibility model causing confusion
- Data sovereignty and compliance issues in multi-cloud environments
    h) Cyber-Physical Systems Security:
- Protecting systems where digital and physical worlds intersect
- Potential for cyber attacks to cause physical harm

11. The Future of Cybersecurity

Looking ahead, several factors are likely to shape the future of cybersecurity:

    a) Quantum Computing:
- Potential to break current encryption methods
- Development of quantum-resistant cryptography
    b) 5G and Beyond:
- New security challenges and opportunities with 5G networks
- Increased attack surface with more connected devices
    c) Biometric Security:
- Advanced biometrics for authentication (e.g., behavioral biometrics)
- Concerns about privacy and potential for biometric data breaches
    d) Autonomous Cybersecurity Systems:
- AI-driven systems capable of autonomous threat detection and response
- Potential for AI vs. AI cyber warfare
    e) Cybersecurity in Space:
- Protecting satellite communications and space-based assets
- Securing future space-based internet systems

f) Brain-Computer Interfaces:
- New frontier of cybersecurity protecting neural data
- Ethical considerations in securing thought-driven interfaces
   g) Regulatory Evolution:
- Increasing government involvement in cybersecurity
- Potential for global cybersecurity treaties and standards
   h) Cybersecurity Education:
- Integration of cybersecurity into core educational curricula
- Continuous learning platforms for keeping skills current

12. Conclusion

Cybersecurity in the digital age is a complex, multifaceted field that touches every aspect of our increasingly connected world. As technology continues to advance, the importance of robust cybersecurity measures only grows. From individual users to large corporations and governments, everyone has a role to play in maintaining a secure digital environment.

The challenges are significant: evolving threats, technological complexity, regulatory pressures, and a persistent skills shortage. However, the field is also marked by rapid innovation, with emerging technologies like AI, quantum computing, and advanced biometrics offering new tools for defense.

Looking to the future, cybersecurity will likely become even more integrated into our daily lives and business operations. As the line between physical and digital worlds continues to blur, cybersecurity will extend beyond traditional IT environments to encompass everything from autonomous vehicles to smart cities and even human-computer interfaces.

Ultimately, success in cybersecurity will require a holistic approach that combines technological solutions with human expertise, strong governance, and a culture of security awareness. As we continue to reap the benefits of our digital age, we must remain vigilant and proactive in protecting our digital assets, identities, and way of life from ever-evolving cyber threats.

CHAPTER SEVEN

BLOCKCHAIN AND DISTRIBUTED LEDGER TECHNOLOGIES

1. Introduction

Blockchain and Distributed Ledger Technologies (DLT) have emerged as transformative forces in the digital landscape, promising to revolutionize how we conduct transactions, manage data, and establish trust in a decentralized world. Since the introduction of Bitcoin in 2008 by the pseudonymous Satoshi Nakamoto, blockchain technology has captured the imagination of technologists, entrepreneurs, and industries alike, expanding far beyond its initial application in cryptocurrencies.

At its core, blockchain is a distributed, immutable ledger that records transactions across a network of computers. This technology enables secure, transparent, and tamper-resistant record-keeping without the need for a central authority. While blockchain is the most well-known form of DLT, the broader category of distributed ledger technologies encompasses various approaches to achieving consensus and maintaining a shared record of information across multiple sites.

The potential applications of blockchain and DLT span numerous sectors, from finance and supply chain management to healthcare and government services. These technologies promise to increase efficiency, reduce costs, enhance transparency, and enable new business models. However, they also face challenges in terms of scalability, energy consumption, regulatory compliance, and widespread adoption.

This comprehensive exploration will delve into the fundamental concepts of blockchain and DLT, examine their key components and variations, and discuss their potential applications and limitations. We will also consider the emerging trends, regulatory landscape, and future prospects of these technologies.

As we navigate through this complex and rapidly evolving field, it becomes clear that blockchain and DLT are not just technological innovations, but catalysts for reimagining how we organize, transact, and collaborate in the digital age. Understanding these technologies is crucial for anyone seeking to grasp the potential future of our increasingly decentralized and interconnected world.

2. Understanding Blockchain Technology

Blockchain technology is fundamentally a distributed ledger of transactions, maintained and verified by a network of participants. Key characteristics include:

a) Decentralization:
- No central authority controls the network
- Participants collectively maintain the ledger

b) Transparency:
- All transactions are visible to network participants
- Enhances trust and auditability

c) Immutability:
- Once recorded, transactions cannot be altered or deleted
- Ensures data integrity and prevents fraud

d) Security:
- Cryptographic techniques secure transactions and user identities
- Resistant to hacking and tampering

e) Consensus:
- Network participants agree on the validity of transactions
- Various mechanisms ensure agreement without central authority

The blockchain operates as a chain of blocks, each containing a set of transactions. Each block is linked to the previous one through a cryptographic hash, creating an unbroken chain of records.

3. Types of Blockchain Networks

Blockchain networks can be categorized into several types:

a) Public Blockchains:
- Open to anyone to participate
- Examples: Bitcoin, Ethereum

- Highly decentralized but can be slower and less efficient
  b) Private Blockchains:
- Restricted to select participants
- Often used in enterprise settings
- More efficient but less decentralized
  c) Permissionless Blockchains:
- Anyone can join and participate without approval
- Typically associated with public blockchains
  d) Permissioned Blockchains:
- Participants need approval to join
- Can be public or private
  e) Consortium or Federated Blockchains:
- Operated by a group of organizations
- Combines elements of public and private blockchains
  f) Hybrid Blockchains:
- Combination of private and public blockchain features
- Allows for customizable transparency and access

Each type has its own advantages and use cases, balancing factors like decentralization, efficiency, and privacy.

4. Distributed Ledger Technology (DLT)

While blockchain is a type of DLT, not all distributed ledgers are blockchains. Key aspects of DLT include:

a) Definition:
- A consensus of replicated, shared, and synchronized digital data
- Geographically spread across multiple sites, countries, or institutions
  b) Types of DLT:
- Blockchain
- Directed Acyclic Graphs (DAG)
- Holochain
- Hashgraph
  c) Key Features:
- Decentralized nature
- No central data store or administration functionality
- Geographical distribution
  d) Differences from Blockchain:
- Not all DLTs group transactions into blocks
- Some DLTs use alternative data structures

e) Advantages:
- Increased efficiency and speed
- Reduced costs by eliminating intermediaries
- Enhanced transparency and auditability

Understanding the broader concept of DLT is crucial for appreciating the full spectrum of decentralized ledger technologies beyond blockchain.

5. Key Components of Blockchain

A blockchain system consists of several key components:

a) Node:
- A computer participating in the blockchain network
- Maintains a copy of the ledger
- Validates and relays transactions

b) Transaction:
- Transfer of value or data between participants
- Basic unit of a blockchain operation

c) Block:
- Collection of transactions over a specific time period
- Contains a reference to the previous block (hash)

d) Chain:
- Sequence of blocks linked cryptographically
- Forms the complete ledger of transactions

e) Cryptographic Hash:
- Unique fingerprint for data
- Ensures data integrity and links blocks together

f) Digital Signatures:
- Proves ownership and authorizes transactions
- Based on public-key cryptography

g) Wallet:
- Stores private keys for transaction authorization
- Interfaces for interacting with the blockchain

h) Mining (in Proof of Work systems):
- Process of creating new blocks
- Involves solving complex mathematical problems

Understanding these components is essential for grasping how blockchain systems operate and interact.

6. Consensus Mechanisms

Consensus mechanisms are crucial for maintaining agreement on the state of the blockchain across all nodes. Common mechanisms include:

a) Proof of Work (PoW):
- Used by Bitcoin and many other cryptocurrencies
- Miners compete to solve complex mathematical puzzles
- Energy-intensive but highly secure

b) Proof of Stake (PoS):
- Validators are chosen based on their stake in the network
- More energy-efficient than PoW
- Examples: Ethereum 2.0, Cardano

c) Delegated Proof of Stake (DPoS):
- Stakeholders vote for "delegates" to validate transactions
- Faster and more efficient than traditional PoS
- Example: EOS

d) Practical Byzantine Fault Tolerance (PBFT):
- Used in some permissioned blockchains
- Relies on a voting system among known validators
- Example: Hyperledger Fabric

e) Proof of Authority (PoA):
- Reputation-based consensus mechanism
- Validators are approved based on their identity
- Often used in private blockchains

f) Proof of Elapsed Time (PoET):
- Developed by Intel for permissioned blockchains
- Uses trusted execution environments to ensure fairness

Each consensus mechanism has its own trade-offs in terms of speed, energy efficiency, decentralization, and security.

7. Smart Contracts

Smart contracts are self-executing contracts with the terms of the agreement directly written into code. They are a crucial feature of many blockchain platforms, particularly Ethereum.

Key aspects of smart contracts:

a) Automation:
- Execute automatically when predefined conditions are met
- Reduce the need for intermediaries

b) Transparency:
- Terms are visible and verifiable on the blockchain
- Reduces disputes and increases trust

c) Immutability:
- Once deployed, cannot be altered

- Ensures contract integrity
    d) Efficiency:
- Streamline processes and reduce transaction costs
- Enable complex, multi-step transactions
    e) Use Cases:
- Financial services (loans, insurance)
- Supply chain management
- Real estate transactions
- Voting systems
    f) Challenges:
- Difficulty in updating or fixing bugs
- Potential for exploits if not properly coded
- Legal status and enforceability in some jurisdictions

Smart contracts are a key driver of blockchain adoption beyond cryptocurrencies, enabling more complex and automated interactions on blockchain networks.

8. Blockchain vs. Traditional Databases

While blockchain shares some similarities with traditional databases, there are key differences:

a) Structure:
- Blockchain: Distributed, linked blocks of data
- Traditional: Centralized, table-based structure
    b) Control:
- Blockchain: Decentralized, shared control
- Traditional: Centralized administration
    c) Immutability:
- Blockchain: Highly resistant to alterations
- Traditional: Can be modified with proper access
    d) Transparency:
- Blockchain: Inherently transparent to all participants
- Traditional: Typically restricted access
    e) Consensus:
- Blockchain: Requires network-wide agreement
- Traditional: Controlled by central authority
    f) Performance:
- Blockchain: Generally slower for read/write operations
- Traditional: Typically faster for high-volume transactions

g) Use Cases:

- Blockchain: Ideal for multi-party scenarios requiring trust and transparency

- Traditional: Efficient for centralized data management and high-speed transactions

Understanding these differences is crucial for determining when blockchain is an appropriate solution compared to traditional database systems.

9. Use Cases and Applications

Blockchain and DLT have potential applications across various industries:

a) Financial Services:

- Cryptocurrencies and digital assets
- Cross-border payments and remittances
- Trade finance and settlement systems

b) Supply Chain Management:

- Product traceability and provenance
- Inventory management
- Supplier verification

c) Healthcare:

- Electronic health records
- Drug traceability
- Clinical trial management

d) Government and Public Sector:

- Digital identity management
- Voting systems
- Land registry and property records

e) Energy Sector:

- Peer-to-peer energy trading
- Renewable energy certificates
- Grid management

f) Education:

- Academic credential verification
- Lifelong learning records
- Copyright and digital rights management

g) Internet of Things (IoT):

- Secure device-to-device communications
- Decentralized IoT networks

- Data integrity for sensor networks
    h) Media and Entertainment:
- Royalty distribution
- Content licensing and rights management
- Anti-piracy measures

These use cases demonstrate the versatility of blockchain and DLT across different sectors, although many are still in early stages of development or adoption.

10. Challenges and Limitations

Despite their potential, blockchain and DLT face several challenges:
    a) Scalability:
- Limited transaction throughput in many public blockchains
- Blockchain bloat as the ledger grows over time
    b) Energy Consumption:
- High energy usage, particularly in Proof of Work systems
- Environmental concerns about blockchain's carbon footprint
    c) Interoperability:
- Lack of standards between different blockchain networks
- Challenges in cross-chain communication and asset transfer
    d) Privacy:
- Public blockchains' transparency can be a privacy concern
- Need for advanced privacy-preserving techniques
    e) Regulatory Uncertainty:
- Unclear or evolving regulations in many jurisdictions
- Compliance challenges, especially in highly regulated industries
    f) User Experience:
- Complex interfaces and technical barriers to entry
- Difficulty in key management and recovery
    g) Oracle Problem:
- Challenges in securely bringing off-chain data onto the blockchain
- Potential centralization point in otherwise decentralized systems
    h) Quantum Computing Threat:
- Future quantum computers could potentially break current cryptographic systems

Addressing these challenges is crucial for the widespread adoption and long-term viability of blockchain and DLT systems.

11. Emerging Trends in Blockchain and DLT

The field of blockchain and DLT is rapidly evolving. Some key trends include:

a) Decentralized Finance (DeFi):
- Blockchain-based financial services without traditional intermediaries
- Includes lending, borrowing, trading, and asset management

b) Non-Fungible Tokens (NFTs):
- Unique digital assets represented on blockchains
- Applications in art, collectibles, gaming, and digital ownership

c) Central Bank Digital Currencies (CBDCs):
- Government-backed digital currencies using blockchain or DLT
- Potential to revolutionize monetary systems

d) Layer 2 Scaling Solutions:
- Off-chain solutions to improve blockchain scalability
- Examples: Lightning Network, Polygon, Optimistic Rollups

e) Blockchain Interoperability:
- Projects focusing on cross-chain communication and asset transfers
- Examples: Polkadot, Cosmos, Chainlink

f) Decentralized Identity:
- Self-sovereign identity solutions using blockchain
- Potential to give individuals control over their personal data

g) Tokenization of Real-World Assets:
- Representing physical assets as digital tokens on a blockchain
- Applications in real estate, commodities, and financial instruments

h) Enterprise Blockchain Adoption:
- Increased implementation of private and consortium blockchains in business settings
- Focus on supply chain, finance, and data sharing use cases

These trends highlight the expanding scope and potential of blockchain and DLT beyond their initial applications in cryptocurrencies.

12. Regulatory Landscape

The regulatory environment for blockchain and DLT is complex and evolving:

a) Cryptocurrency Regulations:
- Varying approaches across jurisdictions, from embracing to banning
- Focus on anti-money laundering (AML) and know-your-customer (KYC) compliance

b) Securities Laws:
- Classification of certain tokens as securities

- Regulatory implications for initial coin offerings (ICOs) and token sales
    c) Data Protection and Privacy:
- Intersection with regulations like GDPR
- Challenges in reconciling data immutability with "right to be forgotten"
    d) Smart Contract Legality:
- Questions about legal enforceability of smart contracts
- Efforts to integrate smart contracts into existing legal frameworks
    e) Central Bank Policies:
- Regulatory approaches to CBDCs and stablecoins
- Impact on monetary policy and financial stability
    f) Industry-Specific Regulations:
- Blockchain applications in regulated industries (e.g., healthcare, finance)
- Need for compliance with existing regulatory frameworks
    g) International Coordination:
- Efforts towards global standards and regulatory cooperation
- Challenges due to differing national approaches

The regulatory landscape continues to evolve as governments and international bodies grapple with the implications of these new technologies.

13. Environmental Considerations

The environmental impact of blockchain, particularly energy consumption, is a growing concern:
    a) Energy Usage in Proof of Work:
- High electricity consumption of Bitcoin and other PoW networks
- Debates about the sustainability of PoW in the long term
    b) Shift to More Sustainable Consensus Mechanisms:
- Move towards Proof of Stake and other energy-efficient alternatives
- Example: Ethereum's transition from PoW to PoS
    c) Green Blockchain Initiatives:
- Use of renewable energy for mining operations
- Development of inherently low-energy blockchain protocols
    d) Carbon Footprint Tracking:
- Blockchain applications for monitoring and reducing carbon emissions
- Tokenization of carbon credits and offsets
    e) E-Waste Concerns:
- Environmental impact of specialized mining hardware
- Need for responsible disposal and recycling practices

Balancing the benefits of blockchain technology with environmental sustainability remains an important challenge for the industry.

14. Future Outlook

The future of blockchain and DLT is likely to be shaped by several factors:

a) Technological Advancements:
- Improvements in scalability and energy efficiency
- Integration with emerging technologies like AI and IoT

b) Mainstream Adoption:
- Increased use in everyday applications and services
- Potential for blockchain to become "invisible" infrastructure

c) Regulatory Developments:
- Clearer regulatory frameworks globally
- Potential impact on innovation and adoption rates

d) Evolving Business Models:
- New decentralized organizational structures (DAOs)
- Transformation of traditional industries

e) Education and Skill Development:
- Growing demand for blockchain and DLT expertise
- Integration of blockchain studies into academic curricula

f) Global Economic Impact:
- Potential reshaping of financial systems and global trade
- Implications for economic inclusion and development

g) Ethical and Social Implications:
- Addressing issues of digital divide and technology access
- Balancing decentralization with societal needs and governance

The future of blockchain and DLT holds both exciting possibilities and significant challenges, requiring ongoing innovation, collaboration, and responsible development.

15. Conclusion

Blockchain and Distributed Ledger Technologies represent a paradigm shift in how we conceptualize trust, transparency, and decentralization in the digital world. From their origins in cryptocurrency to their expanding applications across various sectors, these technologies have demonstrated their potential to revolutionize existing systems and create entirely new possibilities.

While challenges remain, particularly in areas of scalability, energy consumption, regulatory compliance, and widespread adoption, ongoing technological advancements and increasing understanding of these technologies are addressing many of these issues. The integration of blockchain and DLT with other emerging technologies like AI, IoT, and 5G networks promises to unlock even greater potential in the coming years.

As we look to the future, it's clear that blockchain and DLT will play a significant role in shaping our digital landscape. Their impact extends beyond mere technological innovation, touching on fundamental questions of trust, privacy, and the organization of economic and social systems in the digital age.

The full potential of blockchain and DLT is yet to be realized, but it's evident that these technologies will be instrumental in building a more transparent, efficient, and decentralized world. As development continues, it will be crucial to address challenges responsibly, ensuring that the benefits of these technologies are realized while mitigating potential risks and negative impacts.

CHAPTER EIGHT

EXTENDED REALITY (XR): AR, VR, AND MR

1. Introduction to Extended Reality (XR)

Extended Reality (XR) is an umbrella term encompassing a spectrum of immersive technologies that blend the physical and digital worlds. This includes Virtual Reality (VR), Augmented Reality (AR), and Mixed Reality (MR). These technologies are rapidly evolving and have the potential to revolutionize how we interact with information, each other, and our environment.

XR technologies are transforming various sectors, from entertainment and education to healthcare and manufacturing. They offer new ways to visualize data, train professionals, design products, and create immersive experiences. As these technologies continue to advance, they are blurring the lines between the physical and digital realms, opening up new possibilities for human-computer interaction.

The concept of XR is not entirely new, with its roots tracing back to the mid-20th century. However, recent advancements in computing power, display technology, and software development have accelerated the growth and adoption of XR technologies. Today, XR is no longer confined to research labs or niche applications; it's becoming increasingly accessible to consumers and businesses alike.

In this comprehensive exploration of XR, we will delve into each of its primary components: Virtual Reality, Augmented Reality, and Mixed Reality. We'll examine their definitions, historical development, underlying technologies, applications, and challenges. Furthermore, we'll discuss the XR ecosystem, its impact on various industries, and contemplate the future of these transformative technologies.

As we embark on this journey through the world of Extended Reality, we'll uncover how these technologies are not just changing the way we interact with digital content, but also how they're reshaping our perception of reality itself.

2. Virtual Reality (VR)

2.1 Definition and Concepts

Virtual Reality (VR) is a technology that creates a fully immersive digital environment, replacing the user's real-world surroundings with a simulated one. It typically involves wearing a head-mounted display (HMD) that blocks out the physical world and presents a 360-degree digital environment to the user. The key characteristics of VR include:

- Immersion: The feeling of being present in a digital environment.
- Interactivity: The ability to manipulate and interact with objects in the virtual world.
- Sensory feedback: Providing visual, auditory, and sometimes haptic feedback to enhance realism.

2.2 History and Evolution

The concept of VR has roots dating back to the 1960s:
- 1960s: Ivan Sutherland created the first head-mounted display system.
- 1970s-1980s: VR research continued in academic and military settings.
- 1990s: VR gained public attention but failed to meet expectations due to technological limitations.
- 2010s: Resurgence of VR with the development of Oculus Rift and other consumer-grade HMDs.
- 2020s: Ongoing improvements in resolution, field of view, and haptic feedback.

2.3 VR Hardware

Key components of modern VR systems include:
- Head-Mounted Displays (HMDs): Devices like Oculus Quest, HTC Vive, and PlayStation VR.
- Motion Controllers: Hand-held devices for interacting with the virtual environment.
- Tracking Systems: Technologies that monitor the user's position and movement.
- Haptic Feedback Devices: Tools that provide tactile sensations to enhance immersion.

2.4 VR Software and Content

VR software encompasses:

- Development Platforms: Tools like Unity and Unreal Engine for creating VR content.
- Content Distribution Platforms: Stores like Steam VR and Oculus Store for distributing VR applications.
- Applications: Games, educational software, therapeutic tools, and professional applications.

2.5 Applications of VR

VR has found applications in numerous fields:

- Gaming and Entertainment: Immersive gaming experiences and virtual theme parks.
- Education and Training: Simulations for medical procedures, flight training, and hazardous work environments.
- Healthcare: Pain management, phobia treatment, and rehabilitation.
- Architecture and Design: Virtual walkthroughs of buildings and product prototypes.
- Social VR: Platforms for virtual meetings and social interactions.

2.6 Challenges and Limitations

Despite its potential, VR faces several challenges:

- Motion Sickness: Some users experience nausea due to sensory mismatch.
- Hardware Limitations: Current devices still have limitations in resolution and field of view.
- Content Creation: Developing high-quality VR content is time-consuming and expensive.
- Isolation: Full immersion can disconnect users from their physical surroundings.
- Accessibility: Cost and physical requirements can limit widespread adoption.

3. Augmented Reality (AR)

3.1 Definition and Concepts

Augmented Reality (AR) is a technology that overlays digital content onto the real world, enhancing the user's perception of their physical environment. Unlike VR, AR doesn't replace the real world but augments it with computer-generated information. Key characteristics of AR include:

- Real-world integration: Digital content coexists with physical objects.
- Real-time interaction: Users can interact with both physical and digital elements simultaneously.
- Spatial awareness: AR systems understand and respond to the user's

environment.

3.2 History and Evolution

The development of AR has been ongoing for several decades:

- 1968: Ivan Sutherland created the first AR head-mounted display system.

- 1990s: AR research gained momentum in academic and industrial settings.

- 2000s: Early mobile AR applications emerged.

- 2010s: Widespread adoption of AR in mobile apps and specialized devices.

- 2020s: Advancements in AR glasses and integration with AI and 5G technologies.

3.3 AR Hardware

AR can be experienced through various devices:

- Smartphones and Tablets: The most common AR platforms due to their ubiquity.

- AR Glasses: Devices like Microsoft HoloLens and Magic Leap offer hands-free AR experiences.

- Head-up Displays (HUDs): Used in automotive and aviation industries.

- Projection-based AR: Systems that project digital information onto physical surfaces.

3.4 AR Software and Development

AR software ecosystem includes:

- AR Development Kits: Tools like ARKit (Apple) and ARCore (Google) for creating AR applications.

- 3D Modeling and Animation Software: Used to create AR content.

- Computer Vision Libraries: Enable AR systems to recognize and track real-world objects.

- Cloud Services: Provide data storage and processing capabilities for AR applications.

3.5 Applications of AR

AR has found applications in various fields:

- Retail: Virtual try-on for clothing, makeup, and furniture placement.

- Education: Interactive learning experiences and visualizations.

- Navigation: Enhanced GPS systems and indoor navigation.

- Industrial: Assembly instructions, maintenance guidance, and remote expert assistance.

- Entertainment: AR games like Pokémon GO and AR filters in social media apps.

- Marketing: Interactive advertisements and product visualizations.

3.6 Challenges and Limitations

AR faces several challenges in its development and adoption:

- Hardware Limitations: Current AR glasses often have limited field of view and battery life.

- Environmental Understanding: Accurate recognition and tracking of real-world environments can be challenging.

- Social Acceptance: Privacy concerns and the conspicuous nature of AR devices.

- Content Creation: Developing high-quality, contextually relevant AR content is complex.

- Interoperability: Lack of standardization across different AR platforms and devices.

4. Mixed Reality (MR)

4.1 Definition and Concepts

Mixed Reality (MR) is a technology that blends elements of both Virtual Reality and Augmented Reality, creating environments where physical and digital objects coexist and interact in real-time. Key characteristics of MR include:

- Seamless integration: Digital objects appear to be part of the physical world.

- Advanced spatial mapping: MR systems have a deep understanding of the physical environment.

- Natural interactions: Users can interact with digital objects using natural gestures and movements.

4.2 Distinguishing MR from AR and VR

While MR shares characteristics with both AR and VR, it differs in several ways:

- Compared to AR: MR offers more sophisticated integration of digital content with the physical world.

- Compared to VR: MR maintains a connection to the physical environment rather than replacing it entirely.

- Interactivity: MR allows for more complex interactions between physical and digital elements.

4.3 MR Hardware

MR hardware typically includes:

- Head-mounted displays: Devices like Microsoft HoloLens and Magic Leap One.

- Sensors: Depth sensors, cameras, and inertial measurement units for environmental tracking.

- Processing units: Powerful onboard computers to handle real-time rendering and spatial mapping.

- Input devices: Hand tracking systems, eye tracking, and sometimes additional controllers.

4.4 MR Software and Development

The MR software ecosystem includes:

- Development platforms: Tools like Microsoft's Mixed Reality Toolkit and Unity's XR Foundation.

- Spatial mapping software: For creating detailed 3D maps of the physical environment.

- AI and machine learning algorithms: For object recognition and predictive interactions.

- Content creation tools: Specialized software for creating 3D assets and interactions for MR environments.

4.5 Applications of MR

MR has potential applications across various industries:

- Healthcare: Surgical planning and guidance, medical training simulations.

- Engineering and Design: Collaborative 3D modeling and prototyping.

- Education: Interactive learning experiences with 3D models and simulations.

- Manufacturing: Assembly line guidance and quality control.

- Architecture: On-site visualization of building designs and modifications.

- Entertainment: Immersive gaming experiences that blend with the real world.

4.6 Challenges and Limitations

MR faces several challenges in its development and adoption:

- Technical complexity: Integrating digital content seamlessly with the real world is highly challenging.

- Cost: Current MR devices are often expensive, limiting widespread adoption.

- Processing power: Rendering high-quality graphics while maintaining low latency requires significant computational resources.

- Field of view: Many current MR devices offer a limited field of view, affecting immersion.

- Content creation: Developing compelling MR experiences requires specialized skills and tools.

- User experience: Balancing immersion with awareness of the physical environment can be challenging.

5. The XR Ecosystem

5.1 XR Platforms and Frameworks

The XR ecosystem is supported by various platforms and frameworks that enable developers to create immersive experiences:

- Unity and Unreal Engine: Game engines that offer robust XR development capabilities.
- WebXR: A set of standards for creating XR experiences that run in web browsers.
- ARKit and ARCore: AR development frameworks for iOS and Android devices respectively.
- OpenXR: An open standard for XR development, aiming to reduce fragmentation in the industry.
- Vuforia and Wikitude: Platforms specifically designed for AR development.

5.2 Content Creation for XR

Creating content for XR involves several specialized tools and processes:

- 3D Modeling: Software like Blender, Maya, and 3ds Max for creating 3D assets.
- Photogrammetry: Techniques for creating 3D models from photographs.
- 360° Video: Specialized cameras and software for creating immersive video content.
- Spatial Audio: Tools for creating and implementing 3D sound in XR environments.
- Interactive Design: Prototyping tools for designing user interfaces in 3D space.

5.3 XR and Artificial Intelligence

The integration of AI with XR is opening up new possibilities:

- Computer Vision: AI algorithms for object recognition and tracking in AR and MR.
- Natural Language Processing: Enabling more natural interactions with virtual assistants in XR environments.
- Machine Learning: Personalizing XR experiences based on user behavior and preferences.
- AI-generated Content: Using AI to create or modify virtual environments and objects dynamically.
- Predictive Rendering: AI-driven techniques to optimize performance in

XR applications.

5.4 XR Hardware Ecosystem

The XR hardware landscape is diverse and rapidly evolving:

- Head-mounted Displays: From high-end VR headsets to lightweight AR glasses.
- Haptic Devices: Gloves, suits, and controllers that provide tactile feedback.
- Motion Capture Systems: For tracking user movements in VR and MR applications.
- Eye-tracking Technology: Enhancing immersion and enabling foveated rendering.
- Brain-Computer Interfaces: Experimental technologies for direct neural interaction with XR systems.

5.5 XR Standards and Interoperability

Efforts are underway to create standards that ensure interoperability across XR platforms:

- OpenXR: An open standard for XR systems, supported by major industry players.
- WebXR: Enabling XR experiences through web browsers.
- glTF: A standard file format for 3D models used in XR applications.
- Spatial Web: Emerging concepts for standardizing the integration of digital content with physical spaces.

5.6 XR Analytics and User Data

As XR technologies become more prevalent, data analytics play a crucial role:

- User Behavior Analysis: Tracking how users interact with XR environments.
- Performance Metrics: Monitoring and optimizing XR application performance.
- Biometric Data: Collecting and analyzing physiological responses in XR experiences.
- Privacy Considerations: Addressing concerns about data collection in immersive environments.

This cha;ter has provided an overview of the broader XR ecosystem, including the technologies, tools, and considerations that support the development and implementation of XR experiences.

CHAPTER NINE

Big Data and Analytics

1. Introduction to Big Data and Analytics

In the digital age, data has become one of the most valuable assets for organizations across all sectors. The exponential growth in data generation, coupled with advancements in storage and processing capabilities, has given rise to the era of Big Data. This vast amount of information, when properly analyzed, can provide unprecedented insights, driving innovation, improving decision-making, and creating new opportunities for businesses and society at large.

Big Data refers to extremely large datasets that cannot be processed using traditional data processing applications. These datasets are characterized by their volume, variety, and velocity – often referred to as the three V's of Big Data. As technology evolves, two more V's – veracity and value – have been added to this definition, emphasizing the importance of data quality and the insights derived from it.

Analytics, on the other hand, is the process of examining data sets to draw conclusions about the information they contain. In the context of Big Data, analytics involves advanced applications of statistics, computer programming, and operations research to derive meaningful patterns and knowledge from vast and diverse data sources.

The combination of Big Data and Analytics has revolutionized how organizations operate, compete, and create value. From predicting customer behavior to optimizing supply chains, from personalizing healthcare treatments to enhancing cybersecurity, Big Data Analytics is transforming industries and shaping our future.

This comprehensive exploration of Big Data and Analytics will delve into the core concepts, technologies, applications, and challenges associated with this field. We will examine the underlying architectures that support Big Data systems, discuss various analytical techniques and their applications, and explore the ethical considerations that arise from the use of Big Data.

As we navigate through this vast and complex topic, we'll uncover how Big Data and Analytics are not just technological trends, but powerful tools that have the potential to solve some of the world's most pressing problems and drive innovation across all sectors of society.

2. Understanding Big Data

2.1 Definition and Characteristics

Big Data refers to datasets that are so large and complex that traditional data processing applications are inadequate to deal with them. It is characterized by the following key attributes, often referred to as the 5 V's:

1. Volume: The sheer amount of data generated and collected.

2. Velocity: The speed at which new data is generated and moves through systems.

3. Variety: The diverse types of data, including structured, semi-structured, and unstructured data.

4. Veracity: The trustworthiness and quality of the data.

5. Value: The ability to turn the data into meaningful insights and actions.

2.2 Types of Big Data

Big Data can be categorized into three main types:

1. Structured Data: This is data that has a predefined data model and is easily searchable. Examples include relational databases and spreadsheets.

2. Semi-structured Data: This type of data doesn't conform to a rigid structure but has some organizational properties. Examples include XML and JSON files.

3. Unstructured Data: This is data that doesn't have a predefined data model. It includes text documents, images, videos, social media posts, and sensor data.

2.3 Sources of Big Data

Big Data comes from a variety of sources, including:

1. Social Media: Platforms like Facebook, Twitter, and Instagram generate vast amounts of user data.

2. Internet of Things (IoT): Connected devices and sensors continuously produce data about their environment and usage.

3. Transactional Data: Business systems record numerous transactions daily, from point-of-sale to inventory management.

4. Machine-Generated Data: Log files from computers, servers, and other machines contribute significantly to Big Data.

5. Scientific Research: Fields like genomics, climate science, and particle physics generate enormous datasets.

6. Public Records: Governments and public institutions release large datasets for public use.

7. Multimedia: Audio, video, and image files constitute a significant portion of Big Data.

Understanding these characteristics, types, and sources of Big Data is crucial for developing effective strategies to collect, store, process, and analyze this information. The diverse nature of Big Data presents both opportunities and challenges, requiring sophisticated technologies and methodologies to extract meaningful insights.

As we move forward, we'll explore the technologies that enable organizations to harness the power of Big Data, transforming raw information into actionable intelligence.

3. Big Data Technologies

The management and analysis of Big Data require specialized technologies designed to handle large volumes of diverse data at high speeds. These technologies can be broadly categorized into three main areas: storage solutions, processing frameworks, and data integration tools.

3.1 Storage Solutions

Traditional relational databases are often insufficient for storing and managing Big Data. As a result, several alternative storage solutions have emerged:

1. Hadoop Distributed File System (HDFS): A distributed file system designed to store very large datasets across multiple commodity servers.

2. NoSQL Databases: These databases provide flexible schemas for unstructured data. Examples include:
- Document stores (e.g., MongoDB, Couchbase)
- Key-value stores (e.g., Redis, Amazon DynamoDB)
- Column-family stores (e.g., Apache Cassandra, HBase)
- Graph databases (e.g., Neo4j, Amazon Neptune)

3. Data Lakes: Repositories that store raw data in its native format until it's needed. Examples include Amazon S3 and Azure Data Lake.

4. Cloud Storage: Scalable storage solutions provided by cloud providers, such as Google Cloud Storage and Microsoft Azure Blob Storage.

3.2 Processing Frameworks

To process and analyze Big Data efficiently, several frameworks have been developed:

1. Apache Hadoop: An open-source framework for distributed storage and processing of large datasets using the MapReduce programming model.

2. Apache Spark: A fast, in-memory data processing engine that provides APIs in Java, Scala, Python, and R.

3. Apache Flink: A framework for stateful computations over unbounded and bounded data streams.

4. Apache Storm: A real-time computation system for processing fast, large streams of data.

5. Apache Kafka: A distributed streaming platform that can publish, subscribe to, store, and process streams of records in real-time.

6. Presto: An open-source distributed SQL query engine for running interactive analytic queries against data sources of all sizes.

3.3 Data Integration Tools

These tools help in extracting, transforming, and loading (ETL) data from various sources into Big Data systems:

1. Apache NiFi: An easy-to-use, powerful, and reliable system to process and distribute data.

2. Talend: An open-source data integration platform.

3. Informatica PowerCenter: A comprehensive data integration platform for accessing, discovering, and integrating data from various systems.

4. Apache Airflow: A platform to programmatically author, schedule, and monitor workflows.

5. Streamsets: A data collector that helps you ingest, process, and deliver streaming and batch data.

3.4 Analytics and Visualization Tools

Once data is stored and processed, these tools help in analyzing and visualizing the insights:

1. Apache Zeppelin: A web-based notebook that enables data-driven, interactive data analytics and collaborative documents.

2. Jupyter Notebooks: An open-source web application that allows you to create and share documents containing live code, equations, visualizations, and narrative text.

3. Tableau: A powerful data visualization tool that helps in creating interactive, shareable dashboards.

4. Power BI: Microsoft's business analytics service for interactive visualizations and business intelligence capabilities.

5. Elasticsearch and Kibana: Elasticsearch is a search and analytics engine, while Kibana lets you visualize your Elasticsearch data.

These technologies form the backbone of Big Data systems, enabling organizations to store, process, and analyze vast amounts of data efficiently. The choice of specific technologies depends on the organization's needs, existing infrastructure, and the nature of the data being handled.

As the field of Big Data continues to evolve, new technologies and tools are constantly emerging, offering improved performance, scalability, and ease of use. Staying updated with these technological advancements is crucial for organizations looking to leverage Big Data effectively.

4. Data Analytics

Data Analytics is the process of examining datasets to draw conclusions about the information they contain. In the context of Big Data, analytics involves advanced applications of statistics, computer programming, and operations research to derive meaningful patterns and knowledge from vast and diverse data sources.

4.1 Types of Analytics

There are four main types of analytics, each providing different insights and value:

1. Descriptive Analytics: This type answers the question "What happened?" It involves summarizing historical data to provide insights into past events. Techniques include data aggregation and data mining.

2. Diagnostic Analytics: This type answers "Why did it happen?" It involves examining data to understand the causes of past outcomes. Techniques include drill-down, data discovery, data mining, and correlations.

3. Predictive Analytics: This type answers "What is likely to happen?" It uses historical data to forecast future outcomes. Techniques include statistical modeling, forecasting, and machine learning.

4. Prescriptive Analytics: This type answers "What should be done?" It suggests actions to take to achieve desired outcomes or prevent undesired ones. This often involves optimization and simulation techniques.

4.2 Analytical Techniques and Methods

Several techniques are employed in Big Data analytics:

1. Statistical Analysis: Includes methods like regression analysis, factor analysis, and time series analysis.

2. Data Mining: The process of discovering patterns in large datasets involving methods at the intersection of machine learning, statistics, and database systems.

3. Text Analytics: Also known as text mining, this involves deriving high-quality information from text data.

4. Network Analysis: Examines the structure of relationships between entities in a network.

5. Cluster Analysis: Groups similar data points together to discover underlying patterns.

6. Sentiment Analysis: Determines the emotional tone behind a series of words, used to understand attitudes and opinions.

7. Predictive Modeling: Develops models to predict future outcomes based on historical data.

4.3 Machine Learning in Analytics

Machine Learning (ML) has become an integral part of Big Data analytics. It involves developing algorithms that can learn from and make predictions or decisions based on data. Key areas of ML in analytics include:

1. Supervised Learning: Algorithms learn from labeled training data. Examples include classification and regression problems.

2. Unsupervised Learning: Algorithms find hidden patterns in unlabeled data. Clustering and dimensionality reduction are common applications.

3. Reinforcement Learning: Algorithms learn to make decisions by interacting with an environment.

4. Deep Learning: A subset of ML based on artificial neural networks, particularly effective for processing unstructured data like images and text.

4.4 Real-time Analytics

With the increasing velocity of data, real-time analytics has gained prominence. This involves analyzing data as soon as it enters the system, allowing for immediate insights and actions. Technologies like Apache Kafka, Apache Flink, and Apache Storm are often used for real-time data processing and analytics.

4.5 Self-Service Analytics

Self-service analytics tools empower non-technical users to perform queries and generate reports on their own, with minimal IT support. Tools like Tableau, Power BI, and Google Data Studio have made data analytics more accessible to business users.

4.6 Augmented Analytics

This emerging field uses machine learning and natural language processing to automate data preparation, insight discovery, and insight sharing. It aims to make analytics more accessible and user-friendly, potentially transforming how we interact with data.

By leveraging these analytical techniques and methods, organizations can extract valuable insights from their Big Data, enabling data-driven decision making and uncovering new opportunities for innovation and growth.

5. Big Data Architecture

Big Data architecture refers to the framework designed to handle the ingestion, processing, and analysis of data that is too large or complex for traditional database systems. A well-designed Big Data architecture should be able to handle the volume, velocity, and variety of Big Data while ensuring data quality, security, and accessibility.

5.1 Data Ingestion

This is the first layer of the Big Data architecture, responsible for collecting data from various sources:

1. Batch Ingestion: For large volumes of data collected over time.

2. Real-time Ingestion: For streaming data that needs to be processed immediately.

3. Data Integration Tools: ETL (Extract, Transform, Load) or ELT (Extract, Load, Transform) processes.

Technologies used: Apache Kafka, Apache Flume, Apache NiFi, AWS Kinesis.

5.2 Data Storage

This layer handles the storage of raw and processed data:

1. Distributed File Systems: For storing large volumes of unstructured data.

2. NoSQL Databases: For flexible schema and horizontal scalability.

3. Data Warehouses: For structured data optimized for analytics.

4. Data Lakes: For storing raw data in its native format.

Technologies used: Hadoop Distributed File System (HDFS), Apache Cassandra, Amazon S3, Google BigQuery.

5.3 Data Processing

This layer is responsible for cleaning, transforming, and preparing data for analysis:

1. Batch Processing: For processing large volumes of static data.

2. Stream Processing: For real-time processing of streaming data.

3. Lambda Architecture: Combines batch and stream processing.

4. Kappa Architecture: Uses stream processing for both real-time and batch analytics.

Technologies used: Apache Hadoop, Apache Spark, Apache Flink, Apache Storm.

5.4 Data Analysis and Visualization

This layer focuses on deriving insights from the processed data and presenting them in an understandable format:

1. Analytics Engines: For running complex queries and machine learning algorithms.

2. Business Intelligence Tools: For creating reports and dashboards.

3. Data Visualization Tools: For creating interactive visual representations of data.

Technologies used: Apache Spark MLlib, TensorFlow, Tableau, Power BI.

5.5 Data Governance and Security

This cross-cutting concern ensures data quality, privacy, and security throughout the architecture:

1. Data Catalogs: For metadata management and data discovery.

2. Access Control: For managing user permissions and data access.

3. Data Encryption: For protecting sensitive data.

4. Data Lineage: For tracking the data's origin and transformations.

Technologies used: Apache Atlas, Apache Ranger, AWS IAM.

5.6 Orchestration and Workflow Management

This layer manages and coordinates the various components of the Big Data architecture:

1. Job Scheduling: For managing and scheduling data processing tasks.

2. Workflow Management: For defining and managing complex data pipelines.

3. Resource Management: For allocating computational resources efficiently.

Technologies used: Apache Airflow, Apache Oozie, Kubernetes.

5.7 Monitoring and Logging

This layer provides visibility into the performance and health of the Big Data system:

1. System Monitoring: For tracking system performance and resource utilization.

2. Log Management: For collecting and analyzing system and application logs.

3. Alerting: For notifying administrators of issues or anomalies.

Technologies used: Prometheus, ELK Stack (Elasticsearch, Logstash, Kibana), Grafana.

A well-designed Big Data architecture should be scalable, flexible, and resilient. It should be able to handle increasing data volumes and evolving business requirements. The specific technologies and components used may vary depending on the organization's needs, existing infrastructure, and the nature of the data being processed.

As Big Data technologies continue to evolve, architectures are becoming more modular and cloud-native, leveraging containerization and microservices to provide greater flexibility and scalability.

6. Challenges in Big Data and Analytics

While Big Data and Analytics offer tremendous opportunities, they also present significant challenges. Organizations must address these challenges to fully leverage the potential of their data assets.

6.1 Data Quality and Consistency

Ensuring data quality is crucial for deriving accurate insights:

- Data Cleansing: Identifying and correcting inaccurate or incomplete data.

- Data Integration: Combining data from multiple sources while maintaining consistency.

- Data Governance: Establishing policies and procedures for data management.

- Data Lineage: Tracking the origin and transformations of data throughout its lifecycle.

6.2 Privacy and Security

As data becomes more valuable, protecting it becomes increasingly important:

- Data Encryption: Securing data both at rest and in transit.

- Access Control: Implementing robust authentication and authorization mechanisms.

- Compliance: Adhering to regulations like GDPR, CCPA, and industry-specific standards.

- Data Anonymization: Protecting individual privacy in large datasets.

6.3 Scalability and Performance

Managing and processing ever-increasing volumes of data efficiently:

- Infrastructure Scalability: Designing systems that can grow with data volume and user demand.
- Query Performance: Optimizing data structures and algorithms for faster data retrieval and analysis.
- Real-time Processing: Handling streaming data and providing real-time insights.
- Cost Management: Balancing performance requirements with infrastructure costs.

6.4 Skill Gap

The shortage of professionals with Big Data and Analytics expertise:

- Data Scientists: High demand for individuals who can derive insights from complex data.
- Data Engineers: Need for professionals who can design and maintain Big Data infrastructures.
- Analytics Translators: Requirement for individuals who can bridge the gap between technical teams and business stakeholders.
- Continuous Learning: Keeping up with rapidly evolving technologies and methodologies.

6.5 Data Silos

Overcoming organizational and technological barriers to data sharing:

- Cross-departmental Collaboration: Encouraging data sharing across different business units.
- Legacy Systems Integration: Connecting modern Big Data systems with existing enterprise applications.
- Data Standardization: Establishing common data formats and definitions across the organization.

6.6 Ethical Considerations

Addressing the ethical implications of Big Data and AI:

- Algorithmic Bias: Ensuring that analytics models don't perpetuate or amplify existing biases.
- Transparency: Providing explanations for AI-driven decisions, especially in sensitive areas.
- Data Ownership: Clarifying rights and responsibilities regarding data usage and sharing.

6.7 Data Overload

Managing the sheer volume and complexity of available data:

- Data Relevance: Identifying which data is truly valuable for decision-making.

- Information Overload: Presenting insights in a clear, actionable manner to avoid overwhelming users.
- Storage Optimization: Balancing data retention needs with storage costs and performance.

6.8 Technology Evolution

Keeping pace with rapidly changing Big Data technologies:

- Technology Selection: Choosing the right tools and platforms from a crowded marketplace.
- Integration Challenges: Ensuring new technologies work seamlessly with existing systems.
- Obsolescence: Managing the risk of technologies becoming outdated quickly.

6.9 Return on Investment (ROI)

Demonstrating the value of Big Data initiatives:

- Measuring Impact: Developing metrics to quantify the benefits of data-driven decisions.
- Project Prioritization: Focusing on high-value use cases that align with business objectives.
- Change Management: Encouraging adoption of data-driven practices across the organization.

Addressing these challenges requires a combination of technological solutions, organizational changes, and strategic planning. As the field of Big Data and Analytics continues to evolve, new challenges will emerge, requiring ongoing adaptation and innovation.

7. Applications of Big Data Analytics

Big Data Analytics has found applications across various industries, transforming how organizations operate and make decisions. Here are some key areas where Big Data Analytics is making a significant impact:

7.1 Business and Finance

- Customer Analytics: Understanding customer behavior, preferences, and predicting future needs.
- Risk Management: Identifying and mitigating financial, operational, and market risks.
- Fraud Detection: Using anomaly detection techniques to identify fraudulent transactions.
- Algorithmic Trading: Analyzing market data in real-time to make automated trading decisions.
- Supply Chain Optimization: Improving efficiency and reducing costs in

logistics and inventory management.

7.2 Healthcare

- Predictive Diagnostics: Using patient data to predict potential health issues before they become critical.
- Personalized Medicine: Tailoring treatments based on individual patient characteristics and genetic makeup.
- Epidemiology: Tracking disease spread and predicting outbreaks.
- Drug Discovery: Analyzing large datasets to identify potential new drugs and treatments.
- Hospital Administration: Optimizing resource allocation and improving patient care processes.

7.3 Manufacturing and Industry 4.0

- Predictive Maintenance: Analyzing sensor data to predict equipment failures before they occur.
- Quality Control: Using real-time data analysis to identify and correct production issues.
- Supply Chain Optimization: Improving inventory management and logistics.
- Energy Management: Optimizing energy consumption in production processes.
- Product Development: Using customer data to inform new product design and features.

7.4 Smart Cities and IoT

- Traffic Management: Analyzing traffic patterns to optimize signal timing and reduce congestion.
- Energy Grid Optimization: Balancing energy supply and demand in real-time.
- Public Safety: Using predictive analytics to allocate law enforcement resources efficiently.
- Waste Management: Optimizing garbage collection routes and schedules.
- Urban Planning: Using data to inform city development decisions.

7.5 E-commerce and Digital Marketing

- Personalized Recommendations: Suggesting products based on user behavior and preferences.
- Dynamic Pricing: Adjusting prices in real-time based on demand, competition, and other factors.
- Customer Segmentation: Dividing customers into groups for targeted marketing campaigns.

- Sentiment Analysis: Analyzing social media and customer feedback to gauge brand perception.
- Conversion Rate Optimization: Analyzing user behavior to improve website design and functionality.

7.6 Telecommunications

- Network Optimization: Analyzing network traffic to improve service quality and efficiency.
- Churn Prediction: Identifying customers likely to switch providers and taking preventive action.
- Fraud Detection: Identifying unusual usage patterns that may indicate fraudulent activity.
- Infrastructure Planning: Using data to inform decisions about network expansion and upgrades.

7.7 Education

- Personalized Learning: Tailoring educational content and pace to individual student needs.
- Student Performance Prediction: Identifying students at risk of falling behind or dropping out.
- Curriculum Optimization: Analyzing student performance data to improve course content and delivery.
- Resource Allocation: Optimizing the use of educational resources based on demand and effectiveness.

7.8 Agriculture

- Precision Farming: Using data from sensors, satellites, and weather forecasts to optimize crop management.
- Livestock Management: Monitoring animal health and optimizing feeding strategies.
- Yield Prediction: Using historical data and machine learning to forecast crop yields.
- Supply Chain Optimization: Improving the efficiency of food production and distribution.

7.9 Sports and Entertainment

- Performance Analytics: Analyzing player and team performance data to inform strategy.
- Fan Engagement: Personalizing content and experiences based on fan preferences and behavior.
- Content Recommendation: Suggesting movies, music, or games based on user preferences and behavior.

- Ticket Pricing: Dynamically adjusting ticket prices based on demand and other factors.

These applications demonstrate the wide-ranging impact of Big Data Analytics across various sectors. As technology continues to advance and more data becomes available, we can expect to see even more innovative applications emerge, further transforming industries and creating new opportunities for value creation.

8. Future Trends in Big Data and Analytics

As technology continues to evolve, several trends are shaping the future of Big Data and Analytics:

8.1 Edge Computing

Edge computing involves processing data closer to where it's generated, rather than in a centralized data-processing warehouse:

- Reduced Latency: Enables real-time processing for time-sensitive applications.
- Bandwidth Conservation: Reduces the amount of data that needs to be transmitted to central locations.
- Enhanced Privacy: Allows for local processing of sensitive data.
- IoT Integration: Facilitates more efficient processing of data from IoT devices.

8.2 AI and Deep Learning Integration

The integration of Artificial Intelligence and Deep Learning with Big Data is becoming more sophisticated:

- Automated Machine Learning (AutoML): Makes machine learning more accessible to non-experts.
- Natural Language Processing (NLP): Enables more advanced text analysis and human-computer interaction.
- Computer Vision: Enhances the ability to extract insights from image and video data.
- Reinforcement Learning: Allows systems to learn optimal behaviors through interaction with their environment.

8.3 Quantum Computing

While still in early stages, quantum computing has the potential to revolutionize Big Data processing:

- Complex Problem Solving: Could solve certain types of problems exponentially faster than classical computers.
- Cryptography: May lead to new encryption methods and potentially break existing ones.

- Optimization: Could significantly improve optimization algorithms used in various industries.

8.4 Augmented Analytics

This emerging field uses machine learning and AI to enhance how data is analyzed and how insights are shared:

- Automated Insights: AI-driven systems that can automatically identify and explain key findings in data.

- Natural Language Generation: Translating complex data insights into easy-to-understand narratives.

- Augmented Data Preparation: AI-assisted tools for data cleaning, integration, and feature engineering.

8.5 Data Fabric Architecture

Data fabric provides a unified architecture for data management across diverse environments:

- Seamless Integration: Enables smooth data flow between on-premises, multi-cloud, and edge environments.

- Data Democratization: Makes it easier for non-technical users to access and work with data.

- Adaptive Governance: Provides flexible, context-aware data governance across different environments.

8.6 Explainable AI (XAI)

As AI systems become more complex, there's a growing need for transparency and interpretability:

- Model Interpretability: Developing techniques to understand how AI models make decisions.

- Regulatory Compliance: Meeting growing regulatory requirements for AI transparency.

- Trust Building: Increasing user confidence in AI-driven systems.

8.7 Data as a Service (DaaS)

The concept of offering data products and services is gaining traction:

- Data Marketplaces: Platforms for buying and selling data sets.

- API-driven Data Access: Making it easier to integrate external data sources into applications.

- Specialized Data Products: Curated datasets for specific industries or use cases.

8.8 Continuous Intelligence

This involves the integration of real-time analytics into business operations:

- Real-time Decision Making: Enabling immediate responses to changing conditions.
- Predictive Operations: Anticipating issues and opportunities before they occur.
- Automated Actions: Systems that can make decisions and take actions without human intervention.

8.9 Data Ethics and Privacy

As data becomes more pervasive, ethical considerations are becoming increasingly important:

- Privacy-preserving Analytics: Techniques like federated learning that allow analysis without exposing raw data.
- Ethical AI Frameworks: Guidelines and tools for developing AI systems that are fair and unbiased.
- Data Sovereignty: Addressing concerns about data ownership and cross-border data flows.

8.10 Blockchain in Big Data

Blockchain technology is being explored for its potential in data management and analytics:

- Data Provenance: Tracking the origin and transformations of data.
- Decentralized Analytics: Enabling secure, distributed data processing.
- Smart Contracts: Automating data sharing and usage agreements.

These trends indicate that the field of Big Data and Analytics is poised for significant advancements in the coming years. As these technologies mature, they promise to deliver more powerful, efficient, and accessible data-driven solutions across various industries.

9. Ethical Considerations in Big Data

As Big Data becomes increasingly integral to business operations and decision-making processes, it raises significant ethical questions that organizations must address:

9.1 Data Privacy

Protecting individual privacy is a primary ethical concern in Big Data:

- Informed Consent: Ensuring individuals understand how their data will be used and have given permission for its collection and use.
- Data Minimization: Collecting only the data necessary for specific purposes.
- Right to be Forgotten: Allowing individuals to request the deletion of their personal data.
- Anonymization and Pseudonymization: Techniques to protect individual

identities in datasets.

9.2 Data Security

Safeguarding data from unauthorized access and breaches:

- Encryption: Protecting data both at rest and in transit.
- Access Controls: Implementing robust authentication and authorization mechanisms.
- Data Breach Response: Having plans in place to respond to potential data breaches.
- Regular Security Audits: Continuously assessing and improving security measures.

9.3 Algorithmic Bias

Ensuring that data analytics and AI systems don't perpetuate or amplify existing biases:

- Diverse Training Data: Using representative datasets to train AI models.
- Bias Detection: Implementing tools and processes to identify potential biases in algorithms.
- Fairness Metrics: Developing and applying metrics to assess the fairness of algorithmic decisions.
- Human Oversight: Maintaining human involvement in critical decision-making processes.

9.4 Transparency and Explainability

Making data processes and algorithmic decision-making understandable:

- Explainable AI: Developing AI models that can provide explanations for their decisions.
- Data Lineage: Tracking the sources and transformations of data used in analytics.
- Algorithmic Transparency: Providing clear information about how automated systems make decisions.
- Right to Explanation: Giving individuals the ability to understand decisions made about them by automated systems.

9.5 Data Ownership and Control

Clarifying rights and responsibilities regarding data:

- Data Ownership: Defining who owns data, especially in complex ecosystems involving multiple parties.
- Data Portability: Allowing individuals to transfer their data between different service providers.
- Terms of Service: Ensuring clear and fair terms for data usage in user agreements.

- Data Stewardship: Responsible management of data on behalf of individuals and organizations.

9.6 Digital Divide and Data Equity

Addressing inequalities in data access and benefits:

- Data Accessibility: Ensuring equal access to data and analytics tools across different groups.
- Representative Data: Ensuring datasets represent diverse populations.
- Capacity Building: Promoting data literacy and skills across different communities.
- Inclusive Design: Developing data systems and applications that consider diverse user needs.

9.7 Surveillance and Data Collection

Balancing security needs with individual privacy rights:

- Proportionality: Ensuring data collection is proportionate to its intended use.
- Transparency: Being clear about what data is being collected and why.
- Oversight: Implementing checks and balances on data collection practices.
- Purpose Limitation: Using data only for the purposes for which it was collected.

9.8 Ethical Use of Predictive Analytics

Ensuring responsible use of predictive models:

- Impact Assessment: Evaluating the potential consequences of predictive models on individuals and society.
- Avoiding Discrimination: Ensuring predictive models don't lead to unfair treatment of certain groups.
- Human in the Loop: Maintaining human oversight in critical predictive systems.
- Model Validation: Regularly testing and validating predictive models for accuracy and fairness.

9.9 Cross-Border Data Flows

Addressing ethical issues in global data transfers:

- Data Sovereignty: Respecting national laws and regulations regarding data.
- International Standards: Working towards global ethical standards for data handling.
- Cultural Sensitivity: Considering cultural differences in attitudes towards data privacy and use.

9.10 Environmental Impact

Considering the ecological footprint of Big Data operations:

- Energy Efficiency: Optimizing data centers and analytics processes for energy efficiency.

- Sustainable Practices: Implementing environmentally friendly practices in data management.

- E-Waste Management: Responsibly disposing of outdated hardware used in Big Data operations.

Addressing these ethical considerations is crucial for building trust in Big Data systems and ensuring that the benefits of data analytics are realized without compromising individual rights or societal values. Organizations need to develop robust ethical frameworks, engage in ongoing dialogue with stakeholders, and stay adaptable as new ethical challenges emerge in this rapidly evolving field.

10. Implementing Big Data Analytics

Successfully implementing Big Data Analytics requires a strategic approach that aligns technology, processes, and people. Here are key considerations for organizations looking to leverage Big Data:

10.1 Strategy Development

- Define Clear Objectives: Identify specific business goals that Big Data can address.

- Assess Current State: Evaluate existing data infrastructure, skills, and processes.

- Develop a Roadmap: Create a phased plan for implementing Big Data initiatives.

- Align with Business Strategy: Ensure Big Data initiatives support overall business objectives.

10.2 Data Governance

- Establish Policies: Define rules for data collection, storage, use, and disposal.

- Ensure Data Quality: Implement processes to maintain data accuracy and consistency.

- Define Roles and Responsibilities: Clarify who is responsible for various aspects of data management.

- Compliance: Ensure adherence to relevant regulations (e.g., GDPR, CCPA).

10.3 Infrastructure Setup

- Choose Technologies: Select appropriate tools and platforms based on specific needs.

- Scalability: Design infrastructure to handle growing data volumes and user demands.

- Integration: Ensure new systems integrate with existing IT infrastructure.

- Security: Implement robust security measures to protect data and systems.

10.4 Data Collection and Integration

- Identify Data Sources: Determine relevant internal and external data sources.

- Data Ingestion: Implement processes for efficient data collection and storage.

- Data Integration: Combine data from various sources into a unified view.

- Real-time vs. Batch Processing: Determine appropriate processing methods for different data types.

10.5 Analytics Capabilities

- Choose Analytics Tools: Select tools that match your organization's needs and skill levels.

- Develop Models: Create analytical models to derive insights from data.

- Automation: Implement automated analytics processes where appropriate.

- Visualization: Develop effective ways to present insights to stakeholders.

10.6 Building an Analytics Team

- Skill Assessment: Identify required skills and any gaps in current capabilities.

- Recruitment: Hire key roles such as data scientists, data engineers, and analytics translators.

- Training: Provide ongoing training to keep the team updated with latest technologies and methodologies.

- Collaboration: Foster a culture of collaboration between technical teams and business units.

10.7 Change Management

- Stakeholder Engagement: Involve key stakeholders throughout the implementation process.

- Communication: Clearly communicate the benefits and changes brought by Big Data initiatives.

- Training: Provide training to end-users on new tools and data-driven processes.

- Cultural Shift: Foster a data-driven culture across the organization.

10.8 Measuring Success

- Define KPIs: Establish clear metrics to measure the success of Big Data initiatives.

- Regular Evaluation: Continuously assess the performance and impact of

Big Data projects.

- Feedback Loop: Use insights from evaluations to refine and improve Big Data strategies.

- ROI Analysis: Quantify the business value generated by Big Data analytics.

10.9 Ethical Considerations

- Develop Ethics Guidelines: Establish clear guidelines for ethical data use.

- Privacy Protection: Implement strong data privacy measures.

- Transparency: Be open about how data is collected and used.

- Bias Mitigation: Implement processes to detect and mitigate bias in data and algorithms.

10.10 Continuous Improvement

- Stay Informed: Keep up with the latest trends and technologies in Big Data.

- Experiment: Encourage experimentation with new analytics techniques and tools.

- Scalability: Plan for scaling successful pilots across the organization.

- Adapt and Evolve: Continuously refine your Big Data strategy based on learnings and changing business needs.

Implementing Big Data Analytics is a complex undertaking that requires careful planning, significant resources, and ongoing commitment. However, when done effectively, it can provide organizations with powerful insights, driving innovation, improving decision-making, and creating competitive advantages.

The key to success lies in viewing Big Data Analytics not as a one-time project, but as a fundamental shift in how an organization operates and makes decisions. It requires ongoing investment, adaptation, and a commitment to fostering a data-driven culture throughout the organization.

DIGITAL TRANSFORMATION AND BUSINESS MODELS

1. Introduction

Digital transformation has become a pivotal force reshaping the global business landscape in the 21st century. As technological advancements continue to accelerate at an unprecedented pace, organizations across all sectors are compelled to adapt and evolve their operational strategies, customer engagement approaches, and fundamental business models. This comprehensive exploration delves into the multifaceted realm of digital transformation and its profound impact on business models.

The concept of digital transformation extends far beyond mere digitization of existing processes. It encompasses a fundamental reimagining of how an organization delivers value to its customers, leveraging digital technologies to create new or modify existing business processes, culture, and customer experiences. This transformation is not just about technology adoption; it's a strategic, cultural change that requires organizations to continually challenge the status quo, experiment, and get comfortable with failure.

As we navigate through this chapter, we will explore the core concepts of digital transformation, its influence on traditional and emerging business models, and the key technologies driving this change. We will examine how companies across various industries are adapting their business models to thrive in the digital age, supported by real-world case studies of successful transformations. Additionally, we will address the challenges and risks associated with digital transformation and look ahead to future trends that will shape the business landscape.

The significance of this topic cannot be overstated. In an era where digital natives like Amazon, Google, and Uber have disrupted entire industries, established companies must embrace digital transformation to remain competitive. However, this journey is complex and fraught with challenges. By understanding the principles, strategies, and pitfalls of digital transformation, organizations can better position themselves to succeed in an increasingly digital world.

This chapter aims to provide a comprehensive overview of digital transformation and its impact on business models, offering insights and strategies for organizations embarking on or continuing their digital transformation journey. Through this exploration, we hope to equip readers with the knowledge and understanding necessary to navigate the digital future confidently and successfully.

2. Understanding Digital Transformation

Digital transformation is a comprehensive and strategic approach to leveraging digital technologies and capabilities to fundamentally change how businesses operate and deliver value to customers. It goes beyond simply digitizing existing processes or implementing new technologies; it involves a cultural shift that requires organizations to continually challenge the status quo, experiment with new approaches, and embrace change.

Key Aspects of Digital Transformation:

1. Customer Experience: At the heart of digital transformation is the focus on enhancing customer experience. This involves using digital technologies to better understand customer needs, personalize interactions, and create seamless omnichannel experiences.

2. Operational Agility: Digital transformation enables organizations to become more agile and responsive to market changes. This includes automating processes, leveraging data for decision-making, and adopting flexible work models.

3. Business Model Innovation: Digital technologies often enable entirely new business models or significant modifications to existing ones. This might involve creating new revenue streams, entering new markets, or fundamentally changing how value is delivered to customers.

4. Cultural and Organizational Change: Successful digital transformation requires a shift in organizational culture towards one that embraces innovation, continuous learning, and adaptability.

5. Data-Driven Decision Making: Leveraging big data and analytics to inform strategic decisions is a crucial component of digital transformation.

Stages of Digital Transformation:

1. Digitization: The process of converting analog information into digital form. This is often the first step in digital transformation.

2. Digitalization: Using digital technologies to change business processes. This goes beyond mere digitization to actually modify how work is done.

3. Digital Transformation: The most comprehensive stage, involving fundamental changes to business models and organizational structures based on digital capabilities.

Drivers of Digital Transformation:

1. Changing Customer Expectations: Customers now expect personalized, seamless, and instant experiences across all touchpoints.

2. Technological Advancements: Emerging technologies like AI, IoT, and blockchain are creating new possibilities for business innovation.

3. Competitive Pressure: As digital natives disrupt traditional industries, established companies must transform to remain competitive.

4. Operational Efficiency: Digital technologies offer opportunities for significant cost savings and efficiency improvements.

5. Market Disruption: Digital transformation can help companies stay ahead of market disruptions or even become the disruptors themselves.

Impact on Different Business Functions:

1. Marketing: Digital transformation enables more targeted, personalized marketing efforts and better measurement of marketing effectiveness.

2. Sales: Digital tools can enhance the sales process through better lead generation, customer relationship management, and sales analytics.

3. Customer Service: AI-powered chatbots, self-service portals, and data analytics are revolutionizing customer service.

4. Operations: IoT, robotics, and AI are transforming how companies manage their supply chains and production processes.

5. Human Resources: Digital transformation impacts talent acquisition, employee engagement, and workforce management.

6. Finance: Automation, blockchain, and advanced analytics are changing how financial processes are managed and how financial decisions are made.

Measuring Digital Transformation:

To effectively gauge the success of digital transformation efforts, organizations need to establish clear metrics. These may include:

1. Customer Satisfaction and Engagement Metrics

2. Operational Efficiency Indicators

3. Revenue Growth from Digital Initiatives

4. Employee Productivity and Satisfaction Measures

5. Innovation Metrics (e.g., number of new products/services launched)

6. Digital Adoption Rates

Understanding digital transformation is crucial for businesses to navigate the complexities of the digital age successfully. It requires a holistic approach that goes beyond technology adoption to encompass strategy, culture, and organizational structure. As we move forward, we'll explore how this understanding translates into tangible changes in business models and operations.

3. Impact of Digital Transformation on Business Models

Digital transformation has a profound impact on business models, often necessitating fundamental changes in how companies create, deliver, and capture value. This section explores the ways in which digital transformation is reshaping business models across industries.

Redefinition of Value Proposition:

Digital transformation often leads to a redefinition of a company's value proposition. With access to vast amounts of data and advanced analytics, businesses can offer more personalized, efficient, and innovative products and services. For example:

1. Netflix transformed from a DVD rental service to a streaming platform, leveraging data to provide personalized content recommendations.

2. John Deere evolved from a farming equipment manufacturer to a precision agriculture company, offering data-driven insights to improve crop yields.

Shift to Platform-Based Models:

Many businesses are adopting platform-based models, which create value by facilitating exchanges between two or more interdependent groups. This model, popularized by companies like Uber and Airbnb, allows for rapid scaling and network effects. Key characteristics include:

1. Multi-sided markets connecting producers and consumers

2. Network effects that increase value as more users join

3. Data as a key asset for improving the platform and user experience

Servitization of Products:

Digital transformation is enabling the shift from product-centric to service-centric business models. This "servitization" involves offering products as a service, often with a subscription-based revenue model. Examples include:

1. Adobe's shift from selling packaged software to offering cloud-based subscriptions (Software as a Service)

2. Rolls-Royce's "Power by the Hour" model for jet engines, where airlines pay for engine operating time rather than purchasing the engines outright

Ecosystem Orchestration:

Digital technologies allow companies to create and manage complex business ecosystems, integrating various partners to provide comprehensive solutions. This model is exemplified by:

1. Apple's ecosystem of hardware, software, and services

2. Amazon's expansion from e-commerce to cloud services, entertainment, and beyond

Data Monetization:

As data becomes an increasingly valuable asset, many companies are finding ways to monetize their data. This can involve:

1. Selling anonymized data to third parties

2. Offering data analytics as a service

3. Using data to create new products or enhance existing ones

Shift to Direct-to-Consumer (D2C) Models:

Digital channels are enabling manufacturers and producers to bypass traditional intermediaries and sell directly to consumers. This D2C approach offers benefits such as:

1. Higher margins by eliminating middlemen

2. Direct relationship with customers, leading to better insights and loyalty

3. Greater control over brand experience and messaging

Emergence of "As-a-Service" Models:

Beyond Software-as-a-Service (SaaS), many industries are adopting "as-a-service" models. Examples include:

1. Transportation-as-a-Service (e.g., ride-sharing and car-sharing services)

2. Manufacturing-as-a-Service (e.g., on-demand manufacturing platforms)

Collaborative and Sharing Economy Models:

Digital platforms have enabled the rise of collaborative consumption and sharing economy models. These models often involve:

1. Peer-to-peer transactions facilitated by a digital platform

2. Utilization of underused assets (e.g., spare rooms, idle cars)

3. Trust mechanisms such as user ratings and reviews

Freemium and Micropayment Models:

Digital transformation has popularized new pricing models, including:

1. Freemium: Offering basic services for free while charging for premium features

2. Micropayments: Enabling small, often impulse-driven purchases (e.g., in-app purchases in mobile games)

Blockchain-Enabled Business Models:

Emerging blockchain technology is enabling new decentralized business models, characterized by:

1. Disintermediation of traditional intermediaries

2. Increased transparency and traceability

3. New forms of value exchange and tokenization

The impact of digital transformation on business models is far-reaching and continually evolving. Companies must be prepared to reassess and potentially overhaul their business models to remain competitive in the digital age. This often involves experimenting with multiple models, being open to cannibalizing existing revenue streams, and maintaining flexibility to adapt to rapidly changing market conditions.

4. Key Technologies Driving Digital Transformation

Digital transformation is propelled by a constellation of emerging technologies that are reshaping business processes, customer experiences, and entire industries. Understanding these key technologies is crucial for organizations seeking to leverage them effectively in their digital transformation journey.

1. Artificial Intelligence (AI) and Machine Learning (ML):

AI and ML are perhaps the most transformative technologies driving digital change. They enable:

- Predictive analytics for better decision-making
- Personalization of customer experiences
- Automation of complex tasks and processes
- Natural language processing for chatbots and virtual assistants
- Computer vision for image and video analysis

Example: Amazon's recommendation engine uses ML to analyze customer behavior and provide personalized product suggestions, significantly boosting sales.

2. Internet of Things (IoT):

IoT connects physical devices to the internet, enabling data collection and exchange. Applications include:

- Smart manufacturing and predictive maintenance
- Connected vehicles and smart transportation systems
- Smart homes and cities
- Health monitoring devices

Example: Rolls-Royce uses IoT sensors in its jet engines to collect real-time data, enabling predictive maintenance and improving operational efficiency.

3. Cloud Computing:
Cloud technologies provide scalable, on-demand computing resources, enabling:
- Increased agility and flexibility in IT infrastructure
- Cost-effective scaling of operations
- Enhanced collaboration and remote work capabilities
- Platform for developing and deploying new applications rapidly

Example: Netflix leverages AWS cloud services to handle massive amounts of streaming data and scale its operations globally.

4. Big Data Analytics:
The ability to process and analyze vast amounts of data provides:
- Deep insights into customer behavior and preferences
- Improved decision-making and strategy formulation
- Enhanced operational efficiency
- New revenue streams through data monetization

Example: UPS uses big data analytics to optimize delivery routes, saving millions in fuel costs and improving efficiency.

5. Blockchain:
While still emerging, blockchain technology offers potential for:
- Enhanced security and transparency in transactions
- Streamlined supply chain management
- New forms of digital assets and cryptocurrencies
- Decentralized applications and smart contracts

Example: Walmart uses blockchain to improve food traceability in its supply chain, enhancing food safety and reducing waste.

6. 5G Networks:
The fifth generation of cellular network technology enables:
- Ultra-fast data transfer speeds
- Low latency for real-time applications
- Massive device connectivity for IoT
- Enhanced mobile broadband experiences

Example: Ericsson is partnering with manufacturing companies to implement 5G-enabled smart factories, improving efficiency and enabling new capabilities.

7. Augmented Reality (AR) and Virtual Reality (VR):
These immersive technologies are transforming:
- Customer experiences in retail and entertainment
- Training and education
- Product design and prototyping
- Remote collaboration and assistance

Example: IKEA's AR app allows customers to visualize furniture in their homes before purchasing, enhancing the shopping experience.

8. Robotic Process Automation (RPA):
RPA technologies automate repetitive tasks, offering:
- Increased efficiency and accuracy in business processes
- Cost reduction in operations
- Freeing up human resources for more strategic tasks

Example: Bank of America implemented RPA to automate various banking processes, improving efficiency and reducing errors.

9. Edge Computing:
This distributed computing paradigm brings computation closer to data sources, providing:
- Reduced latency for real-time applications
- Enhanced data security and privacy
- Improved reliability in areas with limited connectivity

Example: General Electric uses edge computing in its wind turbines to process data locally, enabling real-time adjustments and improved efficiency.

10. Quantum Computing:
While still in early stages, quantum computing promises:
- Solving complex problems exponentially faster than classical computers
- Breakthroughs in areas like cryptography, drug discovery, and financial modeling

Example: IBM is working on quantum computing applications in finance for portfolio optimization and risk analysis.

These technologies are not isolated but often work in conjunction to drive digital transformation. For instance, IoT devices generate big data, which is then processed using AI and ML algorithms, all supported by cloud computing infrastructure. Organizations must consider how these technologies can be integrated strategically to create new value and transform their business models.

As these technologies continue to evolve, they will unlock new possibilities for innovation and disruption across industries. Companies that can effectively harness these technologies will be well-positioned to lead in the digital economy.

5. Case Studies of Successful Digital Transformations

To illustrate the practical application and impact of digital transformation, let's examine several case studies of companies that have successfully navigated this process.

1. Adobe: From Boxed Software to Cloud-Based Subscription

Background: Adobe was primarily known for its boxed software products like Photoshop and Acrobat.

Transformation:

- Shifted to a cloud-based subscription model (Creative Cloud) in 2011
- Developed new cloud-native applications
- Leveraged data analytics to improve user experience and product development

Results:

- Recurring revenue increased from 19% in 2011 to 89% in 2019
- Stock price increased by over 950% from 2011 to 2021
- Improved ability to update software and combat piracy

Key Lesson: Willingness to cannibalize existing revenue streams for long-term growth.

2. Disney: From Traditional Media to Direct-to-Consumer Streaming

Background: Disney was a traditional media company with theme parks, movie studios, and TV networks.

Transformation:

- Invested heavily in streaming technology
- Acquired key assets (BAMTech, 21st Century Fox)
- Launched Disney+ streaming service in 2019
- Reorganized company structure to prioritize streaming

Results:

- Reached 100 million Disney+ subscribers in just 16 months
- Stock price doubled between streaming announcement (2017) and 2021
- Successfully pivoted during COVID-19 pandemic when theme parks were closed

Key Lesson: Bold, decisive moves can help traditional companies compete with digital natives.

3. Microsoft: From Software Giant to Cloud Leader

Background: Microsoft dominated the PC software market but was losing ground in the mobile and cloud era.

Transformation:

- Shifted focus to cloud computing with Azure
- Adopted a "mobile-first, cloud-first" strategy
- Embraced open-source technologies
- Transitioned Office to a cloud-based subscription model (Office 365)

Results:

- Azure became the second-largest cloud platform globally
- Market cap surpassed $1 trillion in 2019
- Successfully diversified revenue streams

Key Lesson: Large, established companies can successfully pivot if they're willing to embrace new technologies and business models.

4. Domino's Pizza: From Traditional Pizza Chain to Tech-Enabled Food Delivery

Background: Domino's was struggling with poor product quality and outdated ordering systems.

Transformation:

- Invested heavily in digital ordering technology
- Introduced innovative ordering methods (e.g., emoji ordering, zero-click app)
- Leveraged data analytics for store performance and customer preferences
- Implemented GPS tracking for deliveries

Results:

- Digital sales grew from 20% in 2010 to over 65% in 2019
- Stock price increased by over 2,000% from 2010 to 2020
- Became the largest pizza company globally by retail sales

Key Lesson: Digital transformation can revolutionize even traditional, brick-and-mortar businesses.

5. Ping An: From Traditional Insurer to Tech-Driven Financial Services Ecosystem

Background: Ping An was a traditional insurance company in China.

Transformation:

- Invested heavily in AI, blockchain, and cloud technologies
- Created a comprehensive financial services ecosystem

- Launched multiple successful fintech and healthtech spinoffs
    Results:
- Became one of the world's largest and most valuable insurance companies
- Tech investments now contribute significantly to revenue and growth
- Successfully expanded into healthcare, automotive services, and smart city solutions

Key Lesson: Digital transformation can enable expansion into adjacent industries and creation of new revenue streams.

These case studies demonstrate that successful digital transformation often involves:

1. Willingness to disrupt one's own business model

2. Significant investment in new technologies and capabilities

3. Customer-centric approach to innovation

4. Leveraging data and analytics for decision-making

5. Creating new revenue streams and business models

6. Organizational restructuring to support digital initiatives

It's important to note that digital transformation is an ongoing process rather than a one-time event. Even these successful companies continue to evolve and adapt to new technological advancements and market changes.

6. Challenges and Risks in Digital Transformation

While digital transformation offers significant opportunities, it also presents numerous challenges and risks that organizations must navigate:

1. Cultural Resistance:
- Challenge: Employees may resist changes to established processes and ways of working.
- Risk: Failure to address cultural issues can lead to low adoption rates of new technologies and processes.
- Mitigation: Foster a culture of innovation, provide comprehensive training, and ensure clear communication about the benefits of transformation.

2. Legacy Systems and Technical Debt:
- Challenge: Outdated IT infrastructure can be difficult and expensive to integrate with new technologies.
- Risk: Maintaining legacy systems alongside new technologies can lead to increased complexity and costs.
- Mitigation: Develop a clear roadmap for system modernization, considering cloud migration and microservices architecture where appropriate.

3. Data Security and Privacy:
- Challenge: Digital transformation often involves handling more customer data and connecting previously isolated systems.
- Risk: Increased vulnerability to data breaches and non-compliance with data protection regulations.
- Mitigation: Implement robust cybersecurity measures, ensure compliance with regulations like GDPR, and foster a culture of data responsibility.

4. Skill Gaps:
- Challenge: Many organizations lack the in-house talent to implement and manage new digital technologies.
- Risk: Reliance on external consultants can be costly and may not build long-term organizational capabilities.
- Mitigation: Invest in training and development programs, consider strategic hiring, and foster partnerships with universities and tech companies.

5. Return on Investment (ROI) Pressure:
- Challenge: Digital transformation initiatives often require significant upfront investment with unclear immediate returns.
- Risk: Pressure for quick ROI can lead to rushed implementations or abandonment of crucial long-term initiatives.
- Mitigation: Set realistic expectations, focus on incremental improvements, and develop clear KPIs to measure progress.

6. Pace of Technological Change:
- Challenge: The rapid evolution of technology makes it difficult to choose the right solutions and keep up with changes.
- Risk: Investments in technology may become obsolete quickly.
- Mitigation: Focus on building adaptable systems and cultivating a culture of continuous learning and innovation.

7. Customer Adoption:
- Challenge: New digital offerings may not align with all customer preferences or capabilities.
- Risk: Low customer adoption can lead to failed initiatives and wasted resources.
- Mitigation: Conduct thorough market research, involve customers in the design process, and provide support for customer transition.

8. Disruption to Existing Business Models:
- Challenge: Digital initiatives may cannibalize existing revenue streams.
- Risk: Internal resistance to changes that threaten established business

units.
- Mitigation: Clearly communicate the long-term vision, manage the transition carefully, and be prepared to evolve the overall business model.

9. Regulatory Compliance:
- Challenge: Digital transformation often outpaces regulatory frameworks, especially in highly regulated industries.
- Risk: Non-compliance can lead to fines, reputational damage, and forced cessation of new initiatives.
- Mitigation: Engage proactively with regulators, build compliance considerations into transformation plans from the outset.

10. Integration and Interoperability:
- Challenge: Ensuring new digital systems work seamlessly with each other and with existing systems.
- Risk: Siloed systems can lead to inefficiencies and poor user experiences.
- Mitigation: Prioritize interoperability in technology selection, use APIs and microservices architecture to enhance integration.

Addressing these challenges requires a holistic approach to digital transformation, involving not just IT departments but also leadership, HR, legal, and other key stakeholders. Organizations must be prepared to continually reassess and adjust their digital transformation strategies in response to these evolving challenges and risks.

7. Conclusion

Digital transformation has emerged as a critical imperative for businesses across all sectors, fundamentally reshaping how organizations create, deliver, and capture value. Throughout this exploration, we've seen how digital technologies are not just tools for efficiency, but catalysts for reimagining entire business models and customer experiences.

Key takeaways from our discussion include:

1. Comprehensive Nature: Digital transformation is not merely about technology adoption; it's a holistic change that encompasses strategy, culture, and operations.

2. Customer-Centricity: Successful digital transformation efforts are often driven by a focus on enhancing customer experiences and meeting evolving customer expectations.

3. Business Model Innovation: Digital technologies enable entirely new business models, from platform-based ecosystems to subscription services and data monetization strategies.

4. Technological Drivers: A constellation of technologies, including AI, IoT, cloud computing, and blockchain, are driving this transformation, often working in concert to create new possibilities.

5. Successful Case Studies: Companies like Adobe, Disney, and Microsoft demonstrate that even large, established organizations can successfully navigate digital transformation with the right approach.

6. Challenges and Risks: While the potential benefits are significant, organizations must navigate challenges such as cultural resistance, legacy systems, data security, and the rapid pace of technological change.

7. Future Trends: Emerging technologies and concepts like quantum computing, extended reality, and human-AI collaboration promise to further accelerate the pace of change and create new opportunities for innovation.

As we look to the future, it's clear that digital transformation will continue to be a defining factor in business success. Organizations that can effectively leverage digital technologies to create new value propositions, enhance operational efficiency, and deliver superior customer experiences will be best positioned to thrive in an increasingly digital world.

However, it's crucial to remember that digital transformation is not a one-time event, but an ongoing process. The most successful organizations will be those that cultivate a culture of continuous innovation and adaptation, always looking for new ways to leverage technology to create value and stay ahead of the competition.

Moreover, as digital technologies become increasingly pervasive, organizations must also grapple with important ethical considerations. Issues such as data privacy, algorithmic bias, and the societal impacts of automation will require careful consideration and proactive management.

In conclusion, digital transformation represents both a significant challenge and an unprecedented opportunity for businesses. By embracing this change, investing in the right technologies and capabilities, and maintaining a relentless focus on creating value for customers, organizations can position themselves for success in the digital age. The journey of digital transformation is complex and often challenging, but for those who navigate it successfully, the rewards can be transformative.

CHAPTER ELEVEN

GREEN IT AND SUSTAINABILITY

1. Introduction

In an era defined by rapid technological advancement and growing environmental concerns, the concept of Green IT has emerged as a crucial intersection between information technology and sustainability. Green IT, also known as green computing or ICT sustainability, refers to the environmentally responsible and eco-friendly use of computers and related resources. This approach encompasses the design, manufacture, use, and disposal of computing devices in a way that reduces their environmental impact.

The urgency of adopting Green IT practices has never been more apparent. As the digital economy continues to expand, so does the environmental footprint of the IT sector. Data centers alone are projected to consume 20% of the world's electricity by 2025, contributing significantly to global carbon emissions. Moreover, the proliferation of electronic devices has led to an alarming increase in e-waste, with millions of tons of discarded electronics polluting landfills and ecosystems worldwide.

Green IT is not merely about reducing the negative environmental impacts of technology; it's about leveraging IT to drive sustainability across all sectors of the economy. From smart grids that optimize energy distribution to AI-powered systems that minimize resource waste, technology has the potential to be a powerful tool in the fight against climate change and environmental degradation.

This comprehensive exploration of Green IT and Sustainability will delve into the core concepts, strategies, and challenges associated with making our digital world more sustainable. We will examine the key areas where IT intersects with sustainability, including energy-efficient hardware, green data centers, sustainable software development, and responsible e-waste management. Furthermore, we will discuss the measurement of Green IT impacts, the obstacles to implementation, and emerging trends that promise to shape the future of sustainable computing.

As we navigate through this topic, it's important to recognize that Green IT is not just an environmental imperative but also a business opportunity. Companies that effectively implement Green IT strategies often realize significant cost savings through reduced energy consumption and improved resource efficiency. Moreover, as consumers and stakeholders become increasingly environmentally conscious, organizations that demonstrate a commitment to sustainability can enhance their brand image and competitive positioning.

The journey towards a more sustainable digital future requires a collective effort from technology providers, businesses, policymakers, and individual users. By understanding the principles and practices of Green IT, we can all play a part in ensuring that our technological progress aligns with the urgent need for environmental stewardship.

2. Understanding Green IT

Green IT, also referred to as green computing or ICT sustainability, is a multifaceted concept that encompasses the environmentally responsible and efficient use of information technology throughout its lifecycle. It involves designing, manufacturing, using, and disposing of computers, servers, and associated subsystems with minimal impact on the environment.

Key Aspects of Green IT:

1. Energy Efficiency:

- Designing and using hardware and software systems that consume less energy.

- Implementing power management features in devices and data centers.

- Utilizing renewable energy sources for IT operations.

2. Resource Conservation:

- Minimizing the use of rare or harmful materials in IT equipment.

- Extending the lifecycle of IT equipment through upgrades and repairs.

- Virtualizing servers and storage to reduce physical hardware requirements.

3. Responsible Disposal and Recycling:

- Implementing proper e-waste management practices.

- Designing products for easy disassembly and recycling.

- Supporting take-back and recycling programs for used electronics.

    4. Sustainable Software Development:

- Creating software that uses computational resources efficiently.

- Developing applications that enable environmental monitoring and management.

- Implementing algorithms that optimize resource use in various industries.

    5. Green Data Centers:

- Designing energy-efficient data center infrastructure.

- Implementing advanced cooling technologies to reduce energy consumption.

- Optimizing data center operations for maximum energy efficiency.

    6. Telecommuting and Virtual Collaboration:

- Using IT to reduce the need for physical travel and office space.

- Implementing virtual meeting technologies to minimize carbon footprint.

    The Scope of Green IT:

Green IT extends beyond the IT department and impacts various aspects of an organization:

    1. Procurement: Choosing energy-efficient and environmentally friendly IT equipment.

2. Operations: Implementing practices to reduce energy consumption in day-to-day IT use.

3. Strategy: Incorporating sustainability goals into overall IT and business strategies.

4. Innovation: Developing new technologies and solutions that promote sustainability.

5. Corporate Social Responsibility: Demonstrating commitment to environmental stewardship.

    Historical Context:

The concept of Green IT emerged in the late 1990s and gained significant traction in the mid-2000s. Key milestones include:

    1992: The Energy Star program is launched by the U.S. Environmental Protection Agency.

2003: The EU introduces the Restriction of Hazardous Substances (RoHS) directive.

2006: Google begins investing heavily in renewable energy for its data centers.

2009: The Green Grid consortium establishes the Power Usage Effectiveness (PUE) metric for data centers.

2010: The IEEE launches the Green ICT initiative to promote sustainable computing.

Motivations for Green IT:

Organizations adopt Green IT practices for various reasons:

1. Cost Reduction: Energy-efficient IT operations can significantly lower operational costs.

2. Regulatory Compliance: Meeting increasingly stringent environmental regulations.

3. Corporate Social Responsibility: Demonstrating commitment to sustainability to stakeholders.

4. Market Demand: Responding to consumer preferences for eco-friendly products and services.

5. Resource Scarcity: Preparing for potential future shortages in energy and raw materials.

6. Competitive Advantage: Differentiating from competitors through sustainable practices.

The Business Case for Green IT:

While the environmental benefits of Green IT are clear, there's also a strong business case for its adoption:

1. Cost Savings: Energy-efficient IT can lead to significant reductions in electricity bills.

2. Improved Brand Image: Demonstrating environmental responsibility can enhance reputation.

3. Increased Efficiency: Many Green IT practices also lead to more streamlined operations.

4. Risk Mitigation: Preparing for future environmental regulations and resource constraints.

5. Innovation Opportunities: Developing sustainable technologies can open new market opportunities.

Challenges in Green IT:

Despite its benefits, implementing Green IT is not without challenges:

1. Initial Costs: Some Green IT solutions require significant upfront investment.

2. Complexity: Integrating sustainable practices across complex IT systems can be challenging.

3. Lack of Standards: The field of Green IT is still evolving, with varying standards and metrics.

4. Rapid Technological Change: The fast pace of IT innovation can make

long-term planning difficult.

5. Balancing Performance and Sustainability: Ensuring that green solutions don't compromise on performance.

Understanding Green IT is the first step towards implementing sustainable practices in an organization's IT operations. As we delve deeper into specific strategies and applications, it's important to keep in mind that Green IT is not just about reducing environmental impact, but also about creating value and driving innovation in a resource-constrained world.

3. The Importance of Sustainability in IT

As the digital economy continues to grow, the importance of sustainability in IT has become increasingly critical. This section explores why sustainability should be a key consideration in IT strategies and operations.

Environmental Impact of IT:

1. Energy Consumption:
- The IT sector consumes about 7% of global electricity, a figure projected to rise to 20% by 2025.
- Data centers alone accounted for about 1% of global electricity use in 2020.

2. Carbon Emissions:
- The IT industry is responsible for 2-3% of global carbon emissions, comparable to the aviation industry.
- Without intervention, this could rise to 14% by 2040.

3. E-waste:
- Global e-waste reached 53.6 million metric tons in 2019 and is growing by about 2 million tons per year.
- Only 17.4% of e-waste is formally collected and recycled.

4. Resource Depletion:
- IT hardware manufacturing requires significant amounts of rare earth elements and precious metals.
- The extraction of these materials often has severe environmental and social impacts.

Key Reasons for Prioritizing Sustainability in IT:

1. Climate Change Mitigation:
- IT has a significant carbon footprint, and reducing this is crucial for global climate change efforts.
- Green IT practices can contribute to meeting national and international climate goals.

2. Resource Conservation:
- Sustainable IT practices help conserve finite resources, including rare earth elements and water.
- Extending the life of IT equipment reduces demand for new resources.

3. Regulatory Compliance:
- Many countries are introducing stricter environmental regulations for the IT sector.
- Proactive adoption of sustainable practices can help avoid future compliance issues.

4. Cost Reduction:
- Energy-efficient IT operations can significantly reduce operational costs.
- Proper asset management and recycling can recover value from old equipment.

5. Innovation Driver:
- The push for sustainability often leads to innovative solutions and new business opportunities.
- Green IT can drive efficiency improvements across various business processes.

6. Corporate Social Responsibility (CSR):
- Demonstrating commitment to sustainability enhances corporate reputation.
- It can improve relationships with stakeholders, including customers, investors, and employees.

7. Risk Management:
- Sustainable IT practices help mitigate risks associated with resource scarcity and price volatility.
- They also address reputational risks related to environmental issues.

8. Employee Engagement:
- Many employees, especially younger generations, prefer to work for environmentally responsible companies.
- Green IT initiatives can boost employee morale and attract talent.

9. Market Demand:
- Consumers are increasingly favoring eco-friendly products and services.
- B2B customers often consider sustainability in their procurement decisions.

10. Ecosystem Health:
- Reducing e-waste and toxic materials in IT equipment helps protect ecosystems and biodiversity.

- Sustainable IT practices contribute to overall environmental health.

IT as an Enabler of Sustainability:

Beyond reducing its own environmental impact, IT plays a crucial role in enabling sustainability across various sectors:

1. Smart Grids: IT enables more efficient energy distribution and integration of renewable sources.

2. Building Management Systems: IT-driven systems optimize energy use in buildings.

3. Transportation: IT enables route optimization, vehicle sharing, and traffic management systems that reduce emissions.

4. Agriculture: Precision agriculture techniques use IT to optimize resource use and reduce waste.

5. Manufacturing: IT enables more efficient production processes and supply chain management.

6. Environmental Monitoring: IT systems are crucial for tracking and analyzing environmental data.

7. Remote Work: IT enables telecommuting, reducing transportation-related emissions.

8. Circular Economy: IT facilitates tracking and management of resources in circular economy models.

The Role of IT Leaders in Driving Sustainability:

Given the importance of sustainability in IT, CIOs and IT leaders have a critical role to play:

1. Strategy Integration: Incorporating sustainability into overall IT strategy and governance.

2. Measurement and Reporting: Implementing systems to measure and report on IT sustainability metrics.

3. Innovation: Driving the development and adoption of sustainable IT solutions.

4. Collaboration: Working with other departments to leverage IT for organization-wide sustainability efforts.

5. Education: Raising awareness about the importance of sustainable IT practices among staff and stakeholders.

6. Vendor Management: Ensuring that IT suppliers adhere to sustainability standards.

In conclusion, sustainability in IT is not just an environmental imperative but a business necessity. It offers opportunities for cost savings, innovation, and value creation while addressing critical environmental challenges. As the digital economy continues to grow, the importance of aligning IT operations with sustainability principles will only increase.

4. Key Strategies for Implementing Green IT

Implementing Green IT requires a comprehensive approach that addresses various aspects of IT operations, procurement, and management. Here are key strategies organizations can adopt to make their IT practices more sustainable:

1. Energy-Efficient Hardware:
- Procure Energy Star certified equipment
- Implement power management features on all devices
- Use thin clients or zero clients where appropriate
- Adopt low-power displays and peripherals
- Consider the use of ARM-based processors for certain applications

2. Virtualization and Cloud Computing:
- Implement server virtualization to reduce physical hardware requirements
- Utilize cloud services to benefit from economies of scale in energy efficiency
- Implement storage virtualization to optimize storage resource use
- Use desktop virtualization to extend the life of older hardware

3. Data Center Optimization:
- Implement hot aisle/cold aisle configurations
- Use free cooling where climate permits
- Adopt modular data center designs for scalability and efficiency
- Implement Data Center Infrastructure Management (DCIM) tools
- Consider liquid cooling for high-density server environments

4. Sustainable Software Development:
- Develop software with efficient algorithms to minimize resource use
- Implement automatic scaling in cloud-native applications
- Use green coding practices to reduce computational intensity
- Design applications with power management in mind

5. Lifecycle Management:
- Implement a comprehensive IT asset management program
- Extend the lifecycle of IT equipment through upgrades and repairs
- Adopt a circular economy approach to IT procurement and disposal
- Implement proper e-waste management and recycling programs

6. Green Printing Practices:
- Implement pull printing to reduce waste
- Use energy-efficient, multi-function printers

- Encourage paperless workflows where possible
- Set double-sided printing as the default
    7. Remote Work and Collaboration Tools:
- Implement robust remote work technologies to reduce commuting
- Use video conferencing and virtual collaboration tools to minimize travel
- Adopt cloud-based productivity suites for efficient resource use
    8. Green Networking:
- Implement network equipment with energy-efficient features
- Use Power over Ethernet (PoE) to reduce cabling and improve efficiency
- Implement software-defined networking for more efficient network management
    9. Renewable Energy Integration:
- Procure renewable energy for data centers and office IT operations
- Implement on-site renewable energy generation where feasible
- Participate in green energy programs offered by utility providers
    10. IT-Enabled Sustainability Initiatives:
- Implement smart building management systems
- Use IT to optimize logistics and transportation
- Leverage IoT for environmental monitoring and resource management
    11. Green Procurement Policies:
- Establish sustainability criteria for IT vendor selection
- Consider Total Cost of Ownership (TCO) including energy costs in procurement decisions
- Prioritize vendors with take-back and recycling programs
    12. Employee Engagement and Training:
- Provide training on green IT practices to all employees
- Implement gamification to encourage sustainable IT behaviors
- Recognize and reward employees for green IT initiatives
    13. Measurement and Reporting:
- Implement tools to measure IT energy consumption and carbon footprint
- Establish key performance indicators (KPIs) for Green IT initiatives
- Regularly report on Green IT progress to stakeholders
    14. Green IT Governance:
- Establish a Green IT policy and integrate it into overall IT governance
- Assign clear responsibilities for Green IT initiatives
- Include sustainability considerations in all IT decision-making processes
    15. Continuous Improvement:
- Regularly audit IT operations for efficiency improvements

- Stay informed about emerging Green IT technologies and practices
- Participate in industry groups and standards organizations focused on Green IT

Implementation Approach:

To effectively implement these strategies, organizations should consider the following approach:

1. Assessment: Conduct a comprehensive assessment of current IT operations and their environmental impact.

2. Strategy Development: Based on the assessment, develop a Green IT strategy aligned with overall business and sustainability goals.

3. Prioritization: Identify quick wins and high-impact initiatives to prioritize implementation.

4. Pilot Projects: Start with pilot projects to demonstrate value and gain organizational buy-in.

5. Scaling: Gradually scale successful initiatives across the organization.

6. Monitoring and Reporting: Continuously monitor progress and report on outcomes.

7. Review and Adapt: Regularly review the Green IT strategy and adapt to changing technologies and business needs.

By implementing these strategies, organizations can significantly reduce the environmental impact of their IT operations while often realizing cost savings and operational efficiencies. The key is to approach Green IT not as a one-time project, but as an ongoing commitment to sustainability integrated into all aspects of IT management and operations.

5. Green Data Centers

Data centers are at the heart of modern IT infrastructure, but they are also significant consumers of energy and resources. Green data centers aim to minimize environmental impact while maintaining or improving performance. This section explores key strategies and technologies for creating and operating environmentally sustainable data centers.

Energy Efficiency in Data Centers:

1. Power Usage Effectiveness (PUE):
- PUE is a key metric for data center efficiency, measuring the ratio of total facility energy to IT equipment energy.
- The ideal PUE is 1.0; world-class facilities achieve PUEs of 1.1 to 1.2.
- Strategies to improve PUE include optimizing cooling, using efficient power distribution, and maximizing IT equipment efficiency.

2. Cooling Optimization:
- Hot aisle/cold aisle configuration to improve airflow management.
- Use of containment systems to separate hot and cold air.
- Raised floor designs for more efficient air distribution.
- Implementation of free cooling or economizers where climate permits.
- Use of liquid cooling for high-density server environments.

3. Power Management:
- Use of high-efficiency Uninterruptible Power Supply (UPS) systems.
- Implementation of DC power distribution to reduce conversion losses.
- Adoption of renewable energy sources, including on-site solar or wind power.
- Use of intelligent power management software to optimize energy use.

4. IT Equipment Efficiency:
- Deployment of energy-efficient servers and storage systems.
- Implementation of server virtualization to increase utilization.
- Use of power management features in IT equipment.
- Regular refresh of IT equipment to benefit from efficiency improvements.

Green Data Center Design:

1. Modular Data Center Design:
- Allows for scalable growth and more efficient use of space and resources.
- Enables easier implementation of the latest energy-efficient technologies.

2. Building Design:
- Use of sustainable building materials.
- Implementation of green roofs or solar panels.
- Optimized building orientation for natural cooling.

3. Location Selection:
- Choosing locations with access to renewable energy sources.
- Selecting climates that allow for free cooling.
- Considering proximity to end-users to reduce network latency and energy use.

4. Water Management:
- Implementation of water-efficient cooling technologies.
- Use of rainwater harvesting and recycling systems.
- Adoption of waterless cooling technologies where appropriate.

Advanced Technologies for Green Data Centers:

1. Artificial Intelligence and Machine Learning:
- Use of AI for predictive maintenance and optimization of cooling systems.
- ML algorithms for workload balancing and energy use optimization.

2. Edge Computing:

- Distributing computing resources closer to end-users can reduce overall energy consumption.

- Enables more efficient use of local renewable energy sources.

3. Immersion Cooling:

- Submerging servers in dielectric fluid for more efficient heat removal.

- Can significantly reduce or eliminate the need for air conditioning.

4. Fuel Cells:

- Use of fuel cells as a cleaner alternative to diesel generators for backup power.

- Some data centers are experimenting with fuel cells as primary power sources.

5. Advanced Power Management:

- Use of lithium-ion batteries for more efficient energy storage.

- Implementation of smart grid technologies for better integration with the power grid.

Green Data Center Certifications and Standards:

1. LEED (Leadership in Energy and Environmental Design):

- Provides a framework for healthy, highly efficient, and cost-saving green buildings.

2. ISO 50001:

- International standard for energy management systems.

3. ENERGY STAR for Data Centers:

- U.S. EPA program that certifies energy-efficient data centers.

4. The Green Grid's Data Center Maturity Model:

- Provides a comprehensive model for improving data center sustainability.

Case Studies:

1. Google: Achieved a PUE of 1.10 across all its data centers, using AI to optimize cooling.

2. Microsoft: Experimenting with underwater data centers (Project Natick) for natural cooling.

3. Facebook: Built a data center in Lulea, Sweden, that uses 100% renewable energy and free cooling.

4. Apple: All its data centers run on 100% renewable energy, with on-site generation where possible.

Challenges and Future Directions:

1. Balancing Performance and Efficiency: Ensuring that sustainability efforts don't compromise on performance and reliability.

2. Handling Increasing Data Volumes: Managing the environmental impact of exponential data growth.

3. Regulatory Compliance: Navigating evolving environmental regulations across different regions.

4. Technology Refresh Cycles: Balancing the benefits of new, more efficient technology with the environmental impact of frequent hardware replacements.

5. Renewable Energy Integration: Overcoming challenges in integrating variable renewable energy sources into data center operations.

Green data centers represent a critical frontier in sustainable IT. By implementing these strategies and technologies, organizations can significantly reduce the environmental impact of their data center operations while often realizing substantial cost savings. As technology continues to evolve, we can expect to see even more innovative approaches to creating truly sustainable data centers.

6. E-waste Management

E-waste, or electronic waste, refers to discarded electrical or electronic devices. As the use of technology continues to grow, so does the amount of e-waste generated globally. Proper management of e-waste is crucial for minimizing environmental impact and recovering valuable resources.

The E-waste Challenge:

1. Volume: Global e-waste generation reached 53.6 million metric tons in 2019 and is growing by about 2 million tons annually.

2. Toxicity: E-waste often contains hazardous materials like lead, mercury, and flame retardants.

3. Resource Loss: Improper disposal results in the loss of valuable materials like gold, silver, and rare earth elements.

4. Environmental Impact: Improper e-waste disposal can lead to soil, water, and air pollution.

Key Strategies for E-waste Management:

1. Reduce:

- Extend the lifespan of electronic devices through proper maintenance and upgrades.

- Implement IT asset management systems to track and optimize device usage.

- Encourage the use of multifunctional devices to reduce the overall number of devices needed.

2. Reuse:
- Implement internal redeployment programs for IT equipment.
- Donate functional but outdated equipment to schools or nonprofits.
- Explore refurbishment options for used equipment.
3. Recycle:
- Partner with certified e-waste recyclers to ensure proper handling of discarded equipment.
- Implement take-back programs for end-of-life devices.
- Use recyclers that adhere to standards like R2 (Responsible Recycling) or e-Stewards.
4. Responsible Procurement:
- Choose products designed for easy disassembly and recycling.
- Prefer vendors with established take-back and recycling programs.
- Consider leasing options that include end-of-life management.
5. Employee Education:
- Train employees on the importance of proper e-waste disposal.
- Provide clear guidelines for handling end-of-life IT equipment.
6. Data Security:
- Implement secure data wiping procedures before disposal or recycling.
- Use certified data destruction services when necessary.
7. Compliance:
- Stay informed about e-waste regulations in all operating jurisdictions.
- Maintain proper documentation of e-waste handling and disposal.
8. Circular Economy Approach:
- Support the development of products designed for circularity.
- Participate in industry initiatives promoting circular economy principles in electronics.
Best Practices for Organizations:
1. Develop a comprehensive e-waste management policy.
2. Conduct regular e-waste audits to track generation and disposal.
3. Set targets for e-waste reduction and recycling rates.
4. Include e-waste management in sustainability reporting.
5. Explore innovative recycling technologies and partnerships.
Challenges in E-waste Management:
1. Rapid technological change leading to faster obsolescence.
2. Complexity of modern devices making recycling more challenging.
3. Lack of standardization in device design and materials.
4. Illegal export of e-waste to countries with weak environmental

regulations.

5. Consumer awareness and behavior regarding e-waste disposal.

Future Trends:

1. Increased producer responsibility for end-of-life product management.

2. Development of more efficient recycling technologies.

3. Growth of the refurbished electronics market.

4. Integration of IoT and blockchain for better tracking of electronic devices throughout their lifecycle.

5. Shift towards more modular and easily repairable device designs.

Effective e-waste management is crucial for mitigating the environmental impact of the IT industry. By implementing comprehensive e-waste strategies, organizations can not only reduce their environmental footprint but also recover value from end-of-life equipment and enhance their sustainability credentials.

7. Green Software Development

Green software development refers to the practice of designing, developing, and maintaining software applications with environmental sustainability in mind. This approach aims to minimize the energy consumption and resource usage of software throughout its lifecycle.

Key Principles of Green Software Development:

1. Energy Efficiency:

- Optimize algorithms to reduce computational complexity.

- Minimize unnecessary background processes and idle time.

- Implement efficient data structures and storage methods.

2. Resource Optimization:

- Reduce memory usage and storage requirements.

- Optimize network usage to minimize data transfer.

- Implement efficient caching strategies.

3. Hardware Efficiency:

- Design software that can run efficiently on older hardware.

- Utilize hardware acceleration features when available.

- Implement power management features in software.

4. Cloud Optimization:

- Design for efficient use of cloud resources.

- Implement auto-scaling to match resource allocation with demand.

- Utilize serverless architectures where appropriate.

5. User Behavior:
- Design interfaces that encourage energy-efficient user behavior.
- Implement default settings that prioritize energy efficiency.

Strategies for Green Software Development:

1. Code Optimization:
- Conduct regular code reviews focusing on efficiency.
- Use profiling tools to identify and address performance bottlenecks.
- Implement lazy loading and on-demand resource allocation.

2. Efficient Algorithms:
- Choose algorithms with lower time and space complexity.
- Implement parallel processing where possible.
- Use approximation algorithms when exact solutions aren't necessary.

3. Data Management:
- Implement efficient data compression techniques.
- Use appropriate data types to minimize memory usage.
- Optimize database queries and indexing.

4. UI/UX Design:
- Design dark mode interfaces to reduce energy consumption on OLED screens.
- Minimize animations and dynamic content that consume extra power.
- Implement efficient image and video compression.

5. Testing and Monitoring:
- Include energy consumption metrics in performance testing.
- Implement monitoring tools to track resource usage in production.
- Conduct regular energy audits of software applications.

6. Green Coding Practices:
- Avoid busy-waiting and implement efficient sleep/wake cycles.
- Use compiler optimizations to generate more efficient machine code.
- Implement efficient error handling and logging mechanisms.

7. Sustainable Development Lifecycle:
- Include sustainability considerations in requirements gathering.
- Implement green coding guidelines in the development process.
- Include energy efficiency in code review criteria.

Challenges in Green Software Development:

1. Balancing performance and energy efficiency.
2. Lack of standardized metrics for software energy consumption.
3. Limited developer awareness and training in green coding practices.
4. Difficulty in measuring the environmental impact of software.

Emerging Trends:

1. AI-powered code optimization for energy efficiency.

2. Development of energy-aware programming languages and frameworks.

3. Integration of energy consumption metrics into Integrated Development Environments (IDEs).

4. Growing focus on green software engineering in academic curricula.

Tools and Frameworks:

1. GreenCodeScan: Static code analysis tool for identifying energy inefficiencies.

2. PowerAPI: API for monitoring energy consumption of software.

3. Energy Efficiency Design Impact (EEDI): Framework for assessing software energy efficiency.

By adopting green software development practices, organizations can significantly reduce the energy consumption and environmental impact of their software applications. This not only contributes to sustainability goals but can also lead to improved performance, reduced operational costs, and better user experiences.

8. Measuring the Impact of Green IT

Measuring the impact of Green IT initiatives is crucial for assessing their effectiveness, justifying investments, and identifying areas for improvement. This process involves quantifying both the environmental benefits and the business value of Green IT practices.

Key Metrics for Measuring Green IT Impact:

1. Energy Consumption:
- Total energy consumption of IT operations (kWh)
- Energy consumption per user or per service unit
- Percentage of energy from renewable sources

2. Carbon Emissions:
- Total carbon emissions from IT operations (CO2e)
- Carbon emissions per employee or per unit of revenue
- Carbon emissions avoided through Green IT initiatives

3. E-waste:
- Total e-waste generated (kg or units)
- E-waste recycling rate (%)
- Average lifespan of IT equipment

4. Data Center Efficiency:
- Power Usage Effectiveness (PUE)
- Carbon Usage Effectiveness (CUE)

- Water Usage Effectiveness (WUE)
    5. Resource Utilization:
- Server utilization rates
- Storage utilization rates
- Network capacity utilization
    6. Green Software Metrics:
- Energy consumption per transaction or user session
- CPU and memory usage of applications
- Data transfer volumes
    7. Financial Metrics:
- Cost savings from energy efficiency improvements
- Return on Investment (ROI) of Green IT initiatives
- Total Cost of Ownership (TCO) including energy costs
    Measurement Approaches:
    1. Baselining:
- Establish baseline measurements before implementing Green IT initiatives.
- Use these baselines to track progress and calculate improvements.
    2. Continuous Monitoring:
- Implement real-time monitoring of energy consumption and resource utilization.
- Use IoT sensors and smart meters for accurate data collection.
    3. Life Cycle Assessment (LCA):
- Conduct LCAs to understand the full environmental impact of IT equipment from production to disposal.
    4. Benchmarking:
- Compare metrics against industry standards and best practices.
- Participate in industry benchmarking initiatives.
    5. Reporting and Dashboards:
- Develop comprehensive Green IT dashboards for real-time visibility.
- Include Green IT metrics in sustainability and CSR reports.
    Challenges in Measuring Green IT Impact:
    1. Complexity of IT environments and interdependencies.
2. Difficulty in isolating the impact of specific Green IT initiatives.
3. Lack of standardized measurement methodologies across the industry.
4. Balancing the cost of measurement with the benefits gained.
    Best Practices:

1. Align Green IT metrics with overall organizational sustainability goals.
2. Use a combination of environmental, operational, and financial metrics for a holistic view.
3. Ensure data accuracy and consistency in measurement methodologies.
4. Regularly review and update metrics to reflect changing technologies and priorities.
5. Communicate results to stakeholders to maintain support for Green IT initiatives.

Emerging Trends in Green IT Measurement:
1. AI and machine learning for predictive analysis of Green IT impacts.
2. Blockchain for transparent and verifiable tracking of environmental metrics.
3. Integration of Green IT metrics into overall Enterprise Resource Planning (ERP) systems.
4. Development of industry-wide standards for Green IT measurement and reporting.

By implementing robust measurement practices, organizations can effectively track the impact of their Green IT initiatives, make data-driven decisions, and continuously improve their environmental performance. This not only supports sustainability goals but also helps in identifying cost-saving opportunities and improving overall IT efficiency.

9. Challenges in Implementing Green IT

While the benefits of Green IT are clear, organizations often face significant challenges when implementing sustainable IT practices. Understanding these challenges is crucial for developing effective strategies to overcome them.

1. Initial Cost and ROI Concerns:
- Green IT initiatives often require significant upfront investment.
- The return on investment may not be immediate or easily quantifiable.
- Challenge in justifying costs to stakeholders focused on short-term financial metrics.

2. Technological Complexity:
- Rapidly evolving technology landscape makes it difficult to choose the right solutions.
- Integration of new green technologies with existing legacy systems can be complex.
- Ensuring that green solutions don't compromise on performance or reliability.

3. Lack of Expertise and Skills:
- Shortage of professionals with expertise in both IT and sustainability.
- Need for continuous training and upskilling of IT staff on green technologies.
- Difficulty in finding qualified vendors and partners for Green IT initiatives.

4. Organizational Resistance:
- Resistance to change from employees accustomed to traditional IT practices.
- Lack of buy-in from senior management or other departments.
- Conflicting priorities between IT efficiency and other business objectives.

5. Measurement and Reporting Challenges:
- Lack of standardized metrics for measuring Green IT impact.
- Difficulty in accurately measuring the environmental impact of IT operations.
- Complexity in reporting Green IT metrics in a meaningful way to various stakeholders.

6. Regulatory and Compliance Issues:
- Navigating complex and often changing environmental regulations.
- Ensuring compliance across different geographical regions with varying standards.
- Balancing data privacy and security requirements with green initiatives.

7. Supply Chain Complexities:
- Ensuring sustainability throughout the IT supply chain.
- Limited availability of truly green IT products and services.
- Difficulty in verifying environmental claims of vendors and suppliers.

8. Rapid Technological Obsolescence:
- Fast-paced technological change leading to frequent hardware upgrades.
- Balancing the need for latest, more efficient technology with the environmental impact of frequent replacements.

9. Data Center Challenges:
- Retrofitting existing data centers for improved energy efficiency can be costly and disruptive.
- Balancing increased computing demands with energy efficiency goals.
- Challenges in implementing renewable energy solutions for data centers.

10. User Behavior and Awareness:
- Difficulty in changing user behavior towards more sustainable IT practices.

- Lack of awareness among employees about the importance of Green IT.
- Balancing user experience with energy-saving measures.

11. Global Coordination:
- For multinational organizations, coordinating Green IT efforts across different regions and cultures.
- Dealing with varying levels of infrastructure and technology availability in different countries.

12. Balancing Digital Transformation and Sustainability:
- Ensuring that digital transformation initiatives align with sustainability goals.
- Managing the increasing energy demands of emerging technologies like AI and blockchain.

Addressing these challenges requires a multifaceted approach involving technological solutions, organizational change management, employee education, and strategic planning. Organizations need to develop comprehensive Green IT strategies that address these challenges while aligning with overall business objectives and sustainability goals.

Successful implementation of Green IT often involves starting with pilot projects, building cross-functional teams, securing executive support, and fostering a culture of sustainability throughout the organization. By recognizing and proactively addressing these challenges, organizations can increase their chances of successfully implementing Green IT initiatives and realizing both environmental and business benefits.

10. Future Trends in Green IT and Sustainability

As technology continues to evolve and environmental concerns become increasingly pressing, several trends are emerging that will shape the future of Green IT and sustainability in the tech sector.

1. AI and Machine Learning for Sustainability:
- AI-driven optimization of energy consumption in data centers and IT operations.
- Machine learning algorithms for predictive maintenance, reducing waste and improving efficiency.
- AI-powered smart grids for more efficient energy distribution and use.

2. Edge Computing for Energy Efficiency:
- Shift towards edge computing to reduce data transfer and associated energy consumption.
- Integration of renewable energy sources in edge computing infrastructure.
- Development of energy-efficient edge devices and protocols.

3. Quantum Computing:
- Potential for quantum computers to solve complex sustainability problems.
- Research into energy-efficient quantum computing technologies.
- Use of quantum algorithms for optimizing resource allocation and energy use.

4. Green Software Engineering:
- Growing focus on energy-efficient software design and development.
- Emergence of new programming languages and frameworks optimized for energy efficiency.
- Integration of sustainability metrics into software development lifecycles.

5. Circular Economy in IT:
- Increased focus on designing IT products for longevity, repair, and recycling.
- Growth of IT asset refurbishment and second-hand markets.
- Development of new business models based on product-as-a-service concepts.

6. Sustainable Data Storage:
- Advancements in DNA data storage and other molecular storage technologies.
- Development of more energy-efficient and durable storage media.
- Increased use of cold storage for rarely accessed data.

7. Green Blockchain:
- Development of energy-efficient consensus mechanisms for blockchain.
- Use of blockchain for tracking and verifying sustainability efforts.
- Integration of renewable energy in cryptocurrency mining operations.

8. Bio-inspired Computing:
- Research into computing systems inspired by biological processes for improved efficiency.
- Development of biodegradable electronics and computing components.

9. Advanced Cooling Technologies:
- Liquid immersion cooling becoming mainstream in data centers.
- Development of two-phase immersion cooling for extreme efficiency.
- Exploration of novel materials for passive cooling of electronic devices.

10. Renewable Energy Integration:
- Increased adoption of on-site renewable energy generation for IT operations.
- Development of AI-driven systems for optimal integration of renewable

energy.

- Growth of energy storage technologies to support renewable energy use.

12. IoT for Environmental Monitoring:

- Expansion of IoT networks for real-time environmental data collection.
- Development of ultra-low-power IoT devices for long-term deployment.
- Use of IoT for optimizing resource use across various industries.

12. Virtual and Augmented Reality:

- Use of VR/AR to reduce necd for physical travel and resource-intensive physical products.
- Development of energy-efficient VR/AR devices.
- Application of VR/AR in environmental education and awareness.

13. Green 5G and 6G:

- Focus on energy efficiency in the development of 5G and future 6G networks.
- Use of advanced network slicing for optimizing energy use in telecommunications.

14. Sustainable User Interfaces:

- Growth of dark mode and low-power display technologies.
- Development of UI/UX designs that encourage sustainable user behaviors.

These trends indicate a future where sustainability is deeply integrated into every aspect of IT, from hardware design to software development, and from data center operations to end-user devices. As these technologies evolve, they will not only reduce the environmental impact of IT but also enable new solutions for global sustainability challenges.

11. Conclusion

Green IT and sustainability have evolved from niche concerns to critical priorities in the technology sector. As we've explored throughout this comprehensive overview, the imperative for sustainable IT practices is driven by a combination of environmental urgency, economic benefits, and social responsibility.

Key Takeaways:

1. Holistic Approach: Green IT is not just about energy-efficient hardware; it encompasses all aspects of IT, including software development, data center operations, and end-user practices.

2. Business Value: Implementing Green IT strategies often leads to significant cost savings through reduced energy consumption and improved resource efficiency, demonstrating that sustainability and profitability can go hand in hand.

3. Innovation Driver: The push for sustainability in IT is driving innovation in technologies such as energy-efficient hardware, green software development, and sustainable data center designs.

4. Measurement is Key: Effective implementation of Green IT requires robust measurement and reporting practices to track progress, identify areas for improvement, and demonstrate value to stakeholders.

5. Challenges Persist: Despite progress, significant challenges remain, including initial cost barriers, technological complexity, and the need for organizational change.

6. Future Trends: Emerging technologies like AI, edge computing, and quantum computing present both challenges and opportunities for sustainable IT practices.

7. Circular Economy: The IT industry is gradually moving towards more circular models, focusing on product longevity, repairability, and effective e-waste management.

8. Global Impact: As a significant contributor to global carbon emissions, the IT sector has a crucial role to play in addressing climate change and other environmental challenges.

Looking Ahead:

As we look to the future, it's clear that Green IT will become increasingly integral to the overall strategy of technology companies and IT departments. The convergence of digital transformation and sustainability initiatives will likely accelerate, with IT playing a dual role as both a subject of sustainability efforts and an enabler of sustainability across other sectors.

The rapid pace of technological change presents both opportunities and challenges for Green IT. While new technologies offer the potential for greater efficiency and reduced environmental impact, they also require ongoing adaptation of sustainability strategies.

Call to Action:

For organizations and IT professionals, the message is clear: embracing Green IT is no longer optional but a necessity for long-term success and responsibility. This involves:

1. Integrating sustainability into core IT strategies and decision-making processes.

2. Investing in education and skills development for Green IT practices.

3. Collaborating across industries and with policymakers to develop standards and best practices.

4. Continuously innovating and adapting to leverage new technologies for

sustainability.

5. Fostering a culture of environmental responsibility throughout the organization.

In conclusion, Green IT represents a critical frontier in our collective efforts to create a more sustainable future. By leveraging the power of technology to reduce environmental impact while enabling sustainable practices across all sectors of the economy, the IT industry has the potential to be a leader in the global sustainability movement. The path forward will require commitment, innovation, and collaboration, but the potential rewards – for businesses, society, and the planet – are immense.

CHAPTER TWELVE

THE FUTURE OF WORK IN DIGITAL WORLD

1. Introduction

The world of work is undergoing a profound transformation, driven by rapid advancements in digital technologies, changing social norms, and global economic shifts. As we stand on the cusp of what many call the Fourth Industrial Revolution, the future of work in the digital world presents both exciting opportunities and significant challenges.

Digital technologies are reshaping not just how we work, but also what work we do, where we do it, and the skills required to thrive in this new landscape. Automation and artificial intelligence are taking over routine tasks, while simultaneously creating new roles that didn't exist a decade ago. The traditional nine-to-five office job is giving way to more flexible arrangements, with remote work and the gig economy becoming increasingly prevalent.

This transformation is occurring against a backdrop of broader societal changes. The COVID-19 pandemic has accelerated many trends that were already underway, forcing organizations and individuals to adapt rapidly to new ways of working. Climate change concerns are influencing corporate practices and individual career choices. Demographic shifts, including aging populations in some regions and youth bulges in others, are reshaping the workforce.

The future of work in the digital world touches on numerous interconnected issues:

1. The impact of automation and AI on employment
2. The rise of remote work and digital nomadism
3. The growth of the gig economy and platform work

4. The changing nature of skills required in the workplace

5. The evolution of organizational structures and management practices

6. The blurring of work-life boundaries

7. The ethical implications of new work arrangements and technologies

8. The role of education and lifelong learning in preparing the workforce

9. The policy and governance challenges posed by these changes

As we explore these topics, it's important to recognize that the future of work will not be uniform across all sectors, regions, or demographic groups. While some may benefit greatly from increased flexibility and new opportunities, others may face displacement or precarious employment conditions. Understanding these disparities and working to ensure an inclusive future of work is a critical challenge for policymakers, business leaders, and society as a whole.

This comprehensive exploration will delve into the key trends shaping the future of work in the digital world, examining their implications for individuals, organizations, and society. By understanding these trends and their potential impacts, we can better prepare for and shape a future of work that is productive, fulfilling, and equitable.

2. The Digital Transformation of Work

The digital transformation of work represents a fundamental shift in how businesses operate and how individuals perform their jobs. This transformation is driven by the rapid advancement and integration of digital technologies across all sectors of the economy.

Key Aspects of Digital Transformation:

1. Digitization of Processes:

- Automation of routine tasks and workflows

- Implementation of digital tools for collaboration and communication

- Shift from paper-based to digital documentation and record-keeping

2. Data-Driven Decision Making:

- Increased use of big data analytics in business strategy

- Real-time monitoring and adjustment of operations

- Predictive analytics for forecasting and risk management

3. Customer Experience:

- Personalization of products and services through data analysis

- Omnichannel customer engagement

- AI-powered customer service and support

4. New Business Models:

- Emergence of platform-based businesses

- Subscription and as-a-service models
- Digital marketplaces and ecosystems
    5. Digital Skills and Literacy:
- Growing importance of digital skills across all job roles
- Continuous learning and upskilling to keep pace with technological change
    Impact on Different Sectors:
    1. Manufacturing:
- Industry 4.0 and smart factories
- Internet of Things (IoT) for predictive maintenance and supply chain optimization
- 3D printing and additive manufacturing
    2. Healthcare:
- Telemedicine and remote patient monitoring
- AI-assisted diagnostics and treatment planning
- Electronic health records and data interoperability
    3. Finance:
- Digital banking and mobile payment systems
- Algorithmic trading and robo-advisors
- Blockchain and cryptocurrency technologies
    4. Retail:
- E-commerce and omnichannel retail experiences
- AR/VR for virtual try-ons and product visualization
- AI-powered inventory management and demand forecasting
    5. Education:
- Online learning platforms and MOOCs
- Personalized learning through adaptive technologies
- Virtual and augmented reality in educational experiences
    Challenges of Digital Transformation:
    1. Digital Divide:
- Unequal access to digital technologies and skills
- Risk of leaving behind certain demographics or regions
    2. Cybersecurity:
- Increased vulnerability to cyber attacks and data breaches
- Need for robust security measures and data protection
    3. Privacy Concerns:
- Collection and use of personal data in the workplace
- Balancing surveillance and employee privacy

4. Technological Unemployment:
- Displacement of jobs due to automation
- Need for reskilling and redeployment of workers
    5. Rapid Pace of Change:
- Difficulty in keeping up with technological advancements
- Constant need for updating systems and skills
    Benefits of Digital Transformation:
    1. Increased Productivity:
- Streamlining of processes and reduction of manual errors
- Faster decision-making through real-time data analysis
    2. Enhanced Flexibility:
- Ability to work remotely and collaborate across distances
- Scalable infrastructure through cloud computing
    3. Innovation Opportunities:
- New products, services, and business models enabled by digital technologies
- Improved R&D through data analytics and simulation
    4. Improved Customer Experience:
- Personalized and responsive customer interactions
- 24/7 availability through digital channels
    5. Cost Efficiency:
- Reduction in operational costs through automation
- Optimized resource allocation through data-driven insights
    Future Trends in Digital Transformation:
    1. Artificial Intelligence and Machine Learning:
- Increasing integration of AI in business processes and decision-making
- Development of more sophisticated and autonomous AI systems
    2. Internet of Things (IoT):
- Widespread adoption of IoT in various industries
- Creation of smart, interconnected work environments
    3. 5G and Advanced Connectivity:
- Enhanced mobile work capabilities
- Enablement of new applications requiring high-speed, low-latency connections
    4. Extended Reality (XR):
- Use of AR, VR, and MR for training, collaboration, and customer engagement
- Creation of immersive digital workspaces

5. Quantum Computing:
- Potential for solving complex problems in areas like logistics and financial modeling
- New cybersecurity challenges and opportunities

The digital transformation of work is an ongoing process that will continue to reshape the labor market, business operations, and individual job roles. As this transformation progresses, it will be crucial for organizations and individuals to adapt, continuously learn, and innovate to thrive in the evolving digital landscape.

3. Automation and Artificial Intelligence in the Workplace

Automation and Artificial Intelligence (AI) are at the forefront of transforming work across industries. These technologies are reshaping job roles, creating new opportunities, and challenging traditional notions of human labor.

Key Aspects of Automation and AI in the Workplace:

1. Robotic Process Automation (RPA):
- Automation of repetitive, rule-based tasks
- Applications in data entry, document processing, and customer service
- Potential for 24/7 operation and reduction in human error

2. Machine Learning and Predictive Analytics:
- Data-driven decision making and forecasting
- Personalization of products and services
- Fraud detection and risk assessment

3. Natural Language Processing (NLP):
- Chatbots and virtual assistants for customer service
- Language translation for global business operations
- Text analysis for sentiment analysis and market research

4. Computer Vision:
- Quality control in manufacturing
- Facial recognition for security systems
- Augmented reality for training and maintenance

5. Autonomous Systems:
- Self-driving vehicles in transportation and logistics
- Drones for delivery and inspection
- Robotics in manufacturing and warehousing

Impact on Different Job Categories:

1. Routine Cognitive Tasks:
- High potential for automation (e.g., data entry, basic accounting)

- Shift towards oversight and exception handling roles
    2. Routine Manual Tasks:
- Increasing automation in manufacturing and agriculture
- Growth in roles related to robot maintenance and oversight
    3. Non-Routine Cognitive Tasks:
- AI augmentation rather than replacement (e.g., medical diagnosis, legal research)
- Emphasis on uniquely human skills like creativity and emotional intelligence
    4. Non-Routine Manual Tasks:
- Lower immediate impact, but growing potential for automation
- Examples include eldercare robots and automated construction
    Challenges and Considerations:
    1. Job Displacement:
- Potential for significant job losses in certain sectors
- Need for retraining and transition support for affected workers
    2. Skill Gap:
- Growing demand for AI and data science skills
- Importance of developing AI literacy across the workforce
    3. Ethical Concerns:
- Algorithmic bias and fairness in AI-driven decisions
- Privacy issues related to data collection and analysis
- Transparency and explainability of AI systems
    4. Human-AI Collaboration:
- Designing effective human-AI interfaces
- Balancing automation with the need for human oversight and intervention
    5. Economic Impact:
- Potential for increased productivity and economic growth
- Concerns about wealth concentration and income inequality
    Emerging Trends:
    1. Explainable AI (XAI):
- Development of AI systems that can explain their decision-making processes
- Important for building trust and meeting regulatory requirements
    2. Federated Learning:
- AI training on decentralized data, preserving privacy
- Potential for more personalized AI applications in the workplace

3. AI-Powered Workforce Management:
- Predictive scheduling and resource allocation
- Performance analysis and personalized training recommendations

4. Cognitive Automation:
- AI systems capable of learning and adapting to new tasks
- Potential to automate more complex, non-routine tasks

5. Emotional AI:
- Systems capable of recognizing and responding to human emotions
- Applications in customer service, healthcare, and human resources

Future Outlook:

As automation and AI continue to advance, we can expect:
- A shift in the nature of human work towards tasks requiring creativity, emotional intelligence, and complex problem-solving
- Increased human-AI collaboration, with AI augmenting human capabilities rather than simply replacing them
- The emergence of new job roles focused on developing, maintaining, and overseeing AI systems
- A growing emphasis on continuous learning and adaptability in the workforce
- The need for new governance frameworks to address the ethical and societal implications of AI in the workplace

The integration of automation and AI in the workplace presents both significant opportunities and challenges. While these technologies have the potential to dramatically increase productivity and create new forms of value, they also raise important questions about the future of work, the skills needed to thrive in an AI-driven economy, and the broader societal implications of these changes. Successfully navigating this transition will require thoughtful collaboration between policymakers, business leaders, educators, and workers themselves.

4. Remote Work and Digital Nomadism

The rise of remote work and digital nomadism represents one of the most significant shifts in work culture in recent decades, accelerated by advancements in digital technologies and further catalyzed by the COVID-19 pandemic.

Key Aspects of Remote Work:

1. Flexibility in Work Location:
- Ability to work from home, co-working spaces, or any location with internet access

- Potential for improved work-life balance and reduced commute times

2. Digital Collaboration Tools:

- Video conferencing platforms (e.g., Zoom, Microsoft Teams)

- Project management software (e.g., Asana, Trello)

- Cloud-based document sharing and collaboration (e.g., Google Workspace, Microsoft 365)

3. Changes in Management Practices:

- Shift from time-based to outcome-based performance evaluation

- Need for trust-based management and clear communication

4. Impact on Urban Planning and Real Estate:

- Potential decrease in demand for office space in city centers

- Increased interest in suburban and rural living

Digital Nomadism:

1. Definition: Lifestyle combining remote work with travel, often internationally

2. Enablers:

- Global internet connectivity

- Freelance and contract work opportunities

- Digital skills that are location-independent

3. Challenges:

- Legal and tax implications of working across borders

- Maintaining work-life balance while traveling

- Building professional networks and career progression

Benefits of Remote Work:

1. Increased Productivity: Many workers report higher productivity when working remotely

2. Cost Savings: Reduced expenses for both employers (office space) and employees (commuting)

3. Access to Global Talent: Ability to hire from a worldwide talent pool

4. Environmental Impact: Potential reduction in carbon emissions due to decreased commuting

Challenges:

1. Digital Divide: Unequal access to necessary technology and high-speed internet

2. Work-Life Balance: Difficulty in separating work and personal life

3. Company Culture: Challenges in maintaining team cohesion and corporate culture

4. Mental Health: Potential for isolation and burnout

5. Security Concerns: Increased cybersecurity risks with distributed workforce

Emerging Trends:

1. Hybrid Work Models: Combining remote work with periodic in-office presence

2. Virtual Reality Workspaces: Using VR for immersive remote collaboration

3. "Work from Anywhere" Policies: Companies offering complete location flexibility

4. Remote Work Infrastructure: Growth of services catering to remote workers (e.g., global co-working space memberships)

Future Outlook:

As remote work and digital nomadism continue to evolve, we can expect:

- Further development of technologies to support distributed teams
- Evolution of legal and tax frameworks to accommodate mobile workers
- Increased focus on creating engaging virtual work environments
- Growing emphasis on digital wellness and work-life integration strategies

The shift towards remote work and digital nomadism represents a fundamental change in how we conceive of work, offering new freedoms but also presenting unique challenges. As this trend continues, it will be crucial for organizations, policymakers, and individuals to adapt and create structures that support productive, fulfilling, and sustainable remote work practices.

5. Gig Economy and Platform Work

The gig economy and platform work represent a significant shift in employment structures, characterized by short-term contracts, freelance work, and digital platforms that connect workers with clients or customers.

Key Characteristics:

1. Flexibility: Workers can choose when, where, and how much they work

2. Digital Mediation: Online platforms facilitate connections between workers and clients

3. Task-Based: Work is often project-based or task-oriented rather than ongoing employment

4. Rating Systems: Many platforms use rating systems for both workers and clients

Types of Gig Work:

1. Ride-sharing and Delivery Services: (e.g., Uber, Deliveroo)

2. Freelance Professional Services: (e.g., Upwork, Fiverr)

3. Micro-tasks: (e.g., Amazon Mechanical Turk)

4. Creative and Media Work: (e.g., YouTube content creation, Instagram influencers)

5. Accommodation Sharing: (e.g., Airbnb)

Benefits:

1. Flexibility and Autonomy: Workers can set their own schedules

2. Low Barriers to Entry: Easy to start working in many gig economy roles

3. Supplemental Income: Opportunity to earn additional income alongside traditional jobs

4. Access to Global Market: Ability to work for clients worldwide

Challenges:

1. Income Instability: Fluctuating and unpredictable earnings

2. Lack of Benefits: Often no access to traditional employment benefits (e.g., health insurance, paid leave)

3. Job Insecurity: No guarantees of ongoing work

4. Algorithmic Management: Worker performance often managed by algorithms, raising fairness concerns

5. Skill Development: Limited opportunities for structured career progression

Impact on Traditional Employment:

1. Changing Expectations: Workers increasingly value flexibility and autonomy

2. Competition: Traditional businesses adapting to compete with gig economy models

3. Hybrid Models: Some companies incorporating gig work alongside traditional employment

Legal and Regulatory Issues:

1. Worker Classification: Debates over whether gig workers should be classified as employees or independent contractors

2. Labor Protections: Questions about how to extend labor rights to gig workers

3. Taxation: Challenges in ensuring proper tax compliance in the gig economy

Emerging Trends:

1. Platform Cooperatives: Worker-owned platforms as alternatives to corporate-owned models

2. Gig Work in Traditional Companies: Incorporation of internal gig marketplaces within large organizations

3. Specialized Platforms: Growth of niche platforms for specific industries or skills

4. AI-Powered Matching: More sophisticated algorithms for matching workers with tasks

Future Outlook:

As the gig economy continues to evolve, we can expect:

- Increased regulation to address worker protections and platform responsibilities
- Development of new financial and insurance products tailored to gig workers
- Growing integration of gig work into traditional business models
- Emergence of new types of gig work as technology advances

The gig economy and platform work represent both opportunities and challenges in the future of work. While offering flexibility and new income streams, they also raise important questions about job security, worker rights, and the changing nature of the employer-employee relationship. Balancing the benefits of these new work models with adequate protections and support for workers will be a key challenge for policymakers and society as a whole.

6. Skills for the Future Workforce

As the nature of work evolves in the digital age, the skills required to thrive in the future workforce are also changing rapidly. Both technical and soft skills are becoming increasingly important to navigate the complexities of the modern workplace.

Key Skill Categories:

1. Digital Literacy:
- Basic coding and programming knowledge
- Data analysis and interpretation
- Cybersecurity awareness
- Digital content creation and management

2. Cognitive Abilities:
- Complex problem-solving
- Critical thinking
- Creativity and innovation
- Cognitive flexibility

3. Social and Emotional Intelligence:
- Emotional intelligence
- Cross-cultural communication
- Leadership and social influence
- Empathy and relationship building

4. Adaptability and Continuous Learning:
- Growth mindset
- Self-directed learning
- Adaptability to new technologies and work environments
- Resilience and stress management

5. Specialized Technical Skills:
- Artificial Intelligence and Machine Learning
- Robotics and automation
- Blockchain technology
- Virtual and Augmented Reality

Emerging Skill Trends:

1. Human-AI Collaboration:
- Understanding AI capabilities and limitations
- Ability to work alongside AI systems effectively

2. Data Literacy:
- Basic statistical analysis
- Data visualization
- Ethical use of data

3. Digital Ethics:
- Understanding ethical implications of technology
- Responsible innovation

4. Remote Work Competencies:
- Virtual collaboration
- Self-management in distributed teams
- Digital communication etiquette

5. Entrepreneurial Skills:
- Business model innovation
- Risk assessment and management
- Networking in digital environments

Challenges in Skill Development:

1. Rapid Obsolescence: Skills becoming outdated quickly due to technological advancements
2. Access to Training: Ensuring equitable access to skill development

opportunities

3. Relevance of Education: Aligning educational curricula with future skill needs

4. Mid-Career Transitions: Supporting workers in acquiring new skills later in their careers

Strategies for Skill Development:

1. Lifelong Learning: Fostering a culture of continuous education and skill upgrading

2. Micro-credentials: Offering short, focused courses on specific skills

3. Industry-Education Partnerships: Collaboration between businesses and educational institutions

4. Personalized Learning Paths: Using AI to create tailored learning experiences

5. On-the-Job Training: Integrating skill development into everyday work activities

Future Outlook:

As the future workforce continues to evolve, we can expect:

- Increased emphasis on interdisciplinary skills
- Growing importance of 'human' skills that cannot be easily automated
- More frequent career changes and skill pivots throughout working life
- Development of new assessment methods for emerging skills

The ability to continuously learn and adapt will be crucial in the future workforce. While technical skills will remain important, soft skills like creativity, emotional intelligence, and adaptability will become increasingly valuable. Educational institutions, employers, and individuals all have a role to play in fostering a culture of lifelong learning and ensuring that the workforce is equipped with the skills needed to thrive in the digital future.

7. Impact on Employment and Job Markets

The digital transformation of work is having profound effects on employment patterns and job markets worldwide. These changes are reshaping entire industries, creating new job categories, and altering the very nature of work itself.

Key Trends:

1. Job Displacement:
- Automation leading to the reduction or elimination of certain job roles
- Particularly affecting routine cognitive and manual tasks

2. Job Creation:
- Emergence of new roles related to digital technologies (e.g., AI ethicists,

data scientists)
- Growth in sectors like renewable energy, cybersecurity, and digital health
    3. Job Transformation:
- Existing roles evolving to incorporate new technologies and skills
- Increased human-AI collaboration in many professions
    4. Shift in Skill Demands:
- Growing demand for digital and technological skills across all sectors
- Increased value placed on uniquely human skills (creativity, emotional intelligence)
    5. Changes in Employment Structures:
- Rise of contract and freelance work
- Increase in remote and distributed teams
    Sectoral Impacts:
    1. Manufacturing:
- Reduction in manual labor due to automation
- Increase in roles related to robotics and advanced manufacturing technologies
    2. Services:
- Growth in digital service roles (e.g., online customer support, virtual assistants)
- Transformation of traditional service jobs through technology integration
    3. Knowledge Work:
- AI augmentation of professional roles (law, finance, healthcare)
- Increased emphasis on high-level analysis and strategic thinking
    4. Creative Industries:
- New opportunities in digital content creation
- Disruption of traditional media and entertainment models
    Challenges:
    1. Skills Mismatch:
- Gap between available jobs and workforce skills
- Need for large-scale reskilling and upskilling initiatives
    2. Regional Disparities:
- Concentration of high-tech jobs in urban centers
- Potential for increased economic inequality between regions
    3. Demographic Challenges:
- Aging workforce in some regions struggling to adapt to technological changes
- Youth unemployment in areas with limited digital infrastructure

4. Job Quality:
- Concerns about the quality and stability of newly created jobs
- Issues of underemployment in the gig economy
   Opportunities:
   1. Increased Productivity:
- Potential for economic growth through technology-driven productivity gains
   2. Enhanced Job Satisfaction:
- Automation of routine tasks allowing focus on more meaningful work
   3. Improved Work-Life Balance:
- Flexible work arrangements enabled by digital technologies
   4. Global Labor Market:
- Increased access to global job opportunities through remote work
   Future Outlook:
   As employment and job markets continue to evolve, we can expect:
- A more dynamic job market with frequent career changes
- Growing importance of soft skills and emotional intelligence
- Increased focus on lifelong learning and continuous skill development
- Potential for shorter work weeks as productivity increases
- Need for new social safety nets to address job displacement and transition
   The impact of digital transformation on employment and job markets presents both significant challenges and opportunities. While some job roles may become obsolete, new ones will emerge. The key to navigating this transition successfully will be adaptability, continuous learning, and proactive policies to support workforce transition and development.

8. Workplace Technologies and Tools

The digital workplace is constantly evolving, with new technologies and tools emerging to enhance productivity, collaboration, and overall work experience. These innovations are reshaping how we communicate, manage tasks, and interact with our work environment.
   Key Categories of Workplace Technologies:
   1. Communication and Collaboration Tools:
- Video conferencing platforms (e.g., Zoom, Microsoft Teams, Google Meet)
- Instant messaging and chat applications (e.g., Slack, Discord)
- Virtual whiteboarding and brainstorming tools (e.g., Miro, MURAL)
   2. Project Management and Productivity:
- Task management software (e.g., Asana, Trello, Monday.com)
- Time tracking tools (e.g., Toggl, RescueTime)

- Document collaboration platforms (e.g., Google Workspace, Microsoft 365)

3. Cloud Computing and Storage:
- Cloud storage solutions (e.g., Dropbox, Google Drive, OneDrive)
- Cloud-based software-as-a-service (SaaS) applications

4. Artificial Intelligence and Automation:
- AI-powered virtual assistants (e.g., Alcxa for Business, IBM Watson Assistant)
- Robotic Process Automation (RPA) tools
- AI-enhanced analytics and decision-making tools

5. Virtual and Augmented Reality:
- VR for immersive training and simulations
- AR for remote assistance and maintenance
- Virtual meeting spaces and collaborative environments

6. Internet of Things (IoT):
- Smart office devices for environmental control and energy management
- IoT-enabled asset tracking and management
- Wearable devices for employee health and safety monitoring

7. Cybersecurity Tools:
- Multi-factor authentication systems
- Virtual Private Networks (VPNs)
- Endpoint detection and response (EDR) solutions

Emerging Trends:

1. No-Code/Low-Code Platforms:
- Enabling non-technical employees to create applications and automate processes

2. Workplace Analytics:
- Tools for analyzing employee productivity, engagement, and wellbeing

3. Employee Experience Platforms:
- Integrated systems for managing all aspects of the employee journey

4. Edge Computing:
- Bringing computation and data storage closer to the location where it's needed

5. 5G Technology:
- Enabling faster, more reliable connections for remote and mobile workers

Challenges in Adoption:

1. Integration: Ensuring new tools work seamlessly with existing systems
2. Security: Protecting sensitive data across multiple platforms and devices

3. Training: Providing adequate training for employees to effectively use new tools

4. Overload: Managing the proliferation of tools without overwhelming employees

5. Cost: Balancing the benefits of new technologies with implementation costs

Benefits:

1. Increased Productivity: Streamlining workflows and automating routine tasks

2. Enhanced Collaboration: Facilitating teamwork across geographical boundaries

3. Flexibility: Enabling remote and hybrid work models

4. Data-Driven Decision Making: Providing insights through advanced analytics

5. Improved Employee Experience: Creating more engaging and efficient work environments

Future Outlook:

As workplace technologies continue to evolve, we can expect:

- Greater integration of AI and machine learning into everyday work tools
- More immersive and interactive virtual collaboration environments
- Increased focus on tools that support employee wellbeing and work-life balance
- Growing emphasis on sustainable and environmentally friendly workplace technologies
- Continued blurring of lines between personal and professional technology use

The adoption of these technologies and tools will be crucial for organizations looking to stay competitive in the digital age. However, successful implementation will require careful consideration of user needs, security implications, and the overall impact on work culture and practices.

9. Changes in Organizational Structures and Management

The digital transformation of work is not only changing the tools we use and the skills we need but also fundamentally altering organizational structures and management practices. These changes are driven by the need for greater agility, innovation, and adaptability in a rapidly evolving business environment.

Key Trends in Organizational Structures:

1. Flatter Hierarchies:
- Reduction in middle management layers
- Increased employee empowerment and decision-making authority
    2. Network-based Organizations:
- Shift from rigid hierarchies to more flexible, network-based structures
- Focus on cross-functional teams and project-based work
    3. Holacracy and Self-Management:
- Decentralized authority and self-organizing teams
- Emphasis on roles rather than job titles
    4. Virtual and Distributed Teams:
- Geographically dispersed workforce connected by technology
- Blending of internal employees, freelancers, and gig workers
    5. Ecosystem and Platform Models:
- Organizations operating as platforms connecting various stakeholders
- Increased collaboration with external partners and competitors
    Evolving Management Practices:
    1. Agile Management:
- Adoption of agile methodologies beyond software development
- Focus on iterative processes and continuous improvement
    2. Data-Driven Decision Making:
- Increased use of analytics and AI in management decisions
- Real-time performance monitoring and adjustment
    3. Continuous Feedback:
- Shift from annual performance reviews to ongoing feedback
- Use of digital tools for continuous performance management
    4. Remote Leadership:
- Developing skills for managing distributed teams
- Focus on outcomes rather than time spent working
    5. Employee Experience Management:
- Holistic approach to creating positive work environments
- Use of technology to enhance employee engagement and wellbeing
    Challenges:
    1. Cultural Transformation:
- Resistance to change in traditional organizational cultures
- Need for new leadership skills and mindsets
    2. Trust and Accountability:
- Balancing autonomy with accountability in decentralized structures
- Building trust in virtual and distributed teams

3. Diversity and Inclusion:
- Ensuring diverse perspectives in global, distributed organizations
- Addressing biases in AI-driven management tools
   4. Work-Life Balance:
- Managing boundaries in always-connected work environments
- Preventing burnout in flexible work arrangements
   Opportunities:
   1. Increased Agility:
- Faster response to market changes and customer needs
- Greater capacity for innovation and experimentation
   2. Enhanced Collaboration:
- Breaking down silos between departments and teams
- Leveraging diverse skills and perspectives
   3. Improved Employee Satisfaction:
- Greater autonomy and flexibility for workers
- More opportunities for skill development and career growth
   4. Cost Efficiency:
- Reduction in overhead costs through remote work and lean structures
- More efficient resource allocation through data-driven management
   Future Outlook:

As organizational structures and management practices continue to evolve, we can expect:
- Further blurring of boundaries between different organizational functions
- Increased focus on purpose-driven and values-based management
- Growing importance of soft skills and emotional intelligence in leadership
- More sophisticated use of AI and analytics in organizational design and management
- Continued experimentation with new organizational models and management approaches

These changes in organizational structures and management practices represent a significant shift from traditional models. Success in this new environment will require adaptability, continuous learning, and a willingness to challenge established norms of organizational hierarchy and control.

10. Work-Life Balance in the Digital Age

The digital transformation of work has significantly impacted the concept of work-life balance, blurring the lines between professional and personal life. While digital technologies offer unprecedented flexibility, they also create challenges in managing boundaries and maintaining wellbeing.

Key Aspects:

1. Always-On Culture:
- Constant connectivity leading to expectations of 24/7 availability
- Difficulty in disconnecting from work

2. Flexible Work Arrangements:
- Remote work and flexible hours offering more control over schedules
- Challenges in separating work and personal spaces

3. Digital Overload:
- Information overload and multitasking leading to stress and burnout
- Increased screen time affecting physical and mental health

4. Work-Life Integration:
- Shift from strict work-life balance to work-life integration
- Blending of personal and professional activities throughout the day

Challenges:

1. Burnout:
- Increased risk of burnout due to inability to disconnect
- Difficulty in maintaining boundaries between work and personal life

2. Digital Presenteeism:
- Pressure to appear constantly available and productive
- Overworking to prove value in remote settings

3. Time Management:
- Struggling to allocate time effectively between work and personal activities
- Difficulty in prioritizing tasks in a constantly connected environment

4. Mental Health:
- Increased stress and anxiety related to work pressures
- Isolation and loneliness in remote work settings

Opportunities:

1. Increased Flexibility:
- Ability to design work schedules around personal needs and preferences
- Opportunity for better integration of work with family and personal life

2. Reduced Commute Stress:
- Time and energy saved from eliminating or reducing daily commutes
- Potential for improved quality of life and environmental benefits

3. Personalized Work Environments:
- Ability to create optimal personal work settings

- Potential for increased productivity and job satisfaction
    4. Global Opportunities:
- Access to job opportunities regardless of geographical location
- Potential for diverse work experiences and cultural exchanges
    Emerging Trends:
    1. Digital Wellbeing Tools:
- Apps and features designed to manage screen time and digital habits
- AI-powered tools for personalized work-life balance recommendations
    2. Right to Disconnect:
- Implementation of policies protecting employees' right to disconnect after work hours
- Growing recognition of the importance of digital detox
    3. Four-Day Work Week:
- Experiments with reduced work hours to improve work-life balance
- Focus on productivity rather than time spent working
    4. Workplace Wellness Programs:
- Holistic approaches to employee wellbeing, including mental health support
- Integration of wellness activities into daily work routines
    Future Outlook:
    As work-life balance in the digital age continues to evolve, we can expect:
- Increased emphasis on outcome-based performance rather than hours worked
- Growing importance of digital literacy in managing personal and professional boundaries
- More sophisticated technologies to support work-life integration
- Continued debate and policy development around work hours and availability expectations

Achieving a healthy work-life balance in the digital age requires a combination of personal strategies, organizational policies, and technological solutions. As the nature of work continues to change, finding effective ways to manage the integration of work and personal life will be crucial for individual wellbeing and organizational success.

11. Ethical Considerations in the Future of Work

As the digital transformation reshapes the workplace, it brings forth a host of ethical considerations that organizations, policymakers, and individuals must grapple with. These ethical challenges touch on various aspects of work, from privacy and fairness to the very nature of human labor.

Key Ethical Issues:

1. Workplace Surveillance:
- Ethical implications of monitoring employee activities
- Balancing productivity tracking with privacy rights

2. Algorithmic Management:
- Fairness and transparency in AI-driven decision-making
- Potential for bias in hiring, performance evaluation, and task allocation

3. Data Privacy:
- Ethical use and protection of employee and customer data
- Boundaries between personal and professional data

4. Job Displacement:
- Ethical responsibilities towards workers displaced by automation
- Balancing innovation with social responsibility

5. Digital Divide:
- Addressing inequalities in access to digital skills and opportunities
- Ensuring inclusivity in the evolving job market

6. Gig Economy Ethics:
- Fair treatment and protection of gig workers
- Responsibility of platforms towards their workers

7. AI and Human Augmentation:
- Ethical implications of AI augmentation in the workplace
- Potential for creating new forms of inequality

8. Work-Life Balance:
- Ethical considerations in always-on work cultures
- Responsibility for employee wellbeing in flexible work arrangements

Emerging Ethical Frameworks:

1. Responsible AI:
- Principles for ethical development and deployment of AI in the workplace
- Focus on transparency, accountability, and fairness

2. Stakeholder Capitalism:
- Considering the interests of all stakeholders, not just shareholders
- Balancing profit with social and environmental responsibility

3. Digital Ethics:
- Frameworks for ethical decision-making in digital environments
- Addressing issues of consent, privacy, and digital rights

Challenges in Addressing Ethical Issues:

1. Rapid Technological Change:
- Difficulty in developing ethical frameworks that keep pace with innovation
- Unforeseen ethical implications of new technologies

2. Global Differences:
- Varying cultural and legal perspectives on workplace ethics
- Challenges in implementing global ethical standards

3. Balancing Interests:
- Reconciling business interests with ethical considerations
- Addressing potential conflicts between different stakeholder groups

Future Outlook:

As ethical considerations in the future of work continue to evolve, we can expect:
- Increased focus on ethical AI and algorithmic accountability
- Development of new regulatory frameworks addressing digital work ethics
- Growing importance of ethics training in workplace skills development
- Emergence of new roles focused on workplace ethics and digital rights
- Greater emphasis on transparency in organizational practices and decision-making

Addressing ethical considerations in the future of work will require ongoing dialogue and collaboration between businesses, policymakers, ethicists, and workers. As technology continues to reshape the workplace, ensuring that these changes align with human values and societal ethics will be crucial for creating a fair, inclusive, and sustainable future of work.

12. The Role of Education and Lifelong Learning

As the workplace rapidly evolves in the digital age, education and lifelong learning have become critical components in preparing individuals for the future of work. The traditional model of front-loaded education is giving way to a more dynamic, continuous learning approach throughout one's career.

Key Aspects:

1. Skill-based Learning:
- Focus on developing specific, marketable skills
- Shift from degree-centric to skill-centric hiring practices

2. Micro-credentials and Nanodegrees:
- Short, focused courses on specific topics or skills
- Stackable credentials allowing for flexible learning paths

3. Online and Blended Learning:
- Massive Open Online Courses (MOOCs) and digital learning platforms
- Hybrid models combining online and in-person instruction
    4. Personalized Learning:
- AI-driven adaptive learning systems
- Customized learning paths based on individual needs and goals
    5. Corporate Learning and Development:
- Increased investment in employee upskilling and reskilling
- Integration of learning into daily work routines
    Emerging Trends:
    1. Immersive Learning Technologies:
- Use of VR and AR for experiential learning
- Simulations and gamification in education and training
    2. Peer-to-Peer Learning:
- Platforms facilitating knowledge sharing among professionals
- Collaborative learning communities and networks
    3. Just-in-Time Learning:
- On-demand access to learning resources at the point of need
- Integration of learning tools into workplace technologies
    4. AI-Enhanced Education:
- AI tutors and personalized learning assistants
- Predictive analytics to identify learning needs and opportunities
    Challenges:
    1. Keeping Pace with Technological Change:
- Ensuring curriculum relevance in rapidly evolving fields
- Developing educators' skills to teach emerging technologies
    2. Accessibility and Equity:
- Addressing disparities in access to lifelong learning opportunities
- Ensuring inclusivity in digital learning environments
    3. Recognition and Accreditation:
- Validating and recognizing non-traditional learning experiences
- Developing standards for new forms of credentials
    4. Motivation and Engagement:
- Encouraging continuous learning mindset among workers
- Balancing learning with work and personal commitments
    Future Outlook:
    As education and lifelong learning continue to evolve, we can expect:
- Greater integration of education and work, with more fluid transitions

between learning and applying skills
- Increased collaboration between educational institutions and industry to align curricula with workforce needs
- Development of more sophisticated AI-driven learning systems
- Growing emphasis on soft skills and adaptability alongside technical skills
- Emergence of new models for funding and accessing lifelong learning opportunities

The role of education and lifelong learning in preparing for the future of work cannot be overstated. As the half-life of skills continues to shorten, the ability to continuously learn, unlearn, and relearn will become a critical success factor for individuals and organizations alike. Educational institutions, employers, and policymakers will need to work together to create a robust ecosystem that supports lifelong learning and enables individuals to thrive in the ever-changing world of work.

13. Policy Implications and Governance

The rapidly evolving nature of work in the digital age presents significant challenges for policymakers and governance structures. Addressing these challenges requires innovative approaches to labor laws, social protection, education, and economic policies.

Key Policy Areas:

1. Labor Laws and Worker Protection:
- Adapting employment laws to cover new forms of work (e.g., gig economy)
- Ensuring worker rights and protections in digital and platform-based work

2. Social Safety Nets:
- Redesigning social security systems for more flexible career paths
- Exploring universal basic income as a potential response to job displacement

3. Education and Skills Policy:
- Reforming education systems to emphasize digital skills and lifelong learning
- Developing frameworks for recognizing and accrediting non-traditional learning

4. Digital Infrastructure:
- Ensuring widespread access to high-speed internet and digital technologies
- Addressing the digital divide between urban and rural areas

5. Data Protection and Privacy:
- Developing robust data protection regulations for the digital workplace
- Balancing innovation with privacy rights
6. Competition Policy:
- Addressing market concentration in digital platforms
- Ensuring fair competition in the digital economy
Emerging Policy Approaches:
1. Flexicurity:
- Combining labor market flexibility with strong social security
- Balancing employer needs with worker protection
2. Portable Benefits:
- Developing benefit systems that move with workers across jobs and gig work
3. Skills Forecasting:
- Creating systems to anticipate future skill needs and guide policy
- Aligning education and training programs with projected labor market demands
4. Regulatory Sandboxes:
- Creating controlled environments to test new policy approaches
- Allowing for regulatory experimentation in response to technological change
Challenges in Policy Development:
1. Pace of Change:
- Difficulty in keeping policies relevant amid rapid technological advancement
- Balancing the need for timely action with thorough policy development
2. Global Coordination:
- Addressing the transnational nature of digital work
- Harmonizing policies across different jurisdictions
3. Stakeholder Engagement:
- Ensuring input from diverse stakeholders, including workers, businesses, and civil society
- Balancing competing interests in policy formulation
4. Technological Complexity:
- Developing policies that address the nuances of new technologies
- Ensuring policymakers have sufficient technical understanding
Future Outlook:

As policy and governance for the future of work continue to evolve, we can expect:
- More agile and adaptive policy-making processes
- Increased use of data and AI in policy development and implementation
- Greater emphasis on international cooperation in addressing global workforce challenges
- Evolution of governance structures to better address cross-cutting issues in the digital economy

The development of effective policies and governance structures for the future of work is crucial for ensuring that the benefits of digital transformation are widely shared while mitigating potential negative impacts. This will require innovative thinking, cross-sector collaboration, and a willingness to reimagine traditional approaches to labor market governance.

14. Conclusion and Future Outlook

As we've explored throughout this comprehensive overview, the future of work in the digital world is characterized by rapid change, new opportunities, and significant challenges. The digital transformation is reshaping not just how we work, but the very nature of work itself.

Key Takeaways:

1. Technological Disruption: AI, automation, and digital platforms are fundamentally altering job roles and creating new forms of work.

2. Skill Evolution: The demand for digital skills is growing across all sectors, alongside an increased emphasis on uniquely human skills like creativity and emotional intelligence.

3. Flexible Work Arrangements: Remote work and the gig economy are offering new levels of flexibility but also presenting challenges in terms of job security and worker protections.

4. Lifelong Learning: Continuous skill development and adaptability are becoming crucial for career success in a rapidly evolving job market.

5. Ethical Considerations: The digital workplace raises important ethical questions around privacy, algorithmic bias, and the impact of technology on human workers.

6. Policy Challenges: Governments and organizations face the task of developing agile policies that can keep pace with technological change while ensuring worker protections and social stability.

Future Outlook:

As we look towards the future of work, several trends are likely to shape the landscape:

1. Human-AI Collaboration: We can expect to see more sophisticated integration of AI in the workplace, with a focus on augmenting human capabilities rather than replacing them.

2. Hyper-Personalization: Advanced data analytics and AI will enable more personalized work experiences, from tailored learning paths to customized work environments.

3. Distributed Workforce: The trend towards remote and distributed teams is likely to continue, facilitated by advancements in virtual collaboration technologies.

4. Sustainability Focus: Environmental concerns will increasingly influence work practices, from sustainable office designs to the reduction of business travel through virtual alternatives.

5. Evolving Social Contracts: We may see fundamental shifts in how society views work, with potential experiments in reduced work weeks, universal basic income, or new forms of social safety nets.

6. Technological Wild Cards: Emerging technologies like brain-computer interfaces, advanced robotics, or breakthrough in quantum computing could dramatically reshape the work landscape in unforeseen ways.

The future of work presents both exciting possibilities and significant challenges. Success in this new era will require adaptability, continuous learning, and a willingness to rethink traditional notions of work and careers. For individuals, this means embracing lifelong learning and developing a diverse skill set. For organizations, it involves fostering cultures of innovation and agility. For policymakers, the challenge is to create frameworks that promote innovation while ensuring inclusive growth and worker protections.

As we navigate this transition, it will be crucial to approach the future of work with a human-centric mindset, ensuring that technological advancements serve to enhance human potential and well-being rather than diminish them. By doing so, we can work towards a future where the benefits of digital transformation are widely shared, creating more fulfilling, productive, and inclusive work environments for all.

CHAPTER THIRTEEN

GLOBAL DIGITAL POLICIES AND REGULATIONS

1. Introduction

The rapid advancement of digital technologies has transformed virtually every aspect of modern society, from how we communicate and conduct business to how we access information and engage with government services. This digital revolution has brought unprecedented opportunities for innovation, economic growth, and social progress. However, it has also introduced new challenges and risks that require careful consideration and regulation.

Global digital policies and regulations have emerged as critical tools for governments and international organizations to navigate the complex landscape of the digital age. These policies and regulations aim to harness the benefits of digital technologies while mitigating potential harms and ensuring that the digital ecosystem develops in a way that aligns with societal values and protections.

The scope of digital policies and regulations is vast and continuously evolving, encompassing areas such as:

1. Data protection and privacy
2. Cybersecurity
3. Digital market competition
4. Artificial intelligence governance
5. Internet governance and net neutrality
6. Digital taxation

7. Content moderation and platform liability

8. Digital identity and authentication

9. Cryptocurrency and blockchain

10. Telecommunications and 5G networks

11. Digital trade and e-commerce

12. Children's online protection

These policy arcas are interconnected and often overlap, requiring a holistic approach to digital governance. Moreover, the global nature of the digital ecosystem presents unique challenges for policymakers, as digital activities often transcend national borders, necessitating international cooperation and harmonization of regulations.

The development of digital policies and regulations involves a delicate balancing act. On one hand, there is a need to protect individual rights, ensure fair competition, and safeguard national security. On the other hand, overly restrictive regulations can stifle innovation, impede economic growth, and limit the potential benefits of digital technologies.

This comprehensive exploration will delve into the key areas of global digital policies and regulations, examining current frameworks, emerging trends, and future challenges. We will analyze how different regions and countries approach digital governance, highlight best practices, and discuss the implications of these policies for businesses, individuals, and society at large.

As we navigate through this complex landscape, it's important to recognize that digital policies and regulations are not static. They must continually evolve to keep pace with rapid technological advancements and changing societal needs. Understanding the current state of global digital policies and regulations is crucial for policymakers, business leaders, and citizens alike, as we collectively shape the digital future of our interconnected world.

2. Data Protection and Privacy Regulations

Data protection and privacy regulations have become increasingly prominent in the global digital policy landscape, driven by growing concerns over the collection, use, and sharing of personal data by businesses and governments.

Key Global Frameworks:

1. General Data Protection Regulation (GDPR) - European Union
The GDPR, implemented in 2018, has become a global benchmark for data protection regulations. Key features include:

- Broad territorial scope, applying to any organization processing EU residents' data
- Strict consent requirements for data collection and processing
- Data minimization and purpose limitation principles
- Right to erasure ("right to be forgotten") and data portability
- Significant penalties for non-compliance (up to 4% of global annual turnover)

2. California Consumer Privacy Act (CCPA) - United States
Implemented in 2020, the CCPA is one of the most comprehensive privacy laws in the U.S. Key aspects include:
- Rights for consumers to know what personal information is collected and how it's used
- Right to opt-out of the sale of personal information
- Right to request deletion of personal information
- Special protections for minors

3. Personal Information Protection Law (PIPL) - China
Implemented in 2021, China's PIPL shares similarities with GDPR but has unique features:
- Restrictions on cross-border data transfers
- Requirement for critical information infrastructure operators to store personal information within China
- Stricter rules for processing sensitive personal information

4. Lei Geral de Proteção de Dados (LGPD) - Brazil
Brazil's LGPD, effective from 2020, closely aligns with the GDPR. Key elements include:
- Broad definition of personal data
- Legal bases for data processing, including consent
- Data subject rights, including access, correction, and deletion
- Appointment of Data Protection Officers for certain organizations

Emerging Trends in Data Protection Regulations:

1. Cross-Border Data Flows
Regulations increasingly address the transfer of personal data across national borders:
- EU-U.S. Privacy Shield invalidation and subsequent negotiations
- Adequacy decisions by the EU for countries providing equivalent data protection
- Data localization requirements in countries like Russia and India

2. Biometric Data Protection

Special provisions for the collection and use of biometric data:

- Illinois Biometric Information Privacy Act (BIPA) in the U.S.

- Explicit consent requirements for biometric data in GDPR and LGPD

3. AI and Automated Decision-Making

Regulations addressing the use of AI in processing personal data:

- GDPR's right to explanation for automated decision-making

- Proposed AI regulations in the EU with implications for personal data processing

4. Data Breach Notification

Mandatory breach notification requirements becoming more common:

- 72-hour notification requirement under GDPR

- Various state-level breach notification laws in the U.S.

5. Privacy by Design and Default

Embedding privacy considerations into the development of products and services:

- GDPR's requirements for privacy by design and default

- Similar principles in CCPA and other emerging regulations

Challenges in Global Data Protection Regulation:

1. Harmonization vs. Fragmentation

- Balancing the need for global standards with local legal and cultural contexts

- Challenges for businesses in complying with multiple, sometimes conflicting, regulations

2. Technological Advancements

- Keeping regulations relevant in the face of rapidly evolving technologies like AI and IoT

- Addressing new forms of data collection and processing (e.g., edge computing, federated learning)

3. Balancing Privacy with Innovation

- Ensuring data protection doesn't stifle beneficial innovations in areas like healthcare and smart cities

- Finding the right balance between individual privacy rights and societal benefits of data use

4. Enforcement and Compliance

- Challenges in enforcing regulations across jurisdictions

- Resource constraints for regulatory bodies in monitoring and enforcing compliance

5. Data Sovereignty and National Security
- Tensions between data protection and national security interests
- Debates over government access to personal data, particularly in cross-border scenarios

Future Outlook:

As data continues to be a critical asset in the digital economy, we can expect:
- More countries to adopt comprehensive data protection laws
- Increased focus on interoperability between different regulatory frameworks
- Growing emphasis on individual control over personal data, including data portability and right to erasure
- Evolution of regulations to address emerging technologies and data use cases

The landscape of data protection and privacy regulations continues to evolve rapidly, reflecting the growing importance of personal data in our digital society. As these regulations mature and expand globally, they will play a crucial role in shaping the future of the digital economy and society.

3. Cybersecurity Policies and Frameworks

As digital threats continue to evolve in sophistication and scale, cybersecurity has become a critical concern for governments, businesses, and individuals alike. Global cybersecurity policies and frameworks aim to protect digital assets, infrastructure, and personal data from cyber threats.

Key International Cybersecurity Frameworks:

1. NIST Cybersecurity Framework (United States)

Developed by the National Institute of Standards and Technology, this framework provides a comprehensive approach to managing and reducing cybersecurity risk. Key components include:
- Five core functions: Identify, Protect, Detect, Respond, and Recover
- Flexible and adaptable to various sectors and organization sizes
- Widely adopted internationally as a best practice guide

2. ISO/IEC 27001 (International)

This international standard provides requirements for an information security management system (ISMS). Key features include:
- Risk assessment and treatment
- Security controls across various domains (e.g., access control, cryptography)
- Continuous improvement process

- Certification option for organizations

3. EU Network and Information Security (NIS) Directive

This EU-wide legislation aims to enhance cybersecurity across the bloc. Key elements include:

- Security requirements for operators of essential services and digital service providers
- Incident reporting obligations
- Cross-border cooperation mechanisms

4. China's Multi-Level Protection Scheme (MLPS 2.0)

An updated cybersecurity framework in China that categorizes information systems and mandates security measures. Features include:

- Five-level classification system based on potential impact of security breaches
- Mandatory security requirements for each level
- Focus on emerging technologies like cloud computing and IoT

National Cybersecurity Strategies:

Many countries have developed national cybersecurity strategies to address digital threats:

1. United States: The National Cyber Strategy focuses on securing government networks, critical infrastructure, and combating cybercrime.

2. European Union: The EU Cybersecurity Strategy aims to boost resilience, tackle cybercrime, and promote global cooperation.

3. United Kingdom: The National Cyber Security Strategy emphasizes defense, deterrence, and development of cyber capabilities.

4. Japan: The Cybersecurity Strategy focuses on advancing a free, fair, and secure cyberspace while promoting economic growth.

5. Australia: The Cyber Security Strategy 2020 aims to protect the economy, essential services, and national security from cyber threats.

Emerging Trends in Cybersecurity Policies:

1. Critical Infrastructure Protection

- Increased focus on securing energy, healthcare, financial, and other critical sectors
- Mandatory cybersecurity requirements for critical infrastructure operators

2. Supply Chain Security

- Growing emphasis on securing the entire supply chain, including third-party vendors
- Regulations like the EU's Cybersecurity Act addressing supply chain risks

3. Cyber Threat Information Sharing
- Establishment of Information Sharing and Analysis Centers (ISACs) in various sectors
- Policies encouraging public-private partnerships for threat intelligence sharing
4. Artificial Intelligence and Machine Learning in Cybersecurity
- Policies promoting the use of AI for threat detection and response
- Addressing potential vulnerabilities introduced by AI systems
5. Quantum-Safe Cryptography
- Initiatives to prepare for the potential threat of quantum computing to current encryption methods
- Research and standardization efforts for post-quantum cryptography
6. IoT Security
- Development of security standards and regulations for Internet of Things devices
- Initiatives like the UK's Code of Practice for Consumer IoT Security
7. Cybersecurity Workforce Development
- Policies aimed at addressing the global cybersecurity skills shortage
- Initiatives to promote cybersecurity education and training
Challenges in Global Cybersecurity Policy:
1. Attribution and Response
- Difficulties in attributing cyberattacks to specific actors
- Developing appropriate response mechanisms to state-sponsored cyber activities
2. Balancing Security and Privacy
- Addressing tensions between cybersecurity measures and individual privacy rights
- Debates over encryption and government access to data
3. Rapid Technological Change
- Keeping policies and regulations relevant in the face of evolving technologies and threats
- Addressing emerging risks from technologies like 5G, IoT, and quantum computing
4. International Cooperation vs. Cyber Sovereignty
- Balancing the need for global cooperation with national security interests
- Addressing conflicting approaches to internet governance and cyber norms

5. Public-Private Sector Collaboration

- Encouraging information sharing while protecting sensitive business information
- Defining roles and responsibilities between government and private sector in cybersecurity

Future Outlook:

As cyber threats continue to evolve, we can expect:

- Increased emphasis on proactive and adaptive cybersecurity measures
- Greater international cooperation on cybercrime and cyber norms
- Integration of cybersecurity considerations into broader digital policies
- Focus on resilience and rapid recovery in addition to prevention
- Growing importance of cybersecurity in national security strategies

The landscape of cybersecurity policies and frameworks is dynamic, reflecting the ever-changing nature of cyber threats. As digital technologies become more pervasive, effective cybersecurity governance will be crucial for maintaining trust in the digital ecosystem and ensuring the stability of our increasingly connected world.

4. Digital Market Regulations

As digital platforms and tech giants have grown to dominate various sectors of the economy, governments worldwide have increasingly focused on regulating digital markets to ensure fair competition, protect consumers, and foster innovation.

Key Areas of Digital Market Regulation:

1. Antitrust and Competition Law

- EU's Digital Markets Act (DMA): Aims to curb the power of large tech platforms, introducing new obligations for "gatekeepers."
- U.S. antitrust investigations into major tech companies like Google, Facebook, Amazon, and Apple.
- China's anti-monopoly regulations targeting tech giants like Alibaba and Tencent.

2. Data Portability and Interoperability

- Regulations promoting user data portability between platforms (e.g., GDPR's data portability right).
- Efforts to ensure interoperability between different digital services.

3. App Store Regulations

- Investigations into app store practices of Apple and Google.
- South Korea's law requiring alternative payment systems in app stores.

4. Digital Advertising

- EU's Digital Services Act (DSA) introducing transparency requirements for online advertising.

- Regulations addressing targeted advertising and use of personal data.

5. Platform-to-Business Regulations

- EU's Platform-to-Business Regulation ensuring fairness and transparency in online platform trading practices.

Emerging Trends in Digital Market Regulation:

1. Focus on Data as a Competitive Asset

- Recognition of data's role in market dominance.

- Regulations addressing data accumulation and use by large platforms.

2. Sector-Specific Regulations

- Tailored regulations for sectors like fintech, e-commerce, and digital health.

- Example: Open Banking regulations in various countries.

3. AI and Algorithmic Accountability

- Regulations addressing potential anti-competitive use of AI and algorithms.

- Transparency requirements for algorithmic decision-making.

4. Digital Services Taxes

- Introduction of specific taxes on digital services in countries like France and UK.

- OECD efforts to develop a global framework for digital taxation.

5. Merger Control in Digital Markets

- Increased scrutiny of acquisitions by large tech companies.

- Consideration of data and network effects in merger assessments.

Challenges in Digital Market Regulation:

1. Balancing Innovation and Regulation

- Ensuring regulations don't stifle innovation and economic growth.

- Keeping pace with rapid technological advancements.

2. Jurisdictional Issues

- Addressing the global nature of digital markets within national regulatory frameworks.

- Harmonizing regulations across different jurisdictions.

3. Defining Relevant Markets

- Difficulties in applying traditional market definition concepts to digital ecosystems.

- Addressing multi-sided markets and zero-price services.

4. Enforcement and Remedies

- Developing effective enforcement mechanisms for digital markets.

- Designing appropriate remedies for anti-competitive behavior in fast-moving tech sectors.

Future Outlook:

As digital markets continue to evolve, we can expect:

- More comprehensive and tailored regulations for digital platforms and services.

- Increased international cooperation on digital market regulation.

- Greater focus on data governance as a key aspect of competition policy.

- Evolution of regulatory approaches to address emerging technologies and business models.

The regulation of digital markets remains a complex and rapidly evolving area, requiring a delicate balance between fostering innovation, protecting competition, and safeguarding consumer interests in the digital economy.

5. Artificial Intelligence Governance

As Artificial Intelligence (AI) becomes increasingly pervasive across various sectors, governments and international organizations are developing frameworks and regulations to ensure its ethical and responsible development and use.

Key Areas of AI Governance:

1. Ethical AI Principles

- OECD AI Principles: Adopted by 42 countries, promoting AI that is innovative, trustworthy, and respects human rights.

- EU's Ethics Guidelines for Trustworthy AI: Focusing on lawful, ethical, and robust AI.

2. AI Regulation

- EU's proposed Artificial Intelligence Act: Risk-based approach to regulating AI systems.

- China's New Generation Artificial Intelligence Development Plan: Emphasizing AI ethics and safety.

3. Algorithmic Accountability

- U.S. Algorithmic Accountability Act (proposed): Requiring companies to assess and fix flawed algorithms.

- New York City's algorithmic accountability law for automated employment decision tools.

4. AI in Specific Sectors

- Healthcare: FDA's proposed regulatory framework for AI/ML-based medical devices.

- Finance: Regulations on AI use in financial services (e.g., MiFID II in EU).

5. Facial Recognition and Biometrics

- EU's approach in the AI Act: Strict regulation of biometric identification systems.

- Various city-level bans on facial recognition technology in the U.S.

Emerging Trends in AI Governance:

1. Explainable AI (XAI)

- Increasing focus on transparency and interpretability of AI systems.

- Requirements for human-understandable explanations of AI decisions.

2. AI and Data Protection

- Integration of AI governance with data protection regulations (e.g., GDPR's provisions on automated decision-making).

3. AI Auditing and Impact Assessment

- Development of frameworks for assessing the societal impact of AI systems.

- Canada's Algorithmic Impact Assessment tool for government AI use.

4. International AI Cooperation

- Global Partnership on AI (GPAI): International initiative for responsible AI development.

- UNESCO's Recommendation on the Ethics of AI.

Challenges in AI Governance:

1. Balancing Innovation and Regulation

- Ensuring regulations don't stifle beneficial AI development.

- Keeping pace with rapid advancements in AI technology.

2. Defining AI for Regulatory Purposes

- Challenges in creating a legal definition of AI that is both comprehensive and future-proof.

3. Global Harmonization

- Addressing varying approaches to AI governance across different jurisdictions.

- Potential for regulatory arbitrage in AI development.

4. Enforcement and Technical Expertise

- Ensuring regulators have the necessary technical expertise to oversee AI systems.

- Developing effective enforcement mechanisms for AI regulations.

5. Addressing AI Bias and Fairness

- Creating frameworks to detect and mitigate bias in AI systems.

- Balancing fairness considerations across different demographic groups.
   Future Outlook:
As AI continues to evolve, we can expect:
- More comprehensive and sector-specific AI regulations.
- Increased focus on AI ethics education and workforce development.
- Growing emphasis on international cooperation in AI governance.
- Evolution of governance approaches to address emerging AI capabilities (e.g., artificial general intelligence).

AI governance is a rapidly evolving field, requiring a multidisciplinary approach that combines technical, ethical, legal, and social considerations. As AI systems become more complex and ubiquitous, effective governance will be crucial to ensure that AI benefits society while minimizing potential risks and harms.

6. Internet Governance and Net Neutrality

Internet governance encompasses the development and application of shared principles, norms, rules, decision-making procedures, and programs that shape the evolution and use of the Internet. Net neutrality, a key principle within this broader framework, refers to the concept that all Internet traffic should be treated equally, without discrimination or preferential treatment.

Key Aspects of Internet Governance:

1. Multi-stakeholder Model
- Internet Corporation for Assigned Names and Numbers (ICANN): Manages domain names and IP addresses.
- Internet Governance Forum (IGF): UN-sponsored platform for multi-stakeholder policy dialogue.

2. Technical Standards
- Internet Engineering Task Force (IETF): Develops and promotes Internet standards.
- World Wide Web Consortium (W3C): Creates Web standards and guidelines.

3. Cybersecurity and Stability
- Policies aimed at ensuring the security and stability of Internet infrastructure.
- Efforts to combat cybercrime and enhance online safety.

4. Digital Divide and Access
- Initiatives to promote universal Internet access and digital literacy.
- Programs addressing infrastructure development in underserved areas.

Net Neutrality Regulations:

1. United States

- 2015: FCC's Open Internet Order established strong net neutrality rules.
- 2017: FCC repealed these rules, shifting to a "light-touch" regulatory approach.
- Ongoing debates and potential for new federal legislation.

2. European Union

- 2016: EU Net Neutrality Regulations ensuring open Internet access.
- BEREC guidelines on the implementation of net neutrality rules.

3. India

- 2018: Department of Telecommunications approved net neutrality rules.
- Prohibits any form of data discrimination, with exceptions for critical services.

4. Brazil

- 2014: Marco Civil da Internet law enshrined net neutrality principles.
- 2016: Further regulations detailing implementation of net neutrality.

Emerging Trends and Challenges:

1. Content Regulation and Free Speech

- Balancing freedom of expression with efforts to combat misinformation and harmful content.
- Debates over platform liability and content moderation practices.

2. Internet Fragmentation

- Concerns over the "splinternet" - the fragmentation of the global Internet into national or regional networks.
- Tensions between global interoperability and national sovereignty.

3. DNS over HTTPS (DoH) and DNS over TLS (DoT)

- Implications for network management, security, and national regulations.

4. 5G and Network Slicing

- Debates over how net neutrality principles apply to 5G network slicing techniques.

5. Zero-rating and Sponsored Data

- Ongoing discussions about the compatibility of these practices with net neutrality principles.

6. Internet of Things (IoT)

- Challenges in applying net neutrality principles to diverse IoT applications and services.

Future Outlook:

As the Internet continues to evolve, we can expect:

- Ongoing debates and potential policy shifts regarding net neutrality, particularly in the U.S.
- Increased focus on internet governance in the context of emerging technologies (AI, IoT, 5G).
- Growing tensions between global internet governance and national digital sovereignty.
- Evolution of multi-stakeholder governance models to address new challenges.

Internet governance and net neutrality remain complex and contentious areas, reflecting broader debates about the nature of the Internet as a global public resource versus a set of national or commercial interests. Balancing innovation, openness, security, and national priorities will continue to be a key challenge in shaping the future of the Internet.

7. Digital Taxation

The rise of the digital economy has presented significant challenges to traditional taxation systems, leading to efforts to develop new frameworks for taxing digital activities and services. Digital taxation has become a key area of focus for policymakers worldwide, aiming to ensure fair taxation of multinational tech companies and address the erosion of tax bases.

Key Developments in Digital Taxation:

1. OECD/G20 Inclusive Framework on BEPS (Base Erosion and Profit Shifting)
- Pillar One: Reallocation of taxing rights to market jurisdictions for certain digital activities.
- Pillar Two: Global minimum tax to address tax avoidance by multinational enterprises.

2. Unilateral Digital Services Taxes (DSTs)
- France: 3% tax on revenues from digital services.
- UK: 2% tax on revenues of search engines, social media platforms, and online marketplaces.
- Italy: 3% tax on revenues from targeted advertising and digital interface services.

3. EU Digital Levy (Proposed)
- Aimed at addressing tax challenges arising from the digitalization of the economy.
- Designed to be compatible with upcoming OECD agreements.

4. U.S. Approach
- Opposition to unilateral DSTs, viewing them as discriminatory against U.S.

companies.
- Promotion of a global agreement through the OECD framework.
    Key Challenges in Digital Taxation:
    1. Defining the Digital Economy
- Difficulty in clearly delineating digital from traditional economic activities.
- Rapid evolution of business models challenging static definitions.
    2. Nexus and Profit Allocation
- Determining taxable presence in a jurisdiction without physical presence.
- Developing fair methods for allocating profits across jurisdictions.
    3. Data Valuation
- Challenges in valuing data and user contributions for tax purposes.
- Debates over whether and how to tax the collection and use of data.
    4. Double Taxation and Tax Treaties
- Ensuring new digital tax measures don't result in double taxation.
- Navigating existing bilateral tax treaties in the context of new digital tax rules.
    5. Compliance and Administration
- Implementing complex new rules across multiple jurisdictions.
- Developing mechanisms for efficient collection of digital taxes.
    Emerging Trends:
    1. Shift Towards Global Consensus
- Growing momentum for a multilateral approach through OECD efforts.
- Potential phase-out of unilateral measures in favor of global framework.
    2. Expansion of Digital Permanent Establishment Concept
- Broadening the definition of taxable presence to include significant digital presence.
    3. Simplified Tax Regimes for SMEs
- Development of streamlined digital tax compliance for smaller businesses.
    4. Technology-Enabled Tax Administration
- Use of AI and big data analytics in tax collection and auditing.
- Exploration of real-time taxation systems for digital transactions.
    Future Outlook:
As digital taxation evolves, we can expect:
- Continued negotiations towards a global consensus on digital taxation.
- Potential implementation of OECD's two-pillar approach in coming years.
- Ongoing tensions between countries with large digital economies and market jurisdictions.

- Integration of digital taxation with broader reforms of international tax systems.
- Increased focus on taxing the data economy and digital assets (including cryptocurrencies).

Digital taxation remains a complex and contentious area of global economic policy. The outcome of current international negotiations will have significant implications for the future of the digital economy, multinational tech companies, and global tax systems. Balancing national interests, economic efficiency, and fairness in the digital age will continue to be a key challenge for policymakers worldwide.

8. Content Moderation and Platform Liability

As digital platforms have become primary channels for information sharing and communication, the issues of content moderation and platform liability have gained significant importance in digital policy discussions worldwide.

Key Issues:

1. Harmful Content
- Addressing misinformation, hate speech, extremist content, and other forms of harmful material.
- Balancing free speech with the need to protect users and society.

2. Platform Responsibility
- Determining the extent of platforms' responsibility for user-generated content.
- Debates over platforms as publishers vs. neutral intermediaries.

3. Transparency and Accountability
- Ensuring transparency in content moderation practices.
- Providing appeal mechanisms for content removal decisions.

Global Approaches:

1. United States
- Section 230 of the Communications Decency Act: Provides broad immunity to platforms for user-generated content.
- Ongoing debates about potential reforms to Section 230.

2. European Union
- Digital Services Act (DSA): Introduces new obligations for digital platforms, including content moderation and transparency requirements.
- Code of Practice on Disinformation: Voluntary commitments by platforms to combat misinformation.

3. Germany
- Network Enforcement Act (NetzDG): Requires platforms to remove clearly illegal content within 24 hours of notification.

4. Australia
- Online Safety Act 2021: Empowers the eSafety Commissioner to order the removal of harmful online content.

5. India
- Information Technology (Intermediary Guidelines and Digital Media Ethics Code) Rules, 2021: Imposes obligations on social media platforms for content moderation and user grievance redressal.

Emerging Trends:

1. AI in Content Moderation
- Increasing use of AI and machine learning for automated content moderation.
- Challenges in ensuring accuracy and addressing bias in AI systems.

2. Collaborative Content Moderation
- Industry initiatives like the Global Internet Forum to Counter Terrorism (GIFCT).
- Sharing of databases of harmful content across platforms.

3. User Empowerment
- Tools allowing users to customize their content experience and filter unwanted content.

4. Content Authenticity
- Initiatives to verify the authenticity and origin of content, particularly for combating deepfakes.

Challenges:

1. Scale of Content
- Dealing with the enormous volume of user-generated content posted daily.
- Ensuring timely moderation without compromising accuracy.

2. Cultural and Contextual Nuances
- Addressing variations in cultural norms and language nuances in global content moderation.

3. Balancing Rights and Safety
- Navigating the tension between free speech, privacy, and user safety.

4. Regulatory Fragmentation
- Dealing with varying content regulations across different jurisdictions.

5. Transparency and Due Process
- Ensuring fair and transparent processes for content removal and appeals.

Future Outlook:

As content moderation and platform liability issues evolve, we can expect:

- More comprehensive regulations addressing platform responsibilities.
- Increased use of AI in content moderation, coupled with human oversight.
- Greater emphasis on platform transparency and user control.
- Ongoing debates about the balance between platform liability and innovation.

Content moderation and platform liability remain complex issues at the intersection of technology, law, and ethics. As digital platforms continue to play a central role in public discourse, finding effective and balanced approaches to content governance will be crucial for maintaining trust in the digital ecosystem while preserving fundamental rights.

9. Digital Identity and Authentication Policies

Digital identity and authentication policies have become increasingly important as more aspects of our lives move online. These policies aim to provide secure and efficient ways for individuals to prove their identity and access digital services while protecting privacy and preventing fraud.

Key Components:

1. Digital Identity Systems
- National digital ID schemes (e.g., Estonia's e-ID, India's Aadhaar)
- Private sector identity providers (e.g., Google, Facebook)
- Decentralized identity solutions (e.g., blockchain-based systems)

2. Authentication Methods
- Multi-factor authentication (MFA)
- Biometric authentication (fingerprint, facial recognition)
- Risk-based authentication

3. Identity Federation
- Single Sign-On (SSO) systems
- Cross-border identity recognition

Global Approaches:

1. European Union
- eIDAS Regulation: Framework for electronic identification and trust services.
- Proposed update to include a European Digital Identity Wallet.

2. United States
- NIST Digital Identity Guidelines: Provides technical requirements for federal agencies.
- State-level initiatives (e.g., mobile driver's licenses).

3. India
- Aadhaar: World's largest biometric ID system, used for government and private services.
4. Singapore
- SingPass: National digital identity system for accessing government services.
5. Estonia
- e-ID: Comprehensive digital identity system for accessing public and private services.
Emerging Trends:
1. Self-Sovereign Identity (SSI)
- Decentralized identity models giving users control over their identity data.
- Use of blockchain and distributed ledger technologies.
2. Behavioral Biometrics
- Authentication based on user behavior patterns (e.g., typing rhythm, mouse movements).
3. Continuous Authentication
- Ongoing verification of user identity throughout a session, rather than just at login.
4. Identity-as-a-Service (IDaaS)
- Cloud-based identity and access management solutions.
5. Zero Trust Security
- Security model that requires strict identity verification for every person and device.
Challenges:
1. Privacy Concerns
- Balancing robust identity verification with user privacy.
- Addressing concerns about government surveillance and data misuse.
2. Inclusion and Accessibility
- Ensuring digital identity systems don't exclude marginalized populations.
- Providing alternatives for those without access to required technology.
3. Interoperability
- Enabling different identity systems to work together across sectors and borders.
4. Security and Fraud Prevention
- Protecting against identity theft and fraudulent use of digital identities.
- Safeguarding centralized identity databases from breaches.

5. User Experience
- Making authentication processes secure yet user-friendly.
    Future Outlook:
As digital identity systems evolve, we can expect:
- Increased adoption of decentralized and self-sovereign identity models.
- Greater integration of digital identity into various sectors (finance, healthcare, education).
- Evolution of privacy-preserving authentication technologies.
- Efforts towards global standards for digital identity interoperability.

Digital identity and authentication policies play a crucial role in enabling secure and efficient digital interactions. As these systems become more pervasive, policymakers must balance security, privacy, and accessibility considerations to ensure that digital identity solutions serve the needs of all users while protecting against misuse.

10. Cryptocurrency and Blockchain Regulations

The rise of cryptocurrencies and blockchain technology has presented significant challenges to traditional regulatory frameworks. Governments and financial authorities worldwide are grappling with how to regulate these decentralized technologies while balancing innovation, consumer protection, and financial stability.

Key Regulatory Concerns:

1. Financial Stability
- Potential impact of cryptocurrencies on monetary policy and financial systems.
- Systemic risks associated with large-scale adoption of cryptocurrencies.

2. Consumer Protection
- Addressing fraud, scams, and market manipulation in crypto markets.
- Ensuring transparency and disclosure in crypto-related products and services.

3. Anti-Money Laundering (AML) and Countering the Financing of Terrorism (CFT)
- Applying AML/CFT regulations to cryptocurrency transactions.
- Implementing Know Your Customer (KYC) requirements for crypto exchanges.

4. Taxation
- Defining tax treatment of cryptocurrency transactions and holdings.
- Addressing challenges in reporting and enforcing crypto-related taxes.

Global Approaches:

1. United States
- SEC: Regulating certain cryptocurrencies as securities.
- CFTC: Oversight of cryptocurrency derivatives.
- FinCEN: Applying AML regulations to cryptocurrency businesses.
2. European Union
- Markets in Crypto-Assets (MiCA) Regulation: Comprehensive framework for crypto regulation.
- 5th Anti-Money Laundering Directive: Includes virtual currency providers under AML rules.
3. Japan
- Legal recognition of cryptocurrencies as a means of payment.
- Licensing system for cryptocurrency exchanges.
4. China
- Ban on cryptocurrency trading and mining.
- Development of central bank digital currency (Digital Yuan).
5. Switzerland
- Creation of "crypto valley" with supportive regulatory environment.
- FINMA guidelines on ICOs and stable coins.
Emerging Trends:
1. Central Bank Digital Currencies (CBDCs)
- Many countries exploring or piloting CBDCs.
- Potential impact on monetary policy and financial inclusion.
2. Decentralized Finance (DeFi) Regulation
- Addressing regulatory challenges posed by decentralized financial services.
3. Non-Fungible Tokens (NFTs)
- Developing regulatory frameworks for NFT markets and platforms.
4. Stablecoin Regulation
- Increased scrutiny of stablecoins due to their potential impact on financial stability.
Challenges:
1. Jurisdictional Issues
- Dealing with the borderless nature of cryptocurrency transactions.
- Coordinating regulatory efforts across different countries.
2. Technological Complexity
- Ensuring regulators have sufficient technical expertise to oversee crypto markets.
- Keeping pace with rapid technological innovations in the blockchain space.

3. Balancing Innovation and Regulation
- Fostering blockchain innovation while protecting against risks.
- Avoiding regulatory arbitrage between jurisdictions.
    4. Privacy Concerns
- Balancing the need for financial oversight with privacy rights.
- Addressing concerns about government surveillance of financial transactions.

Future Outlook:
As the cryptocurrency and blockchain space continues to evolve, we can expect:
- More comprehensive and tailored regulatory frameworks for different types of crypto assets.
- Increased international cooperation on crypto regulation.
- Growing integration of blockchain technology in traditional financial services.
- Evolution of regulatory approaches to address emerging DeFi and Web3 technologies.

The regulation of cryptocurrencies and blockchain technology remains a complex and rapidly evolving area. As these technologies continue to mature and gain wider adoption, finding the right balance between fostering innovation and mitigating risks will be crucial for realizing the potential benefits of blockchain while maintaining financial stability and consumer protection.

11. Telecom and 5G Policies

The rollout of 5G networks and the evolution of telecommunications infrastructure are reshaping the digital landscape, prompting governments worldwide to develop new policies and regulations to address the opportunities and challenges presented by these technologies.

Key Policy Areas:
    1. Spectrum Allocation
- Assigning and managing radio frequency spectrum for 5G networks.
- Balancing commercial interests with public use and national security considerations.
    2. Infrastructure Development
- Policies to facilitate the deployment of 5G infrastructure (e.g., small cells, fiber optic networks).
- Addressing challenges in rural and underserved areas.

3. Security and Resilience
- Ensuring the security and resilience of 5G networks against cyber threats.
- Managing risks associated with equipment suppliers and foreign influence.
    4. Competition and Market Structure
- Promoting competition in telecom markets.
- Addressing concerns about market concentration and vertical integration.
    Global Approaches:
    1. United States
- FCC's 5G FAST Plan: Focusing on spectrum allocation, infrastructure policy, and regulatory reform.
- Restrictions on the use of equipment from certain foreign suppliers (e.g., Huawei).
    2. European Union
- 5G Action Plan: Coordinated approach to 5G deployment across EU member states.
- EU Toolbox for 5G Security: Guidelines for mitigating security risks in 5G networks.
    3. China
- Ambitious targets for 5G deployment and adoption.
- Strong government support for domestic 5G technology development.
    4. South Korea
- Early adoption and widespread deployment of 5G networks.
- Policies promoting 5G-enabled services and applications.
    5. Japan
- "Beyond 5G" strategy focusing on 6G research and development.
- Policies to promote Open RAN and network virtualization.
    Emerging Trends:
    1. Open Radio Access Network (Open RAN)
- Policies promoting open and interoperable network architectures.
- Efforts to reduce reliance on single-vendor proprietary solutions.
    2. Network Slicing Regulation
- Developing frameworks for regulating 5G network slicing capabilities.
- Addressing net neutrality implications of network slicing.
    3. EMF Exposure Guidelines
- Updating electromagnetic field (EMF) exposure limits for 5G frequencies.
- Addressing public concerns about potential health effects of 5G.
    4. Edge Computing Integration
- Policies to facilitate the integration of edge computing with 5G networks.

- Addressing data localization and privacy concerns in edge computing scenarios.

Challenges:

1. Balancing Innovation and Regulation
- Fostering 5G innovation while addressing security and privacy concerns.
- Adapting regulatory frameworks to keep pace with technological advancements.

2. Digital Divide
- Ensuring equitable access to 5G technologies in rural and underserved areas.
- Addressing affordability concerns for 5G services.

3. Geopolitical Tensions
- Managing international tensions around 5G technology suppliers and standards.
- Balancing national security concerns with global supply chain realities.

4. Spectrum Management
- Efficiently allocating and managing spectrum resources for 5G and beyond.
- Balancing commercial, public safety, and military spectrum needs.

Future Outlook:

As 5G networks continue to evolve and expand, we can expect:
- Increased focus on security and resilience in telecom policies.
- Growing emphasis on Open RAN and vendor diversity.
- Evolution of regulatory approaches to address emerging 5G use cases (e.g., autonomous vehicles, industrial IoT).
- Early discussions and policy planning for 6G technologies.

Telecom and 5G policies play a crucial role in shaping the future of digital infrastructure and services. As these technologies become increasingly central to economic and social development, policymakers must navigate complex technical, economic, and geopolitical considerations to ensure that the benefits of advanced telecommunications are realized while managing associated risks and challenges.

12. Digital Trade and E-commerce Regulations

The rapid growth of digital trade and e-commerce has necessitated the development of new regulatory frameworks to govern cross-border digital transactions, data flows, and online business practices.

Key Areas of Regulation:

1. Cross-Border Data Flows
- Policies governing the transfer of data across national borders.
- Balancing free flow of data with privacy and security concerns.

2. Digital Services and Goods
- Defining and regulating digital products and services.
- Addressing challenges in applying traditional trade rules to digital goods.

3. Consumer Protection
- Ensuring consumer rights in online transactions.
- Addressing issues like product safety, fraud prevention, and dispute resolution.

4. Digital Taxation
- Developing frameworks for taxing digital transactions and services.
- Addressing challenges in determining tax jurisdiction for digital businesses.

5. Intellectual Property Rights
- Protecting and enforcing IP rights in the digital domain.
- Addressing challenges like digital piracy and counterfeit goods in e-commerce.

Global Approaches:

1. World Trade Organization (WTO)
- Ongoing negotiations on e-commerce rules under the Joint Statement Initiative.
- Discussions on extending the moratorium on customs duties on electronic transmissions.

2. United States-Mexico-Canada Agreement (USMCA)
- Includes provisions on digital trade, prohibiting data localization requirements and customs duties on digital products.

3. European Union
- Digital Single Market strategy to reduce barriers to e-commerce within the EU.
- Geoblocking Regulation to prevent discrimination based on customer location.

4. Asia-Pacific Economic Cooperation (APEC)
- Cross-Border Privacy Rules (CBPR) system for data protection in cross-border data flows.

5. African Continental Free Trade Area (AfCFTA)
- Negotiations on a protocol on e-commerce to facilitate digital trade across Africa.

Emerging Trends:

1. Platform Regulation

- Developing rules for large online platforms and marketplaces.
- Addressing issues of market dominance and fair competition.

2. Digital Trade Facilitation

- Implementing paperless trading and e-customs systems.
- Developing interoperable digital identity systems for cross-border trade.

3. Blockchain in Trade

- Exploring the use of blockchain for supply chain transparency and trade finance.
- Developing regulatory frameworks for blockchain-based trade solutions.

4. AI and Automated Decision-Making

- Addressing the implications of AI in international trade and e-commerce.
- Developing guidelines for transparent and fair use of algorithms in e-commerce.

Challenges:

1. Regulatory Fragmentation

- Dealing with varying and sometimes conflicting regulations across jurisdictions.
- Balancing national sovereignty with the need for global harmonization.

2. Technological Neutrality

- Crafting regulations that remain relevant as technology evolves.
- Balancing specificity with flexibility in regulatory approaches.

3. Digital Divide

- Ensuring developing countries can participate effectively in digital trade.
- Addressing infrastructure and capacity gaps in e-commerce readiness.

4. Cybersecurity and Trust

- Building trust in digital trade systems and platforms.
- Addressing cybersecurity risks in cross-border digital transactions.

Future Outlook:

As digital trade and e-commerce continue to grow, we can expect:

- Increased efforts towards international harmonization of digital trade rules.
- Greater focus on inclusive e-commerce policies to bridge the digital divide.
- Evolution of regulations to address emerging technologies in trade (AI, IoT, blockchain).
- Growing emphasis on sustainability and ethical considerations in digital trade policies.

Digital trade and e-commerce regulations are crucial for fostering a fair, secure, and inclusive global digital economy. As the digital landscape continues to evolve, policymakers must balance the need for clear rules with the flexibility to accommodate technological innovation and changing business models.

13. Children's Online Protection Policies

As children increasingly engage with digital technologies, governments and organizations worldwide have developed policies and regulations aimed at protecting minors online while ensuring they can benefit from digital opportunities.

Key Areas of Focus:

1. Age-Appropriate Design

- Ensuring digital services are designed with children's best interests in mind.
- Implementing age verification mechanisms and parental controls.

2. Data Protection

- Special provisions for collecting and processing children's personal data.
- Stricter consent requirements for data collection from minors.

3. Content Filtering

- Measures to protect children from harmful or inappropriate content.
- Age-rating systems for online content and applications.

4. Cyberbullying and Online Harassment

- Policies to prevent and address cyberbullying among children.
- Reporting mechanisms and support systems for victims.

5. Digital Literacy

- Educational initiatives to help children navigate the online world safely.
- Programs to develop critical thinking skills for evaluating online information.

Global Approaches:

1. United States

- Children's Online Privacy Protection Act (COPPA): Regulates collection of personal information from children under 13.
- Broadband Data Improvement Act: Promotes internet safety education.

2. European Union

- General Data Protection Regulation (GDPR): Specific provisions for protecting children's data.
- Audiovisual Media Services Directive: Includes measures to protect minors from harmful content.

3. United Kingdom

- Age Appropriate Design Code: Sets standards for online services to protect children's privacy.
- Online Safety Bill: Proposed legislation to make the UK "the safest place in the world to be online."

4. Australia

- eSafety Commissioner: Dedicated office for online safety, with specific focus on children.
- Online Safety Act 2021: Enhances protections for children against cyberbullying and abuse.

5. China

- Minor Protection Law: Includes provisions for protecting minors online, including gaming time restrictions.

Emerging Trends:

1. AI and Machine Learning for Child Protection

- Using AI to detect and prevent online threats to children.
- Developing age-appropriate AI interactions for children.

2. Digital Wellbeing

- Policies addressing screen time and digital addiction among children.
- Promoting healthy digital habits and balanced use of technology.

3. Virtual and Augmented Reality Safeguards

- Developing safety standards for children in immersive digital environments.

4. Child-Specific Digital Identity

- Exploring secure and privacy-preserving digital identity solutions for minors.

Challenges:

1. Balancing Protection and Empowerment

- Ensuring safety without overly restricting children's access to digital opportunities.
- Adapting protections to different age groups and developmental stages.

2. Global Coordination

- Addressing the borderless nature of the internet in child protection efforts.
- Harmonizing approaches across different jurisdictions.

3. Rapidly Evolving Technology

- Keeping policies relevant in the face of new platforms and technologies.
- Addressing emerging risks in areas like IoT devices and AI assistants.

4. Privacy and Surveillance Concerns
- Balancing child protection with privacy rights.
- Addressing concerns about overreach in monitoring children's online activities.

Future Outlook:
As children's online protection policies continue to evolve, we can expect:
- More comprehensive and nuanced approaches to age-appropriate design.
- Increased use of technology (AI, machine learning) in child protection efforts.
- Greater emphasis on digital literacy and resilience-building among children.
- Evolution of policies to address emerging technologies and online environments.

Children's online protection remains a critical area of digital policy, requiring a delicate balance between safeguarding minors and enabling them to benefit from digital technologies. As the online landscape continues to evolve, policies must adapt to new challenges while empowering children to become safe and responsible digital citizens.

14. Global Cooperation and Challenges in Digital Policymaking

As digital technologies continue to transcend national borders, the need for international cooperation in digital policymaking has become increasingly apparent. However, this cooperation faces numerous challenges due to differing national interests, varying technological capabilities, and divergent views on internet governance.

Key Areas of Global Cooperation:
1. Cybersecurity
- Information sharing on cyber threats
- Development of international norms for responsible state behavior in cyberspace
- Capacity building for cybersecurity in developing countries
2. Data Governance
- Efforts to establish interoperable data protection frameworks
- Addressing challenges in cross-border data flows
- Developing global standards for data ethics and AI governance
3. Digital Trade
- Negotiations on e-commerce rules at the WTO
- Harmonization of digital trade provisions in free trade agreements
- Addressing digital protectionism and promoting open digital markets

4. Internet Governance
- Multi-stakeholder forums like the Internet Governance Forum (IGF)
- Coordination on domain name system management through ICANN
- Debates on the future of internet governance models
    International Initiatives and Forums:
    1. United Nations
- UN Group of Governmental Experts (GGE) on cybersecurity
- Internet Governancc Forum (IGF)
- ITU's World Summit on the Information Society (WSIS) process
    2. G7 and G20
- Digital and Technology Ministers' meetings
- Initiatives on data free flow with trust and digital economy principles
    3. OECD
- Going Digital project
- Work on taxation challenges of the digital economy
    4. Regional Organizations
- EU's Digital Single Market strategy
- APEC's work on digital trade and e-commerce
- African Union's Digital Transformation Strategy
    Challenges in Global Digital Policymaking:
    1. Digital Sovereignty vs. Global Internet
- Tensions between national control and the open, global nature of the internet
- Balancing domestic policy objectives with international cooperation
    2. Technological Divide
- Disparities in digital infrastructure and capabilities between countries
- Ensuring inclusive participation in global digital policymaking
    3. Jurisdictional Issues
- Difficulties in applying traditional jurisdictional concepts to the digital realm
- Addressing conflicts of law in cross-border digital activities
    4. Pace of Technological Change
- Keeping policy discussions relevant in the face of rapid technological advancements
- Balancing the need for timely regulation with thorough deliberation
    5. Diverse Stakeholder Interests
- Balancing interests of governments, private sector, civil society, and technical community

- Ensuring meaningful participation of all stakeholders in policy processes
  6. Geopolitical Tensions
- Impact of broader geopolitical conflicts on digital cooperation
- Competing visions for the future of the internet and digital technologies
  Future Outlook:
As global digital policymaking evolves, we can expect:
- Increased efforts to develop common principles and standards for digital governance
- Growing importance of regional approaches and coalitions in shaping global digital norms
- Continued debates on the appropriate balance between national sovereignty and global interoperability
- Emergence of new forums and mechanisms for addressing cross-border digital challenges

Global cooperation in digital policymaking is essential for addressing the complex challenges of the digital age. While progress has been made in many areas, significant obstacles remain. Overcoming these challenges will require sustained dialogue, innovative governance approaches, and a commitment to balancing diverse interests while preserving the open and global nature of the internet.

15. Conclusion and Future Outlook

As we've explored throughout this comprehensive overview, global digital policies and regulations are evolving rapidly to address the challenges and opportunities presented by the digital age. The landscape of digital governance is complex, multifaceted, and constantly changing, reflecting the dynamic nature of digital technologies themselves.

Key Takeaways:

1. Interconnectedness: Digital policies across various domains are increasingly interconnected, requiring holistic and coordinated approaches.

2. Balancing Act: Policymakers face the ongoing challenge of balancing innovation, economic growth, individual rights, and societal protection.

3. Global vs. Local: There's a constant tension between the need for global harmonization and the desire to maintain national sovereignty in digital governance.

4. Multistakeholder Approach: Effective digital policymaking requires the involvement of diverse stakeholders, including governments, private sector, civil society, and the technical community.

5. Technological Neutrality: Policies must strive to be technologically neutral to remain relevant in the face of rapid innovation.

6. Digital Divide: Addressing disparities in digital access and capabilities remains a critical challenge in global digital governance.

Future Outlook:

As we look to the future of global digital policies and regulations, several trends and challenges are likely to shape the landscape:

1. AI Governance: As artificial intelligence becomes more pervasive, developing ethical and effective governance frameworks for AI will be a top priority.

2. Data Sovereignty: Debates over data localization and cross-border data flows will continue, with potential implications for global digital trade.

3. Cybersecurity Cooperation: Increased international cooperation on cybersecurity will be crucial as cyber threats become more sophisticated and widespread.

4. Digital Identity: The development of interoperable and privacy-preserving digital identity systems will be a key focus area.

5. Emerging Technologies: Policies will need to evolve to address the implications of emerging technologies such as quantum computing, 6G, and brain-computer interfaces.

6. Platform Regulation: The power and influence of large digital platforms will continue to be a central issue in digital policy discussions.

7. Digital Sustainability: Environmental considerations will increasingly factor into digital policies, addressing the carbon footprint of digital technologies.

8. Human-Centric Approach: There will be a growing emphasis on ensuring that digital policies prioritize human rights, dignity, and well-being.

9. Adaptive Regulation: More flexible and responsive regulatory approaches may emerge to keep pace with technological change.

10. Global Digital Norms: Efforts to establish shared global norms and principles for the digital realm will intensify.

In conclusion, the field of global digital policies and regulations is at a critical juncture. As digital technologies become increasingly central to all aspects of society and the economy, the decisions made in digital governance will have far-reaching implications. The challenge for policymakers, industry leaders, and civil society will be to craft policies that foster innovation, protect individual rights, ensure security, and promote inclusive growth in the digital age.

Success in this endeavor will require unprecedented levels of international cooperation, multistakeholder engagement, and adaptive policymaking. By addressing these challenges thoughtfully and collaboratively, we can work towards a digital future that is equitable, secure, and beneficial for all.

CONCLUSION: NAVIGATING THE DIGITAL LANDSCAPE AS A MANAGER

1. Introduction

As we conclude our exploration of global trends in digital technologies, it's clear that managers across all industries face both unprecedented challenges and extraordinary opportunities. The digital landscape is evolving at a breathtaking pace, reshaping business models, customer expectations, and the very nature of work itself.

This concluding chapter aims to synthesize the key insights from our journey through the digital realm and provide a roadmap for managers seeking to navigate this complex terrain successfully. We will explore how the trends we've discussed – from artificial intelligence and the Internet of Things to blockchain and quantum computing – converge to create a new business environment that demands agility, continuous learning, and strategic foresight.

As a manager in this digital age, your role is not just to keep up with technological changes but to harness them for organizational success and societal benefit. This requires a multifaceted approach that encompasses technology adoption, workforce development, ethical considerations, and strategic planning.

In the pages that follow, we will:

1. Recap the major technological trends and their implications for business

2. Discuss the key competencies required for effective digital leadership

3. Explore strategies for fostering innovation and digital transformation

4. Address the ethical considerations and societal impacts of digital technologies

5. Provide a framework for continuous learning and adaptation in the digital age

6. Offer insights into the future trajectory of digital technologies and their potential impacts

By the end of this chapter, you will have a comprehensive understanding of how to navigate the digital landscape as a manager, equipped with the knowledge and strategies needed to thrive in an increasingly digital world.

Let's begin by revisiting the major technological trends that are shaping our digital future and consider their implications for managerial practice.

2. Recapping Major Technological Trends and Their Business Implications

Throughout this book, we've explored a wide array of digital technologies that are reshaping the business landscape. Let's briefly recap these key trends and their implications for managers:

Artificial Intelligence and Machine Learning:

AI and ML have moved from the realm of science fiction to become integral parts of business operations. As a manager, you must understand that:

- AI can automate routine tasks, freeing up human resources for more strategic work.

- Machine learning algorithms can provide deep insights from vast amounts of data, informing decision-making across all business functions.

- The integration of AI requires careful consideration of ethical implications, particularly in areas like hiring, customer service, and product development.

Implication: Managers need to identify opportunities for AI integration while being mindful of its limitations and potential biases.

Internet of Things (IoT):

The proliferation of connected devices is creating new data streams and business opportunities:

- IoT enables real-time monitoring and predictive maintenance in manufacturing and supply chain operations.

- Connected products offer new revenue streams through value-added services and subscription models.

- IoT data can provide unprecedented insights into customer behavior and product usage.

Implication: Managers should explore how IoT can enhance their products, services, and operations while addressing security and privacy concerns.

Blockchain and Distributed Ledger Technologies:
While often associated with cryptocurrencies, blockchain has broader applications:

- It can enhance transparency and traceability in supply chains.
- Smart contracts can automate and secure business agreements.
- Blockchain can revolutionize identity management and data security.

Implication: Managers need to assess how blockchain might disrupt their industry and consider potential applications within their own operations.

5G and Advanced Connectivity:
The rollout of 5G networks is set to accelerate digital transformation:

- Enhanced mobile broadband will enable new applications in augmented and virtual reality.
- Ultra-reliable low latency communications will support critical applications like remote surgery and autonomous vehicles.
- Massive machine-type communications will facilitate large-scale IoT deployments.

Implication: Managers should prepare for a hyper-connected business environment and the opportunities it presents for product and service innovation.

Cloud Computing and Edge Computing:
The evolution of cloud technologies is changing how businesses manage and process data:

- Cloud computing offers scalability, flexibility, and cost-efficiency in IT infrastructure.
- Edge computing brings data processing closer to the source, enabling real-time analytics and reducing latency.
- Hybrid cloud solutions allow businesses to balance security, compliance, and performance needs.

Implication: Managers must develop strategies for cloud adoption that align with their organization's data needs and regulatory requirements.

Extended Reality (XR):
Virtual, Augmented, and Mixed Reality technologies are creating new ways

to interact with digital content:
- XR can enhance training and simulation in various industries.
- It offers new possibilities for product design, visualization, and customer engagement.
- XR has the potential to revolutionize remote collaboration and virtual meetings.

Implication: Managers should explore XR applications in their industry and consider how it might enhance their products, services, or internal processes.

Quantum Computing:
While still in its early stages, quantum computing promises to solve complex problems beyond the capabilities of classical computers:
- It could revolutionize fields like drug discovery, financial modeling, and cryptography.
- Quantum computing may render current encryption methods obsolete, necessitating new approaches to cybersecurity.

Implication: Managers, particularly in tech-intensive industries, should monitor quantum computing developments and consider their long-term strategic implications.

As we can see, these technological trends are not isolated phenomena but interconnected forces shaping the digital landscape. Their convergence is creating a business environment characterized by:
1. Unprecedented data availability and analytical capabilities
2. Increased automation and AI-augmented decision making
3. New models of customer engagement and personalization
4. Disruption of traditional industry boundaries
5. Heightened cybersecurity risks and privacy concerns
6. Rapid cycles of innovation and obsolescence

For managers, navigating this landscape requires not just an understanding of individual technologies, but a holistic view of how they interact and the new possibilities they create. In the following sections, we'll explore how managers can develop the competencies and strategies needed to thrive in this digital future.

3. Key Competencies for Effective Digital Leadership

As we've seen, the digital landscape is complex and ever-evolving. To navigate it successfully, managers must develop a set of key competencies that go beyond traditional management skills. Let's explore these essential competencies for effective digital leadership:

1. Digital Literacy and Technological Fluency:
- Understanding of core digital technologies and their potential applications
- Ability to evaluate new technologies and their relevance to the business
- Skill in using digital tools for productivity and collaboration

As a manager, you don't need to be a technical expert, but you should be comfortable discussing technology and its implications. This involves:
- Regularly engaging with tech news and trends
- Participating in technology demonstrations and workshops
- Fostering relationships with IT teams and external tech partners

2. Data-Driven Decision Making:
- Proficiency in interpreting data and analytics
- Understanding of data collection, storage, and privacy issues
- Ability to translate data insights into strategic action

To enhance this competency:
- Develop a working knowledge of data analytics tools
- Practice making decisions based on data rather than intuition alone
- Encourage a data-driven culture within your team

3. Agile Thinking and Adaptive Leadership:
- Flexibility in the face of rapid change
- Comfort with ambiguity and uncertainty
- Ability to lead iterative, incremental change processes

Cultivate this mindset by:
- Embracing experimentation and learning from failure
- Implementing agile methodologies in project management
- Regularly reassessing and adjusting strategies based on new information

4. Digital Innovation and Design Thinking:
- Ability to identify opportunities for digital innovation
- Skills in leading creative problem-solving processes
- Understanding of user-centered design principles

Enhance your innovation capabilities by:
- Encouraging cross-functional collaboration
- Implementing design thinking workshops
- Creating space for experimentation and prototyping

5. Cybersecurity and Risk Management:
- Understanding of digital security threats and best practices
- Ability to balance innovation with risk mitigation
- Skills in crisis management and digital resilience

Develop this competency through:
- Regular briefings with cybersecurity experts
- Participating in risk assessment exercises
- Staying informed about regulatory changes in data protection

6. Digital Ethics and Responsible Technology Use:
- Awareness of ethical implications of digital technologies
- Ability to make principled decisions in complex digital scenarios
- Understanding of corporate digital responsibility

Strengthen your ethical leadership by:
- Engaging in discussions about tech ethics
- Implementing ethical guidelines for technology use
- Considering diverse perspectives in technology adoption decisions

7. Digital Collaboration and Virtual Leadership:
- Skills in managing remote and distributed teams
- Proficiency in virtual communication and collaboration tools
- Ability to foster engagement and culture in digital environments

Improve these skills by:
- Experimenting with various digital collaboration platforms
- Developing protocols for effective virtual meetings
- Regularly soliciting feedback on virtual leadership effectiveness

8. Continuous Learning and Adaptability:
- Commitment to ongoing personal development in digital areas
- Ability to quickly learn and apply new technologies
- Skills in fostering a learning culture within the organization

Cultivate this mindset through:
- Setting personal learning goals related to digital technologies
- Encouraging and facilitating learning opportunities for your team
- Staying curious and open to new ideas and approaches

9. Strategic Digital Thinking:
- Ability to envision how digital technologies can transform the business
- Skills in developing and implementing digital transformation strategies
- Understanding of digital business models and ecosystems

Enhance this competency by:
- Studying digital transformation case studies
- Engaging in strategic foresight exercises
- Collaborating with other leaders on digital initiatives

By developing these competencies, managers can position themselves as effective digital leaders, capable of guiding their organizations through the complexities of the digital landscape. Remember, the goal is not to become an expert in every technology, but to have enough understanding to make informed decisions, ask the right questions, and lead with confidence in a digital world.

In the next section, we'll explore strategies for fostering innovation and driving digital transformation within your organization.

4. Strategies for Fostering Innovation and Digital Transformation

As a manager in the digital age, one of your key responsibilities is to drive innovation and lead digital transformation initiatives. Here are some strategies to help you foster a culture of innovation and successfully navigate digital transformation:

1. Create a Vision for Digital Transformation:

- Develop a clear, compelling vision of how digital technologies can enhance your organization's value proposition.

- Communicate this vision effectively to all stakeholders, emphasizing the benefits and addressing concerns.

- Align digital initiatives with overall business strategy and goals.

2. Cultivate a Culture of Innovation:

- Encourage experimentation and calculated risk-taking.

- Implement systems for capturing and evaluating ideas from all levels of the organization.

- Celebrate both successes and "intelligent failures" to promote learning.

3. Implement Cross-Functional Collaboration:

- Break down silos between departments to foster innovation.

- Create cross-functional teams for digital projects to bring diverse perspectives.

- Use digital collaboration tools to facilitate communication and idea-sharing.

4. Adopt Agile and Lean Methodologies:

- Implement agile project management practices for digital initiatives.

- Use lean startup principles for testing and iterating on new ideas quickly.

- Foster a mindset of continuous improvement and adaptation.

5. Invest in Employee Skills Development:

- Provide training and resources for employees to develop digital skills.

- Encourage continuous learning through online courses, workshops, and conferences.

- Consider implementing reverse mentoring programs where younger, tech-savvy employees mentor senior staff.

6. Leverage External Partnerships and Ecosystems:
- Collaborate with startups, universities, and tech companies to access new ideas and technologies.
- Participate in industry consortiums and standards bodies to stay ahead of trends.
- Consider open innovation approaches to tap into external expertise.
   7. Establish Digital Innovation Labs or Incubators:
- Create dedicated spaces for experimenting with new technologies and business models.
- Allow these units to operate with more flexibility than the core business.
- Use these labs as a bridge between emerging technologies and practical business applications.
   8. Implement Data-Driven Decision Making:
- Invest in data analytics capabilities and tools.
- Train managers and employees in data interpretation and analysis.
- Use data to inform strategic decisions and measure the impact of digital initiatives.
   9. Focus on Customer-Centric Innovation:
- Use digital technologies to gain deeper insights into customer needs and behaviors.
- Implement design thinking methodologies for product and service innovation.
- Leverage digital channels for continuous customer feedback and co-creation.
   10. Address Organizational Change Management:
- Recognize that digital transformation is as much about people as it is about technology.
- Develop comprehensive change management strategies to address resistance and fear.
- Communicate frequently and transparently about the impact of digital changes.
   11. Secure Executive Support and Alignment:
- Ensure top-level commitment to digital transformation initiatives.
- Align incentives and KPIs with digital transformation goals.
- Create a digital governance structure that includes C-suite representation.
   12. Balance Short-Term Wins with Long-Term Vision:
- Identify and pursue quick wins to build momentum and demonstrate value.

- Maintain focus on long-term strategic goals while delivering incremental improvements.
- Develop a roadmap that outlines both short-term actions and long-term aspirations.

13. Embrace Emerging Technologies Strategically:
- Stay informed about emerging technologies like AI, blockchain, and IoT.
- Assess the potential impact of these technologies on your industry and business model.
- Develop pilot projects to test and learn from new technologies in a controlled environment.

14. Foster a Growth Mindset:
- Encourage employees to view challenges as opportunities for learning and growth.
- Promote resilience and adaptability in the face of rapid technological change.
- Lead by example in embracing new technologies and ways of working.

By implementing these strategies, you can create an environment that nurtures innovation and drives successful digital transformation. Remember that digital transformation is an ongoing journey rather than a destination. It requires continuous adaptation and a willingness to challenge the status quo.

In the next section, we'll address the ethical considerations and societal impacts of digital technologies, an increasingly important aspect of digital leadership.

5. Ethical Considerations and Societal Impacts of Digital Technologies

As digital technologies become increasingly pervasive, managers must grapple with a range of ethical considerations and societal impacts. Navigating these challenges is crucial for maintaining trust, ensuring long-term sustainability, and fulfilling corporate social responsibility. Let's explore some key areas of focus:

1. Data Privacy and Security:
- Ethical data collection and usage practices
- Transparency in how customer data is used and shared
- Robust cybersecurity measures to protect sensitive information

As a manager, you should:
- Implement strict data protection policies and practices
- Regularly audit data usage and security measures
- Foster a culture of privacy awareness among employees

2. AI Ethics and Algorithmic Bias:
- Fairness and non-discrimination in AI-driven decision-making
- Transparency and explainability of AI systems
- Accountability for AI outcomes
    Key actions include:
- Implementing diverse teams in AI development to minimize bias
- Regularly testing AI systems for fairness and unintended consequences
- Developing clear guidelines for ethical AI use within your organization
    3. Digital Inclusion and Accessibility:
- Ensuring digital products and services are accessible to all, including those with disabilities
- Addressing the digital divide in terms of access to technology and digital skills
    Managers should:
- Incorporate accessibility features in digital products from the design phase
- Support initiatives that promote digital literacy and access in underserved communities
- Ensure diverse representation in user testing and product development
    4. Environmental Sustainability:
- Managing the environmental impact of digital technologies
- Leveraging digital solutions to support sustainability goals
    Consider:
- Implementing energy-efficient data centers and IT infrastructure
- Using digital technologies to optimize resource use and reduce waste
- Factoring environmental impact into technology procurement decisions
    5. Workforce Disruption and Reskilling:
- Addressing job displacement due to automation and AI
- Supporting workforce transition and reskilling initiatives
    Managers should:
- Develop proactive strategies for workforce evolution
- Invest in reskilling and upskilling programs for employees
- Collaborate with educational institutions on curriculum development for future skills
    6. Digital Addiction and Well-being:
- Addressing the potential negative impacts of excessive technology use
- Promoting healthy digital habits among employees and customers
    Actions to consider:
- Implementing features that encourage mindful technology use

- Promoting work-life balance in increasingly connected work environments
- Supporting research on the long-term effects of digital technologies on well-being

7. Misinformation and Digital Manipulation:
- Combating the spread of false information
- Addressing concerns about deep fakes and digital manipulation
    Managers should:
- Implement robust fact-checking processes for digital content
- Educate employees and customers about identifying misinformation
- Support initiatives that promote digital literacy and critical thinking

8. Ethical Supply Chain Management:
- Ensuring ethical practices in the production and disposal of digital devices
- Addressing issues like conflict minerals and e-waste
    Consider:
- Implementing transparent supply chain monitoring systems
- Supporting responsible e-waste recycling programs
- Collaborating with suppliers on ethical and sustainable practices

9. Digital Rights and Freedom of Expression:
- Balancing content moderation with free speech
- Addressing issues of digital censorship and surveillance
    Managers should:
- Develop clear, transparent policies on content moderation
- Engage with stakeholders on issues of digital rights and freedom of expression
- Consider the global implications of digital policies across different cultural contexts

10. Responsible Innovation:
- Considering the long-term societal impacts of new technologies
- Engaging in ethical foresight and scenario planning
    Actions include:
- Incorporating ethical impact assessments into the innovation process
- Engaging with diverse stakeholders to understand potential impacts
- Participating in industry initiatives on responsible innovation

By actively addressing these ethical considerations and societal impacts, managers can help ensure that digital technologies are developed and deployed in ways that benefit society as a whole. This approach not only mitigates risks but also builds trust with customers, employees, and other stakeholders.

Remember, ethical leadership in the digital age is not just about compliance with regulations, but about proactively shaping the future in a responsible and sustainable way. As a manager, you play a crucial role in setting the tone for ethical technology use within your organization and contributing to broader societal discussions on these important issues.

In the next section, we'll explore a framework for continuous learning and adaptation in the digital age, essential for staying ahead in this rapidly evolving landscape.

6. Framework for Continuous Learning and Adaptation in the Digital Age

In the rapidly evolving digital landscape, continuous learning and adaptation are not just beneficial—they're essential for survival and success. As a manager, you must not only engage in your own ongoing development but also foster a culture of continuous learning within your organization. Here's a framework to help you approach this challenge:

1. Personal Learning and Development:

a) Self-Assessment:

- Regularly assess your digital skills and knowledge gaps
- Seek feedback from peers, subordinates, and superiors on your digital leadership

b) Set Learning Goals:

- Establish clear, measurable objectives for your digital learning
- Align these goals with your career aspirations and organizational needs

c) Diverse Learning Methods:

- Engage in formal training programs, online courses, and certifications
- Attend industry conferences and webinars
- Participate in peer learning groups or communities of practice
- Read widely: books, journals, industry reports, and reputable online sources

d) Experiential Learning:

- Take on challenging digital projects outside your comfort zone
- Experiment with new technologies in low-risk environments
- Seek mentorship from digital leaders in your industry

2. Fostering Organizational Learning:

a) Learning Culture:

- Promote a growth mindset throughout the organization
- Celebrate learning and curiosity as core values

- Encourage knowledge sharing and cross-functional learning
  b) Learning Infrastructure:
- Implement a robust Learning Management System (LMS)
- Create digital libraries and knowledge bases
- Develop internal platforms for sharing insights and best practices
  c) Tailored Learning Programs:
- Offer personalized learning paths based on role and skill level
- Implement micro-learning initiatives for just-in-time skill development
- Use AI-powered learning platforms for adaptive learning experiences
  d) Collaborative Learning:
- Establish communities of practice around key digital technologies
- Implement peer-to-peer learning programs
- Encourage cross-functional projects to promote knowledge transfer
  3. Adaptive Strategies:
  a) Environmental Scanning:
- Implement systematic processes for monitoring technological trends
- Engage with startups, academia, and thought leaders to stay ahead of the curve
- Use AI-powered tools for trend analysis and predictive insights
  b) Experimentation Culture:
- Allocate resources for small-scale experiments with new technologies
- Implement rapid prototyping and MVP (Minimum Viable Product) approaches
- Create "safe spaces" for testing innovative ideas without fear of failure
  c) Agile Decision Making:
- Develop frameworks for quickly assessing and responding to technological changes
- Implement agile methodologies beyond IT, applying them to strategy and operations
- Foster cross-functional teams that can quickly pivot based on new insights
  d) Feedback Loops:
- Implement systems for continuous feedback on digital initiatives
- Use data analytics to measure the impact of learning and adaptation efforts
- Regularly review and adjust your learning and adaptation strategies
  4. Ecosystem Engagement:
  a) Partner Collaboration:
- Engage in joint learning initiatives with key partners and suppliers
- Participate in industry consortiums focused on digital innovation

- Collaborate with academic institutions on research and development
   b) Customer Co-creation:
- Involve customers in your learning and innovation processes
- Use digital platforms to gather continuous feedback and insights
- Implement co-creation initiatives to develop new digital products and services
   c) Start-up Engagement:
- Establish partnerships or mentorship programs with relevant start-ups
- Consider corporate venturing to stay connected to cutting-edge innovations
- Participate in or host hackathons and innovation challenges
   5. Reflection and Iteration:
   a) Regular Reviews:
- Schedule periodic assessments of your learning and adaptation strategies
- Analyze the effectiveness of different learning methods and adjust accordingly
- Reflect on how new knowledge is being applied and creating value
   b) Future-focused Thinking:
- Engage in scenario planning to anticipate future skill needs
- Regularly update your digital strategy based on new learnings
- Foster a culture of forward-thinking and proactive skill development

By implementing this framework, you create a robust system for continuous learning and adaptation, essential for navigating the digital landscape. Remember, the goal is not just to keep up with change, but to position yourself and your organization to lead and innovate in the digital future.

In our next and final section, we'll offer insights into the future trajectory of digital technologies and their potential impacts, helping you prepare for what's on the horizon.

7. Future Trajectory of Digital Technologies and Potential Impacts

As we look towards the future, it's crucial for managers to anticipate the trajectory of digital technologies and their potential impacts. While predicting the future is inherently challenging, we can identify emerging trends and consider their implications. Here's an overview of what we might expect in the coming years:

   1. Artificial Intelligence and Machine Learning:
- Development of more advanced and autonomous AI systems
- Increased integration of AI in decision-making processes across industries

- Potential emergence of artificial general intelligence (AGI)
    Implications for managers:
- Need for strategies to effectively collaborate with AI systems
- Ethical considerations in AI decision-making will become more complex
- Potential for significant job disruption and the need for workforce reskilling
    2. Quantum Computing:
- Commercialization of quantum computing for specific applications
- Potential breakthroughs in areas like drug discovery, financial modeling, and cryptography
    Implications for managers:
- Need to understand potential impacts on industry-specific processes
- Cybersecurity strategies will need to evolve to address quantum threats
- Opportunities for competitive advantage through early adoption in relevant fields
    3. Extended Reality (XR):
- Mainstream adoption of augmented reality (AR) in daily life
- More immersive and realistic virtual reality (VR) experiences
- Development of the "metaverse" - persistent, shared virtual worlds
    Implications for managers:
- New platforms for marketing, customer engagement, and product showcasing
- Transformation of remote work and collaboration practices
- Potential for new business models in virtual economies
    4. Internet of Things (IoT) and 5G/6G:
- Ubiquitous connectivity with billions of devices
- Ultra-low latency enabling real-time applications
- Integration of AI with IoT (AIoT) for more intelligent systems
    Implications for managers:
- Opportunities for data-driven decision making and predictive maintenance
- Need for robust data management and security strategies
- Potential for new service-based business models
    5. Biotechnology and Digital Health:
- Convergence of digital technologies with healthcare and life sciences
- Personalized medicine based on genetic and real-time health data
- Advanced brain-computer interfaces

Implications for managers:
- Opportunities for innovation at the intersection of tech and health
- Need to navigate complex regulatory environments
- Ethical considerations in handling sensitive health data

6. Sustainable and Green Technologies:
- Increased focus on using digital technologies for environmental sustainability
- Development of more energy-efficient computing systems
- AI-driven solutions for climate change and resource management

Implications for managers:
- Growing importance of environmental considerations in tech decisions
- Opportunities for innovation in sustainable technologies
- Need to balance digital advancement with environmental responsibility

7. Cybersecurity and Privacy:
- More sophisticated cyber threats, including AI-powered attacks
- Evolution of privacy-preserving technologies (e.g., homomorphic encryption)
- Potential for decentralized identity systems

Implications for managers:
- Cybersecurity will become even more critical to business operations
- Need for ongoing investment in security measures and employee training
- Balancing data utilization with privacy concerns will be an ongoing challenge

8. Blockchain and Decentralized Systems:
- Maturation of blockchain technology beyond cryptocurrencies
- Growth of decentralized finance (DeFi) and decentralized autonomous organizations (DAOs)
- Potential disruption of traditional intermediaries in various industries

Implications for managers:
- Need to understand how blockchain might impact industry-specific processes
- Opportunities for increased transparency and efficiency in operations
- Potential for new decentralized business models

9. Human Augmentation:
- Advancements in prosthetics and human-computer interfaces
- Potential for cognitive enhancement technologies
- Ethical debates around human augmentation and equality

Implications for managers:
- Need to consider implications for workforce capabilities and training
- Potential for new products and services in augmentation technologies
- Navigating ethical and regulatory challenges in human augmentation

As these technologies evolve and converge, we can expect to see transformative changes across all sectors of the economy and society. The pace of change is likely to accelerate, requiring managers to be increasingly agile and forward-thinking.

Key considerations for managers in preparing for this future include:

1. Developing a culture of continuous learning and adaptation
2. Fostering ethical decision-making frameworks for emerging technologies
3. Balancing short-term operational needs with long-term strategic positioning
4. Collaborating across industries and sectors to address complex challenges
5. Prioritizing human-centric approaches in technology adoption and development

Remember, the goal is not to predict the future with certainty, but to be prepared for a range of possible scenarios. By staying informed, adaptable, and focused on creating value through responsible innovation, managers can help their organizations thrive in the digital future.

As we conclude this book, it's clear that navigating the digital landscape as a manager is both a significant challenge and an exciting opportunity. By embracing the strategies, developing the competencies, and considering the ethical implications we've discussed, you can position yourself and your organization for success in the digital age.

The future is digital, and it's in your hands to shape it.

Conclusion:

As we close this exploration of global trends in digital technologies, it's clear that we stand at the threshold of a new era. The digital landscape is not just changing; it's evolving at an unprecedented pace, reshaping industries, societies, and the very nature of work itself. As managers, your role in navigating this complex terrain is crucial.

Throughout this book, we've delved into the transformative power of technologies such as artificial intelligence, blockchain, the Internet of Things, and quantum computing. We've explored the challenges and opportunities they present, from ethical considerations to strategic implementation. We've emphasized the importance of continuous learning, adaptability, and ethical leadership in the face of rapid technological change.

The future of work and business in the digital age will be defined by those who can harness these technologies responsibly and innovatively. It will require a delicate balance of technical knowledge, strategic foresight, and human-centric values. As you move forward, remember that your goal is not just to keep pace with technological change, but to leverage it in ways that create value, foster innovation, and contribute positively to society.

The journey ahead is complex and uncertain, but it's also filled with unprecedented opportunities. By embracing a mindset of continuous learning, fostering a culture of innovation, and maintaining a strong ethical compass, you can lead your organizations into a future where technology serves as a powerful tool for progress and positive change.

The digital future is not something that simply happens to us; it's something we actively shape. As managers and leaders in the digital age, you have the power and responsibility to guide this transformation. Embrace the challenges, seize the opportunities, and remember that at the heart of all this technological advancement, the human element remains paramount.

The future is digital, and it's in your hands to make it a future that benefits all. Let this book serve as your guide and inspiration as you navigate the exciting journey ahead in the ever-evolving digital landscape.

Glossary

1. 5G: Fifth-generation cellular network technology, offering faster speeds, lower latency, and more reliable connections than previous generations.

2. Artificial Intelligence (AI): The simulation of human intelligence in machines programmed to think and learn like humans, capable of tasks such as visual perception, speech recognition, and decision-making.

3. API Economy: An ecosystem where businesses expose their services or data through application programming interfaces (APIs), allowing third-party developers to create new applications and services.

4. Augmented Reality (AR): An interactive experience where real-world environments are enhanced with computer-generated information, typically through visual or audio overlays.

5. Big Data: Extremely large data sets that may be analyzed computationally to reveal patterns, trends, and associations, especially relating to human behavior and interactions.

6. Blockchain: A decentralized, distributed ledger technology that records transactions across multiple computers, ensuring transparency, security, and immutability.

7. Citizen Development: A business process where non-professional developers create applications using company-approved technology, often through low-code or no-code platforms.

8. Cloud Computing: The delivery of computing services over the internet, including storage, servers, databases, and software, offering flexible resources and economies of scale.

9. Confidential Computing: The protection of data in use by performing computation in a hardware-based Trusted Execution Environment, enhancing data security and privacy.

10. Cryptocurrency: Digital or virtual currency that uses cryptography for security, operating independently of central banks and often based on blockchain technology.

11. Cybersecurity: The practice of protecting systems, networks, and programs from digital attacks, unauthorized access, and data theft.

12. Data Analytics: The process of examining data sets to draw conclusions about the information they contain, often involving predictive modeling and machine learning techniques.

13. Decentralized Finance (DeFi): Financial services and applications built on blockchain technology, operating without centralized intermediaries like banks or financial institutions.

14. DevOps: A set of practices that combines software development (Dev) and IT operations (Ops) to shorten the systems development life cycle and provide continuous delivery of high-quality software.

15. Digital Ethics: The branch of ethics that deals with the impact of digital technologies on society and individuals, addressing issues such as privacy, bias, and the societal implications of AI.

16. Digital Supply Chain: The application of advanced digital technologies to supply chain operations, improving efficiency, transparency, and responsiveness.

17. Digital Sovereignty: The ability of a state or individual to have control over their own digital destiny – personal data, software, and hardware – free from external interference.

18. Digital Transformation: The integration of digital technology into all areas of a business, fundamentally changing how it operates and delivers value to customers.

19. Digital Twin: A digital replica of a living or non-living physical entity, used for various purposes including simulation, monitoring, and predictive maintenance.

20. Digital Twin of an Organization (DTO): A dynamic software model of any organization that relies on operational and/or other data to understand how it operates and predict future performance.

21. Edge Computing: A distributed computing paradigm that brings computation and data storage closer to the location where it is needed, reducing latency and bandwidth use.

22. Explainable AI (XAI): Artificial intelligence systems whose actions and decisions can be easily understood by humans, promoting transparency and trust in AI applications.

23. Extended Reality (XR): An umbrella term for all immersive technologies, including Augmented Reality (AR), Virtual Reality (VR), and Mixed Reality (MR).

24. Federated Learning: A machine learning technique that trains algorithms across multiple decentralized devices or servers holding local data samples, without exchanging the data itself.

25. Fintech: Financial technology, referring to new tech that seeks to improve and automate the delivery and use of financial services.

26. Homomorphic Encryption: A form of encryption allowing computation on ciphertexts, generating an encrypted result that matches the result of operations performed on the plaintext.

27. Hyper-Automation: The application of advanced technologies like AI, machine learning, and robotic process automation to increasingly automate processes and augment human capabilities.

28. Internet of Things (IoT): The interconnection of everyday devices via the internet, enabling them to send and receive data and creating a network of smart, connected objects.

29. Low-Code/No-Code Platforms: Development platforms that allow for the creation of application software through graphical user interfaces instead of traditional hand-coded computer programming.

30. Machine Learning: A subset of AI that enables systems to learn and improve from experience without being explicitly programmed, often used for pattern recognition and predictive analytics.

31. Natural Language Processing (NLP): A branch of AI that helps computers understand, interpret, and manipulate human language, enabling applications like chatbots and language translation.

32. Neuromorphic Computing: Computing architectures inspired by the human brain, designed to process information more efficiently and potentially achieve human-like cognitive abilities.

33. Non-Fungible Tokens (NFTs): Unique digital assets verified using blockchain technology, often used for digital art, collectibles, and representing ownership of virtual or physical items.

34. Passwordless Authentication: Security methods that enable users to access devices and applications without entering a password, often using biometrics or hardware tokens.

35. Predictive Maintenance: Techniques designed to help determine the condition of in-service equipment to predict when maintenance should be performed, reducing downtime and maintenance costs.

36. Quantum Computing: A type of computing that uses quantum-mechanical phenomena, such as superposition and entanglement, to perform operations on data, potentially solving certain problems much faster than classical computers.

37. Robotic Process Automation (RPA): The use of software robots or "bots" to automate repetitive tasks and processes, improving efficiency and reducing human error.

38. Serverless Computing: A cloud computing execution model where the cloud provider manages the server infrastructure, automatically allocating resources as needed.

39. Smart Cities: Urban areas that use different types of electronic data collection sensors to supply information used to manage assets and resources efficiently, improving quality of life for residents.

40. Software as a Service (SaaS): A software licensing and delivery model where software is licensed on a subscription basis and centrally hosted, allowing users to access applications via the internet.

41. Spatial Computing: The use of space around us as a medium to interact with technology, blending the physical and digital worlds through technologies like AR and VR.

42. Sustainable IT: The practice of manufacturing, using, and disposing of computers and other technological devices in an environmentally friendly manner, minimizing negative impacts on the environment.

43. Synthetic Data: Artificially generated data that mimics real data in terms of essential statistical properties, used for testing, training AI models, and protecting privacy.

44. Virtual Reality (VR): A simulated experience that can be similar to or completely different from the real world, typically achieved through the use of headsets that immerse the user in a digital environment.

45. Zero Trust Security: A security model that requires strict identity verification for every person and device trying to access resources on a network, regardless of whether they are inside or outside the network perimeter.

Bibliography

Chapter 2 : Cloud Computing and Edge Computing

1. Armbrust, M., Fox, A., Griffith, R., Joseph, A. D., Katz, R., Konwinski, A., ... & Zaharia, M. (2010). A view of cloud computing. Communications of the ACM, 53(4), 50-58.

2. Botta, A., De Donato, W., Persico, V., & Pescapé, A. (2016). Integration of cloud computing and internet of things: a survey. Future generation computer systems, 56, 684-700.

3. Buyya, R., Yeo, C. S., Venugopal, S., Broberg, J., & Brandic, I. (2009). Cloud computing and emerging IT platforms: Vision, hype, and reality for delivering computing as the 5th utility. Future Generation computer systems, 25(6), 599-616.

4. Cai, W., Wang, Z., Ernst, J. B., Hong, Z., Feng, C., & Leung, V. C. (2018). Decentralized applications: The blockchain-empowered software system. IEEE Access, 6, 53019-53033.

5. Chen, M., & Zhao, Y. (2020). Edge Computing: Theory and Practice. Springer.

6. Dastjerdi, A. V., & Buyya, R. (2016). Fog computing: Helping the Internet of Things realize its potential. Computer, 49(8), 112-116.

7. El-Sayed, H., Sankar, S., Prasad, M., Puthal, D., Gupta, A., Mohanty, M., & Lin, C. T. (2018). Edge of things: The big picture on the integration of edge, IoT and the cloud in a distributed computing environment. IEEE Access, 6, 1706-1717.

8. Gartner, Inc. (2023). Gartner Identifies the Top 10 Strategic Technology Trends for 2024. Gartner Press Release.

9. Hassan, N., Gillani, S., Ahmed, E., Yaqoob, I., & Imran, M. (2018). The role of edge computing in internet of things. IEEE Communications Magazine, 56(11), 110-115.

10. Hu, P., Dhelim, S., Ning, H., & Qiu, T. (2017). Survey on fog computing: architecture, key technologies, applications and open issues. Journal of network and computer applications, 98, 27-42.

11. Iorga, M., Feldman, L., Barton, R., Martin, M. J., Goren, N., & Mahmoudi, C. (2018). Fog computing conceptual model. National Institute of Standards and Technology.

12. Jamshidi, P., Pahl, C., Mendonça, N. C., Lewis, J., & Tilkov, S. (2018). Microservices: The journey so far and challenges ahead. IEEE Software, 35(3), 24-35.

13. Li, W., Santos, I., Delicato, F. C., Pires, P. F., Pirmez, L., Wei, W., ... & Albert, K. (2017). System modelling and performance evaluation of a three-tier cloud of things. Future Generation Computer Systems, 70, 104-125.

14. Mahmud, R., Kotagiri, R., & Buyya, R. (2018). Fog computing: A taxonomy, survey and future directions. In Internet of everything (pp. 103-130). Springer, Singapore.

15. Mell, P., & Grance, T. (2011). The NIST definition of cloud computing. National Institute of Standards and Technology.

16. Morabito, R., Cozzolino, V., Ding, A. Y., Beijar, N., & Ott, J. (2018). Consolidate IoT edge computing with lightweight virtualization. IEEE Network, 32(1), 102-111.

17. Nunna, S., Kousaridas, A., Ibrahim, M., Dillinger, M., Thuemmler, C., Feussner, H., & Schneider, A. (2015). Enabling real-time context-aware collaboration through 5G and mobile edge computing. In 2015 12th International Conference on Information Technology-New Generations (pp. 601-605). IEEE.

18. Satyanarayanan, M. (2017). The emergence of edge computing. Computer, 50(1), 30-39.

19. Shi, W., Cao, J., Zhang, Q., Li, Y., & Xu, L. (2016). Edge computing: Vision and challenges. IEEE internet of things journal, 3(5), 637-646.

20. Varghese, B., Wang, N., Barbhuiya, S., Kilpatrick, P., & Nikolopoulos, D. S. (2016). Challenges and opportunities in edge computing. In 2016 IEEE International Conference on Smart Cloud (SmartCloud) (pp. 20-26). IEEE.

21. Wang, S., Zhao, Y., Xu, J., Yuan, J., & Hsu, C. H. (2019). Edge server placement in mobile edge computing. Journal of Parallel and Distributed Computing, 127, 160-168.

22. Wu, D., Liu, S., Zhang, L., Terpenny, J., Gao, R. X., Kurfess, T., & Guzzo, J. A. (2017). A fog computing-based framework for process monitoring and prognosis in cyber-manufacturing. Journal of Manufacturing Systems, 43, 25-34.

23. Xu, X., He, S., & Wang, Q. (2018). Orchestration and scheduling in heterogeneous cloud and edge computing. In 2018 IEEE International Conference on Internet of Things (iThings) and IEEE Green Computing and Communications (GreenCom) and IEEE Cyber, Physical and Social Computing (CPSCom) and IEEE Smart Data (SmartData) (pp. 1-8). IEEE.

24. Yang, C., Huang, Q., Li, Z., Liu, K., & Hu, F. (2017). Big Data and cloud computing: innovation opportunities and challenges. International Journal of Digital Earth, 10(1), 13-53.

25. Zhang, Q., Cheng, L., & Boutaba, R. (2010). Cloud computing: state-of-the-art and research challenges. Journal of internet services and applications, 1(1), 7-18.

Chapter 3 : Artificial Intelligence and Machine Learning

1. Alpaydin, E. (2020). Introduction to Machine Learning (4th ed.). MIT Press.

2. Boden, M. A. (2016). AI: Its Nature and Future. Oxford University Press.

3. Chollet, F. (2021). Deep Learning with Python (2nd ed.). Manning Publications.

4. Dieterich, T. G., & Horvitz, E. J. (2015). Rise of concerns about AI: Reflections and directions. Communications of the ACM, 58(10), 38-40.

5. Domingos, P. (2015). The Master Algorithm: How the Quest for the Ultimate Learning Machine Will Remake Our World. Basic Books.

6. Doshi-Velez, F., & Kim, B. (2017). Towards A Rigorous Science of Interpretable Machine Learning. arXiv preprint arXiv:1702.08608.

7. Géron, A. (2019). Hands-On Machine Learning with Scikit-Learn, Keras, and TensorFlow (2nd ed.). O'Reilly Media.

8. Goodfellow, I., Bengio, Y., & Courville, A. (2016). Deep Learning. MIT Press.

9. Haykin, S. (2008). Neural Networks and Learning Machines (3rd ed.). Pearson.

10. Jordan, M. I., & Mitchell, T. M. (2015). Machine learning: Trends, perspectives, and prospects. Science, 349(6245), 255-260.

11. Kaplan, A., & Haenlein, M. (2019). Siri, Siri, in my hand: Who's the fairest in the land? On the interpretations, illustrations, and implications of artificial intelligence. Business Horizons, 62(1), 15-25.

12. LeCun, Y., Bengio, Y., & Hinton, G. (2015). Deep learning. Nature, 521(7553), 436-444.

13. Marcus, G. (2018). Deep Learning: A Critical Appraisal. arXiv preprint arXiv:1801.00631.

14. Minsky, M. (1986). The Society of Mind. Simon & Schuster.

15. Mitchell, T. M. (1997). Machine Learning. McGraw-Hill.

16. Murphy, K. P. (2022). Probabilistic Machine Learning: An Introduction. MIT Press.

17. Ng, A. Y. (2021). Machine Learning Yearning. deeplearning.ai.

18. Pearl, J., & Mackenzie, D. (2018). The Book of Why: The New Science of Cause and Effect. Basic Books.

19. Raschka, S., & Mirjalili, V. (2019). Python Machine Learning (3rd ed.). Packt Publishing.

20. Russell, S., & Norvig, P. (2020). Artificial Intelligence: A Modern Approach (4th ed.). Pearson.

21. Samuel, A. L. (1959). Some Studies in Machine Learning Using the Game of Checkers. IBM Journal of Research and Development, 3(3), 210-229.

22. Silver, D., Hubert, T., Schrittwieser, J., Antonoglou, I., Lai, M., Guez, A., ... & Hassabis, D. (2018). A general reinforcement learning algorithm that masters chess, shogi, and Go through self-play. Science, 362(6419), 1140-1144.

23. Sutton, R. S., & Barto, A. G. (2018). Reinforcement Learning: An Introduction (2nd ed.). MIT Press.

24. Vapnik, V. N. (1998). Statistical Learning Theory. Wiley-Interscience.

25. Witten, I. H., Frank, E., Hall, M. A., & Pal, C. J. (2016). Data Mining: Practical Machine Learning Tools and Techniques (4th ed.). Morgan Kaufmann.

26. Wu, X., Zhu, X., Wu, G. Q., & Ding, W. (2014). Data mining with big data. IEEE Transactions on Knowledge and Data Engineering, 26(1), 97-107.

27. Zhu, X., & Goldberg, A. B. (2009). Introduction to Semi-Supervised Learning. Synthesis Lectures on Artificial Intelligence and Machine Learning, 3(1), 1-130.

28. Zou, J., & Schiebinger, L. (2018). AI can be sexist and racist — it's time to make it fair. Nature, 559(7714), 324-326.

29. Artificial Intelligence Index Report 2023. (2023). Stanford Institute for Human-Centered Artificial Intelligence.

30. Brynjolfsson, E., & McAfee, A. (2017). The Business of Artificial Intelligence. Harvard Business Review, 95(4), 3-11.

Chapter 4 : Internet of Things

1. Atzori, L., Iera, A., & Morabito, G. (2010). The Internet of Things: A survey. Computer Networks, 54(15), 2787-2805.

2. Boyes, H., Hallaq, B., Cunningham, J., & Watson, T. (2018). The industrial internet of things (IIoT): An analysis framework. Computers in Industry, 101, 1-12.

3. Gilchrist, A. (2016). Industry 4.0: The Industrial Internet of Things. Apress.

4. Gubbi, J., Buyya, R., Marusic, S., & Palaniswami, M. (2013). Internet of Things (IoT): A vision, architectural elements, and future directions. Future Generation Computer Systems, 29(7), 1645-1660.

5. Lee, I., & Lee, K. (2015). The Internet of Things (IoT): Applications, investments, and challenges for enterprises. Business Horizons, 58(4), 431-440.

6. Manyika, J., Chui, M., Bisson, P., Woetzel, J., Dobbs, R., Bughin, J., & Aharon, D. (2015). The Internet of Things: Mapping the value beyond the hype. McKinsey Global Institute.

7. Minerva, R., Biru, A., & Rotondi, D. (2015). Towards a definition of the Internet of Things (IoT). IEEE Internet Initiative, 1, 1-86.

8. O'Donovan, P., Leahy, K., Bruton, K., & O'Sullivan, D. T. J. (2015). An industrial big data pipeline for data-driven analytics maintenance applications in large-scale smart manufacturing facilities. Journal of Big Data, 2(1), 25.

9. Sisinni, E., Saifullah, A., Han, S., Jennehag, U., & Gidlund, M. (2018). Industrial internet of things: Challenges, opportunities, and directions. IEEE Transactions on Industrial Informatics, 14(11), 4724-4734.

10. Wortmann, F., & Flüchter, K. (2015). Internet of Things. Business & Information Systems Engineering, 57(3), 221-224.

11. Xu, L. D., He, W., & Li, S. (2014). Internet of Things in industries: A survey. IEEE Transactions on Industrial Informatics, 10(4), 2233-2243.

12. Zanella, A., Bui, N., Castellani, A., Vangelista, L., & Zorzi, M. (2014). Internet of Things for smart cities. IEEE Internet of Things Journal, 1(1), 22-32.

Chapter 5 : 5G and Beyond

1. Agiwal, M., Roy, A., & Saxena, N. (2016). Next Generation 5G Wireless Networks: A Comprehensive Survey. IEEE Communications Surveys & Tutorials, 18(3), 1617-1655.

2. Akyildiz, I. F., Kak, A., & Nie, S. (2020). 6G and Beyond: The Future of Wireless Communications Systems. IEEE Access, 8, 133995-134030.

3. Al-Fuqaha, A., Guizani, M., Mohammadi, M., Aledhari, M., & Ayyash, M. (2015). Internet of Things: A Survey on Enabling Technologies, Protocols, and Applications. IEEE Communications Surveys & Tutorials, 17(4), 2347-2376.

4. Andrews, J. G., Buzzi, S., Choi, W., Hanly, S. V., Lozano, A., Soong, A. C., & Zhang, J. C. (2014). What Will 5G Be? IEEE Journal on Selected Areas in Communications, 32(6), 1065-1082.

5. Boccardi, F., Heath, R. W., Lozano, A., Marzetta, T. L., & Popovski, P. (2014). Five disruptive technology directions for 5G. IEEE Communications Magazine, 52(2), 74-80.

6. Chih-Lin, I., Han, S., Xu, Z., Sun, Q., & Pan, Z. (2016). 5G: Rethink mobile communications for 2020+. Philosophical Transactions of the Royal Society A: Mathematical, Physical and Engineering Sciences, 374(2062), 20140432.

7. Dahlman, E., Parkvall, S., & Skold, J. (2020). 5G NR: The Next Generation Wireless Access Technology. Academic Press.

8. Dang, S., Amin, O., Shihada, B., & Alouini, M. S. (2020). What should 6G be? Nature Electronics, 3(1), 20-29.

9. ETSI. (2021). 5G; NR; Overall description; Stage-2 (3GPP TS 38.300 version 16.5.0 Release 16). ETSI.

10. Foukas, X., Patounas, G., Elmokashfi, A., & Marina, M. K. (2017). Network Slicing in 5G: Survey and Challenges. IEEE Communications Magazine, 55(5), 94-100.

11. Giordani, M., Polese, M., Mezzavilla, M., Rangan, S., & Zorzi, M. (2020). Toward 6G Networks: Use Cases and Technologies. IEEE Communications Magazine, 58(3), 55-61.

12. GSMA. (2022). The Mobile Economy 2022. GSMA Intelligence.

13. Gupta, A., & Jha, R. K. (2015). A Survey of 5G Network: Architecture and Emerging Technologies. IEEE Access, 3, 1206-1232.

14. Huawei. (2021). 6G: The Next Horizon: From Connected People and Things to Connected Intelligence. Huawei White Paper.

15. ITU-R. (2015). IMT Vision – Framework and overall objectives of the future development of IMT for 2020 and beyond. Recommendation ITU-R M.2083-0.

16. Li, R., Zhao, Z., Zhou, X., Ding, G., Chen, Y., Wang, Z., & Zhang, H. (2017). Intelligent 5G: When Cellular Networks Meet Artificial

Intelligence. IEEE Wireless Communications, 24(5), 175-183.

17. Liu, G., Hou, X., Wang, J., Guo, J., Liu, H., & Jiang, T. (2019). 5G-based Internet of Things: Opportunities and Challenges. IEEE Network, 33(6), 144-151.

18. Mahmood, N. H., Alves, H., López, O. A., Shehab, M., Osorio, D. P. M., & Latva-aho, M. (2020). Six Key Features of Machine Type Communication in 6G. 2020 2nd 6G Wireless Summit (6G SUMMIT), 1-5.

19. Nakamura, T., Nagata, S., Benjebbour, A., Kishiyama, Y., Hai, T., Xiaodong, S., ... & Kato, A. (2013). Trends in small cell enhancements in LTE advanced. IEEE Communications Magazine, 51(2), 98-105.

20. Nawaz, S. J., Sharma, S. K., Wyne, S., Patwary, M. N., & Asaduzzaman, M. (2019). Quantum Machine Learning for 6G Communication Networks: State-of-the-Art and Vision for the Future. IEEE Access, 7, 46317-46350.

21. Parkvall, S., Dahlman, E., Furuskar, A., & Frenne, M. (2017). NR: The New 5G Radio Access Technology. IEEE Communications Standards Magazine, 1(4), 24-30.

22. Rappaport, T. S., Sun, S., Mayzus, R., Zhao, H., Azar, Y., Wang, K., ... & Gutierrez, F. (2013). Millimeter Wave Mobile Communications for 5G Cellular: It Will Work! IEEE Access, 1, 335-349.

23. Saad, W., Bennis, M., & Chen, M. (2020). A Vision of 6G Wireless Systems: Applications, Trends, Technologies, and Open Research Problems. IEEE Network, 34(3), 134-142.

24. Shafi, M., Molisch, A. F., Smith, P. J., Haustein, T., Zhu, P., De Silva, P., ... & Wunder, G. (2017). 5G: A Tutorial Overview of Standards, Trials, Challenges, Deployment, and Practice. IEEE Journal on Selected Areas in Communications, 35(6), 1201-1221.

25. Tariq, F., Khandaker, M. R. A., Wong, K. K., Imran, M. A., Bennis, M., & Debbah, M. (2020). A Speculative Study on 6G. IEEE Wireless Communications, 27(4), 118-125.

26. Viswanathan, H., & Mogensen, P. E. (2020). Communications in the 6G Era. IEEE Access, 8, 57063-57074.

27. Yang, P., Xiao, Y., Xiao, M., & Li, S. (2019). 6G Wireless Communications: Vision and Potential Techniques. IEEE Network, 33(4), 70-75.

28. Zhang, Z., Xiao, Y., Ma, Z., Xiao, M., Ding, Z., Lei, X., ... & Fan, P. (2019). 6G Wireless Networks: Vision, Requirements, Architecture, and Key Technologies. IEEE Vehicular Technology Magazine, 14(3), 28-41.

Chapter 6 : Cybersecurity in the Digital Age

1. Andress, J. (2019). The Basics of Information Security: Understanding the Fundamentals of InfoSec in Theory and Practice (3rd ed.). Syngress.

2. Arce, I. (2021). Cybersecurity in the Digital Age: Challenges and Solutions. Springer.

3. Bidgoli, H. (2019). Handbook of Information Security, Information Warfare, Social, Legal, and International Issues and Security Foundations (Volume 2). John Wiley & Sons.

4. Buchanan, B. (2020). The Hacker and the State: Cyber Attacks and the New Normal of Geopolitics. Harvard University Press.

5. Cherdantseva, Y., & Hilton, J. (2013). A Reference Model of Information Assurance & Security. 2013 International Conference on Availability, Reliability and Security, 546-555.

6. Clarke, R. A., & Knake, R. K. (2019). The Fifth Domain: Defending Our Country, Our Companies, and Ourselves in the Age of Cyber Threats. Penguin Press.

7. Cybersecurity and Infrastructure Security Agency. (2023). National Cybersecurity Strategy of the United States of America. The White House.

8. Diogenes, Y., & Ozkaya, E. (2019). Cybersecurity – Attack and Defense Strategies (2nd ed.). Packt Publishing.

9. ENISA. (2022). ENISA Threat Landscape 2022. European Union Agency for Cybersecurity.

10. Furnell, S., & Papadaki, M. (2019). Security Education, Training and Awareness. In Information Security Management Principles (3rd ed.). BCS Learning & Development Limited.

11. Goodman, M. (2015). Future Crimes: Inside the Digital Underground and the Battle for Our Connected World. Anchor.

12. Gordon, L. A., Loeb, M. P., & Zhou, L. (2020). Investing in Cybersecurity: Insights from the Gordon-Loeb Model. Journal of Information Security, 11(4), 215-228.

13. Granger, S. (2021). Cyberwar: How Russian Hackers and Trolls Helped Elect a President. Oxford University Press.

14. Hoffman, W., & Levite, A. E. (2017). Private Sector Cyber Defense: Can Active Measures Help Stabilize Cyberspace? Carnegie Endowment for International Peace.

15. ISO/IEC. (2018). ISO/IEC 27001:2013 Information technology — Security techniques — Information security management systems — Requirements. International Organization for Standardization.

16. Jang-Jaccard, J., & Nepal, S. (2014). A survey of emerging threats in cybersecurity. Journal of Computer and System Sciences, 80(5), 973-993.

17. Kaplan, F. (2016). Dark Territory: The Secret History of Cyber War. Simon & Schuster.

18. Kello, L. (2017). The Virtual Weapon and International Order. Yale University Press.

19. Kim, D., & Solomon, M. G. (2018). Fundamentals of Information Systems Security (3rd ed.). Jones & Bartlett Learning.

20. Krebs, B. (2021). Spam Nation: The Inside Story of Organized Cybercrime-from Global Epidemic to Your Front Door. Sourcebooks.

21. Maurer, T. (2018). Cyber Mercenaries: The State, Hackers, and Power. Cambridge University Press.

22. NIST. (2018). Framework for Improving Critical Infrastructure Cybersecurity, Version 1.1. National Institute of Standards and Technology.

23. Perlroth, N. (2021). This Is How They Tell Me the World Ends: The Cyberweapons Arms Race. Bloomsbury Publishing.

24. Rid, T. (2020). Active Measures: The Secret History of Disinformation and Political Warfare. Farrar, Straus and Giroux.

25. Schneier, B. (2018). Click Here to Kill Everybody: Security and Survival in a Hyper-connected World. W. W. Norton & Company.

26. Singer, P. W., & Friedman, A. (2014). Cybersecurity and Cyberwar: What Everyone Needs to Know. Oxford University Press.

27. Srinivas, J., Das, A. K., & Kumar, N. (2019). Government regulations in cyber security: Framework, standards and recommendations. Future Generation Computer Systems, 92, 178-188.

28. Stallings, W., & Brown, L. (2018). Computer Security: Principles and Practice (4th ed.). Pearson.

29. Verizon. (2023). 2023 Data Breach Investigations Report. Verizon.

30. World Economic Forum. (2023). Global Cybersecurity Outlook 2023. World Economic Forum.

Chapter 7 : Blockchain and Distributed Ledger Technologies

1. Antonopoulos, A. M. (2017). Mastering Bitcoin: Programming the Open Blockchain (2nd ed.). O'Reilly Media.

2. Bashir, I. (2020). Mastering Blockchain: Distributed ledger technology, decentralization, and smart contracts explained (3rd ed.). Packt Publishing.

3. Beck, R., Müller-Bloch, C., & King, J. L. (2018). Governance in the blockchain economy: A framework and research agenda. Journal of the Association for Information Systems, 19(10), 1020-1034.

4. Buterin, V. (2014). Ethereum White Paper: A next-generation smart contract and decentralized application platform. Ethereum Foundation.

5. Casino, F., Dasaklis, T. K., & Patsakis, C. (2019). A systematic literature review of blockchain-based applications: Current status, classification and open issues. Telematics and Informatics, 36, 55-81.

6. Chen, Y., & Bellavitis, C. (2020). Blockchain disruption and decentralized finance: The rise of decentralized business models. Journal of Business Venturing Insights, 13, e00151.

7. Christidis, K., & Devetsikiotis, M. (2016). Blockchains and smart contracts for the internet of things. IEEE Access, 4, 2292-2303.

8. De Filippi, P., & Wright, A. (2018). Blockchain and the Law: The Rule of Code. Harvard University Press.

9. Drescher, D. (2017). Blockchain Basics: A Non-Technical Introduction in 25 Steps. Apress.

10. ENISA. (2022). Distributed Ledger Technology & Cybersecurity. European Union Agency for Cybersecurity.

11. Ethereum Foundation. (2023). Ethereum Whitepaper. ethereum.org.

12. European Commission. (2022). European Blockchain Strategy. Digital Strategy.

13. Ferdous, M. S., Chowdhury, M. J. M., Hoque, M. A., & Colman, A. (2020). Blockchain Consensus Algorithms: A Survey. arXiv preprint arXiv:2001.07091.

14. Financial Stability Board. (2022). Assessment of Risks to Financial Stability from Crypto-assets. FSB.

15. Grigg, I. (2004). The Ricardian Contract. In Proceedings. First IEEE International Workshop on Electronic Contracting, 2004.

16. Haber, S., & Stornetta, W. S. (1991). How to time-stamp a digital document. Journal of Cryptology, 3(2), 99-111.

17. Hughes, A., Park, A., Kietzmann, J., & Archer-Brown, C. (2019). Beyond Bitcoin: What blockchain and distributed ledger technologies mean for firms. Business Horizons, 62(3), 273-281.

18. Hyperledger Foundation. (2023). An Introduction to Hyperledger. The Linux Foundation.

19. Iansiti, M., & Lakhani, K. R. (2017). The truth about blockchain. Harvard Business Review, 95(1), 118-127.

20. Lacity, M. C. (2018). Addressing key challenges to making enterprise blockchain applications a reality. MIS Quarterly Executive, 17(3), 201-222.

21. Nakamoto, S. (2008). Bitcoin: A Peer-to-Peer Electronic Cash System. Bitcoin.org.

22. OECD. (2020). The Tokenisation of Assets and Potential Implications for Financial Markets. OECD Blockchain Policy Series.

23. Pilkington, M. (2016). Blockchain technology: principles and applications. In Research handbook on digital transformations. Edward Elgar Publishing.

24. Puthal, D., Malik, N., Mohanty, S. P., Kougianos, E., & Yang, C. (2018). The blockchain as a decentralized security framework. IEEE Consumer Electronics Magazine, 7(2), 18-21.

25. R3. (2023). Corda: Open Source Blockchain Platform for Business. R3.

26. Ripple. (2023). RippleNet Overview. Ripple.

27. Swan, M. (2015). Blockchain: Blueprint for a New Economy. O'Reilly Media.

28. Szabo, N. (1997). Formalizing and securing relationships on public networks. First Monday, 2(9).

29. Tapscott, D., & Tapscott, A. (2016). Blockchain Revolution: How the Technology Behind Bitcoin Is Changing Money, Business, and the World. Portfolio.

30. Treiblmaier, H. (2018). The impact of the blockchain on the supply chain: a theory-based research framework and a call for action. Supply Chain Management: An International Journal, 23(6), 545-559.

31. Wang, Y., Han, J. H., & Beynon-Davies, P. (2019). Understanding blockchain technology for future supply chains: a systematic literature review and research agenda. Supply Chain Management: An International Journal, 24(1), 62-84.

32. World Economic Forum. (2022). Digital Assets, Distributed Ledger Technology, and the Future of Capital Markets. WEF.

33. Xu, X., Weber, I., & Staples, M. (2019). Architecture for Blockchain Applications. Springer.

34. Yaga, D., Mell, P., Roby, N., & Scarfone, K. (2018). Blockchain technology overview. National Institute of Standards and Technology.

35. Zheng, Z., Xie, S., Dai, H., Chen, X., & Wang, H. (2017). An overview of blockchain technology: Architecture, consensus, and future trends. In 2017 IEEE international congress on big data (BigData congress) (pp. 557-564). IEEE.

Chapter 8 : Extended Reality (XR), including Augmented Reality (AR), Virtual Reality (VR), and Mixed Reality (MR)

1. Aukstakalnis, S. (2016). Practical Augmented Reality: A Guide to the Technologies, Applications, and Human Factors for AR and VR. Addison-Wesley Professional.

2. Azuma, R. T. (1997). A survey of augmented reality. Presence: Teleoperators & Virtual Environments, 6(4), 355-385.

3. Bailenson, J. (2018). Experience on Demand: What Virtual Reality Is, How It Works, and What It Can Do. W. W. Norton & Company.

4. Bardi, J., & Mousavi, M. (2020). Virtual Reality for Dummies. John Wiley & Sons.

5. Billinghurst, M., Clark, A., & Lee, G. (2015). A survey of augmented reality. Foundations and Trends® in Human–Computer Interaction, 8(2-3), 73-272.

6. Boletsis, C. (2017). The New Era of Virtual Reality Locomotion: A Systematic Literature Review of Techniques and a Proposed Typology. Multimodal Technologies and Interaction, 1(4), 24.

7. Bowman, D. A., & McMahan, R. P. (2007). Virtual Reality: How Much Immersion Is Enough? Computer, 40(7), 36-43.

8. Burdea, G. C., & Coiffet, P. (2003). Virtual Reality Technology (2nd ed.). John Wiley & Sons.

9. Caudell, T. P., & Mizell, D. W. (1992). Augmented reality: An application of heads-up display technology to manual manufacturing processes. In Proceedings of the Twenty-Fifth Hawaii International Conference on System Sciences (Vol. 2, pp. 659-669). IEEE.

10. Craig, A. B. (2013). Understanding Augmented Reality: Concepts and Applications. Morgan Kaufmann.

11. Dalton, J. (2021). Reality Check: How Immersive Technologies Can Transform Your Business. Kogan Page.

12. Dey, A., Billinghurst, M., Lindeman, R. W., & Swan, J. E. (2018). A systematic review of 10 years of augmented reality usability studies: 2005 to 2014. Frontiers in Robotics and AI, 5, 37.

13. Diemer, J., Alpers, G. W., Peperkorn, H. M., Shiban, Y., & Mühlberger, A. (2015). The impact of perception and presence on emotional reactions: a review of research in virtual reality. Frontiers in Psychology, 6, 26.

14. Dwivedi, Y. K., Hughes, L., Baabdullah, A. M., Ribeiro-Navarrete, S., Giannakis, M., Al-Debei, M. M., ... & Wamba, S. F. (2022). Metaverse beyond the hype: Multidisciplinary perspectives on emerging challenges, opportunities, and agenda for research, practice and policy. International Journal of Information Management, 66, 102542.

15. Furht, B. (Ed.). (2011). Handbook of Augmented Reality. Springer.

16. Gartner, Inc. (2023). Hype Cycle for Emerging Technologies, 2023. Gartner.

17. Hale, K. S., & Stanney, K. M. (Eds.). (2014). Handbook of Virtual Environments: Design, Implementation, and Applications (2nd ed.). CRC Press.

18. IDC. (2023). Worldwide Augmented and Virtual Reality Spending Guide. International Data Corporation.

19. Jerald, J. (2015). The VR Book: Human-Centered Design for Virtual Reality. Morgan & Claypool.

20. Kim, J., & Hall, W. (2019). Towards Teaching and Learning of Mixed Reality in History Education. In Proceedings of the 2019 ACM International Conference on Interactive Surfaces and Spaces (pp. 371-376).

21. LaValle, S. M. (2019). Virtual Reality. Cambridge University Press.

22. Lupton, D. (2021). Towards critical digital health studies: Reflections on two decades of research in health and the way forward. Health Sociology Review, 30(1), 9-23.

23. Mann, S., Furness, T., Yuan, Y., Iorio, J., & Wang, Z. (2018). All Reality: Virtual, Augmented, Mixed (X), Mediated (X, Y), and Multimediated Reality. arXiv preprint arXiv:1804.08386.

24. Milgram, P., & Kishino, F. (1994). A taxonomy of mixed reality visual displays. IEICE TRANSACTIONS on Information and Systems,

77(12), 1321-1329.

25. Nee, A. Y., Ong, S. K., Chryssolouris, G., & Mourtzis, D. (2012). Augmented reality applications in design and manufacturing. CIRP Annals, 61(2), 657-679.

26. Parisi, T. (2015). Learning Virtual Reality: Developing Immersive Experiences and Applications for Desktop, Web, and Mobile. O'Reilly Media.

27. Poetker, B. (2019). The Very Real History of Virtual Reality. G2.

28. Riva, G., Wiederhold, B. K., & Mantovani, F. (2019). Neuroscience of virtual reality: From virtual exposure to embodied medicine. Cyberpsychology, Behavior, and Social Networking, 22(1), 82-96.

29. Schmalstieg, D., & Hollerer, T. (2016). Augmented Reality: Principles and Practice. Addison-Wesley Professional.

30. Sherman, W. R., & Craig, A. B. (2018). Understanding Virtual Reality: Interface, Application, and Design (2nd ed.). Morgan Kaufmann.

31. Slater, M., & Sanchez-Vives, M. V. (2016). Enhancing our lives with immersive virtual reality. Frontiers in Robotics and AI, 3, 74.

32. Speicher, M., Hall, B. D., & Nebeling, M. (2019). What is Mixed Reality? In Proceedings of the 2019 CHI Conference on Human Factors in Computing Systems (pp. 1-15).

33. Sutherland, I. E. (1968). A head-mounted three dimensional display. In Proceedings of the December 9-11, 1968, fall joint computer conference, part I (pp. 757-764).

34. Tussyadiah, I. P., Wang, D., Jung, T. H., & tom Dieck, M. C. (2018). Virtual reality, presence, and attitude change: Empirical evidence from tourism. Tourism Management, 66, 140-154.

35. World Economic Forum. (2023). State of the Connected World 2023 Edition. WEF.

Chapter 9 : Big Data and Analytics

1. Abbasi, A., Sarker, S., & Chiang, R. H. (2016). Big Data Research in Information Systems: Toward an Inclusive Research Agenda. Journal of the Association for Information Systems, 17(2), 3.

2. Agrawal, D., Bernstein, P., Bertino, E., Davidson, S., Dayal, U., Franklin, M., ... & Widom, J. (2012). Challenges and Opportunities with Big Data: A community white paper developed by leading researchers across the United States. Computing Research Association.

3. Akter, S., & Wamba, S. F. (2016). Big data analytics in E-commerce: a systematic review and agenda for future research. Electronic Markets, 26(2), 173-194.

4. Baesens, B., Bapna, R., Marsden, J. R., Vanthienen, J., & Zhao, J. L. (2016). Transformational issues of big data and analytics in networked business. MIS quarterly, 40(4), 807-818.

5. Barton, D., & Court, D. (2012). Making advanced analytics work for you. Harvard business review, 90(10), 78-83.

6. Bean, R. (2017). How companies say they're using big data. Harvard Business Review Digital Articles, 2-5.

7. Bengio, Y., Courville, A., & Vincent, P. (2013). Representation learning: A review and new perspectives. IEEE transactions on pattern analysis and machine intelligence, 35(8), 1798-1828.

8. Chen, C. P., & Zhang, C. Y. (2014). Data-intensive applications, challenges, techniques and technologies: A survey on Big Data. Information sciences, 275, 314-347.

9. Chen, H., Chiang, R. H., & Storey, V. C. (2012). Business intelligence and analytics: From big data to big impact. MIS quarterly, 36(4), 1165-1188.

10. Davenport, T. H. (2014). Big data at work: dispelling the myths, uncovering the opportunities. Harvard Business Review Press.

11. Davenport, T. H., & Harris, J. G. (2017). Competing on analytics: Updated, with a new introduction: The new science of winning. Harvard Business Press.

12. Dean, J., & Ghemawat, S. (2008). MapReduce: simplified data processing on large clusters. Communications of the ACM, 51(1), 107-113.

13. Dhar, V. (2013). Data science and prediction. Communications of the ACM, 56(12), 64-73.

14. Dumbill, E. (2013). Making sense of big data. Big Data, 1(1), 1-2.

15. Gandomi, A., & Haider, M. (2015). Beyond the hype: Big data concepts, methods, and analytics. International journal of information management, 35(2), 137-144.

16. Gartner, Inc. (2023). Top Strategic Technology Trends for 2024. Gartner.

17. Ghemawat, S., Gobioff, H., & Leung, S. T. (2003). The Google file system. In Proceedings of the nineteenth ACM symposium on Operating systems principles (pp. 29-43).

18. Grover, V., Chiang, R. H., Liang, T. P., & Zhang, D. (2018). Creating strategic business value from big data analytics: A research framework.

Journal of Management Information Systems, 35(2), 388-423.

19. Günther, W. A., Rezazade Mehrizi, M. H., Huysman, M., & Feldberg, F. (2017). Debating big data: A literature review on realizing value from big data. The Journal of Strategic Information Systems, 26(3), 191-209.

20. Jagadish, H. V., Gehrke, J., Labrinidis, A., Papakonstantinou, Y., Patel, J. M., Ramakrishnan, R., & Shahabi, C. (2014). Big data and its technical challenges. Communications of the ACM, 57(7), 86-94.

21. Kitchin, R. (2014). The data revolution: Big data, open data, data infrastructures and their consequences. Sage.

22. LaValle, S., Lesser, E., Shockley, R., Hopkins, M. S., & Kruschwitz, N. (2011). Big data, analytics and the path from insights to value. MIT sloan management review, 52(2), 21-32.

23. Manyika, J., Chui, M., Brown, B., Bughin, J., Dobbs, R., Roxburgh, C., & Byers, A. H. (2011). Big data: The next frontier for innovation, competition, and productivity. McKinsey Global Institute.

24. McAfee, A., Brynjolfsson, E., Davenport, T. H., Patil, D. J., & Barton, D. (2012). Big data: the management revolution. Harvard business review, 90(10), 60-68.

25. O'Neil, C. (2016). Weapons of math destruction: How big data increases inequality and threatens democracy. Broadway Books.

26. Provost, F., & Fawcett, T. (2013). Data Science for Business: What you need to know about data mining and data-analytic thinking. O'Reilly Media, Inc.

27. Russom, P. (2011). Big data analytics. TDWI best practices report, fourth quarter, 19(4), 1-34.

28. Sivarajah, U., Kamal, M. M., Irani, Z., & Weerakkody, V. (2017). Critical analysis of Big Data challenges and analytical methods. Journal of Business Research, 70, 263-286.

29. Tene, O., & Polonetsky, J. (2012). Big data for all: Privacy and user control in the age of analytics. Nw. J. Tech. & Intell. Prop., 11, xxvii.

30. Wamba, S. F., Gunasekaran, A., Akter, S., Ren, S. J. F., Dubey, R., & Childe, S. J. (2017). Big data analytics and firm performance: Effects of dynamic capabilities. Journal of Business Research, 70, 356-365.

31. Ward, J. S., & Barker, A. (2013). Undefined by data: a survey of big data definitions. arXiv preprint arXiv:1309.5821.

32. White, T. (2015). Hadoop: The definitive guide: Storage and analysis at internet scale. O'Reilly Media, Inc.

33. Witten, I. H., Frank, E., Hall, M. A., & Pal, C. J. (2016). Data Mining: Practical machine learning tools and techniques. Morgan Kaufmann.

34. Wu, X., Zhu, X., Wu, G. Q., & Ding, W. (2014). Data mining with big data. IEEE transactions on knowledge and data engineering, 26(1), 97-107.

35. Zikopoulos, P., & Eaton, C. (2011). Understanding big data: Analytics for enterprise class hadoop and streaming data. McGraw-Hill Osborne Media.

Chapter 10 : Digital Transformation and Business Models

1. Westerman, G., Bonnet, D., & McAfee, A. (2014). Leading Digital: Turning Technology into Business Transformation. Harvard Business Review Press.

2. Rogers, D. L. (2016). The Digital Transformation Playbook: Rethink Your Business for the Digital Age. Columbia Business School Publishing.

3. Schwab, K. (2017). The Fourth Industrial Revolution. Currency.

4. Parker, G. G., Van Alstyne, M. W., & Choudary, S. P. (2016). Platform Revolution: How Networked Markets Are Transforming the Economy and How to Make Them Work for You. W. W. Norton & Company.

5. Ross, J. W., Beath, C. M., & Mocker, M. (2019). Designed for Digital: How to Architect Your Business for Sustained Success. MIT Press.

6. Davenport, T. H., & Westerman, G. (2018). Why So Many High-Profile Digital Transformations Fail. Harvard Business Review.

7. Iansiti, M., & Lakhani, K. R. (2020). Competing in the Age of AI: Strategy and Leadership When Algorithms and Networks Run the World. Harvard Business Review Press.

8. Brynjolfsson, E., & McAfee, A. (2014). The Second Machine Age: Work, Progress, and Prosperity in a Time of Brilliant Technologies. W. W. Norton & Company.

9. Gupta, S. (2018). Driving Digital Strategy: A Guide to Reimagining Your Business. Harvard Business Review Press.

10. Kane, G. C., Phillips, A. N., Copulsky, J., & Andrus, G. (2019). The Technology Fallacy: How People Are the Real Key to Digital Transformation. MIT Press.

11. Reis, J., Amorim, M., Melão, N., & Matos, P. (2018). Digital Transformation: A Literature Review and Guidelines for Future Research. In World Conference on Information Systems and Technologies (pp. 411-421). Springer.

12. Vial, G. (2019). Understanding digital transformation: A review and a research agenda. The Journal of Strategic Information Systems, 28(2), 118-144.

13. Berman, S. J. (2012). Digital transformation: opportunities to create new business models. Strategy & Leadership, 40(2), 16-24.

14. Fitzgerald, M., Kruschwitz, N., Bonnet, D., & Welch, M. (2014). Embracing digital technology: A new strategic imperative. MIT Sloan Management Review, 55(2), 1.

15. Gartner. (2020). Gartner Top Strategic Technology Trends for 2021. Retrieved from [URL].

16. McKinsey & Company. (2020). The Next Normal: The recovery will be digital. Retrieved from [URL].

17. World Economic Forum. (2020). Digital Transformation: Powering the Great Reset. Retrieved from [URL].

18. MIT Sloan Management Review and Deloitte. (2015). Strategy, not Technology, Drives Digital Transformation. Retrieved from [URL].

19. Forbes Technology Council. (2021). 16 Essential Elements Of A Successful Digital Transformation Strategy. Forbes. Retrieved from [URL].

20. Harvard Business Review. (2019). Digital Transformation Is Not About Technology. Retrieved from [URL].

Chapter 11 : Green IT and Sustainability

1. Murugesan, S., & Gangadharan, G. R. (2012). Harnessing Green IT: Principles and Practices. John Wiley & Sons.

2. Uddin, M., & Rahman, A. A. (2012). Energy efficiency and low carbon enabler green IT framework for data centers considering green metrics. Renewable and Sustainable Energy Reviews, 16(6), 4078-4094.

3. Belkhir, L., & Elmeligi, A. (2018). Assessing ICT global emissions footprint: Trends to 2040 & recommendations. Journal of Cleaner Production, 177, 448-463.

4. Masanet, E., Shehabi, A., Lei, N., Smith, S., & Koomey, J. (2020). Recalibrating global data center energy-use estimates. Science, 367(6481), 984-986.

5. Forti V., Baldé C.P., Kuehr R., Bel G. (2020). The Global E-waste Monitor 2020: Quantities, flows and the circular economy potential. United Nations University.

6. Ardito, L., & Morisio, M. (2014). Green IT – Available data and guidelines for reducing energy consumption in IT systems. Sustainable Computing: Informatics and Systems, 4(1), 24-32.

7. Tjazizadeh, F., & Garrod, B. (2019). Green information systems for sustainable development: A systematic literature review. Sustainability Accounting, Management and Policy Journal.

8. Laplante, P. A. (2016). Principles of Green Software Design. CRC Press.

9. Jnr, B. A. (2020). Examining the role of green IT/IS innovation in collaborative enterprise-implications in an emerging economy. Technology in Society, 62, 101301.

10. Molla, A., Cooper, V., & Pittayachawan, S. (2011). The Green IT Readiness (G-Readiness) of Organizations: An Exploratory Analysis of a Construct and Instrument. Communications of the Association for Information Systems, 29, 67-96.

11. Gholami, R., Sulaiman, A. B., Ramayah, T., & Molla, A. (2013). Senior managers' perception on green information systems (IS) adoption and environmental performance: Results from a field survey. Information & Management, 50(7), 431-438.

12. Gallard-Perez, J., Hernantes, J., & Serrano, N. (2020). Designing Energy-Aware IT Systems: The GREENSOFT Model. IT Professional, 22(1), 40-48.

13. Kern, E., Dick, M., Naumann, S., & Hiller, T. (2015). Green Software and Green Software Engineering – Definitions, Measurements, and Quality Aspects. Journal of Information and Communication Technology for Human Development, 7(1), 57-74.

14. Bozzelli, P., Gu, Q., & Lago, P. (2013). A systematic literature review on green software metrics. Technical Report: VU University Amsterdam.

15. Accenture & WSP. (2021). The Green Behind the Cloud. Accenture.

16. Google. (2020). Environmental Report 2020. Google LLC.

17. Microsoft. (2021). 2020 Environmental Sustainability Report. Microsoft Corporation.

18. Shehabi, A., Smith, S. J., Horner, N., Azevedo, I., Brown, R., Koomey, J., ... & Lintner, W. (2016). United States data center energy usage report. Lawrence Berkeley National Laboratory.

19. Koomey, J., & Masanet, E. (2021). Does not compute: Avoiding pitfalls assessing the Internet's energy and carbon impacts. Joule, 5(7), 1625-1628.

20. Global e-Sustainability Initiative (GeSI). (2015). #SMARTer2030: ICT Solutions for 21st Century Challenges. Brussels, Belgium.

Chapter 12 : The Future of Work in Digital world

1. Acemoglu, D., & Restrepo, P. (2018). Artificial Intelligence, Automation and Work. National Bureau of Economic Research.

2. Autor, D. H. (2015). Why Are There Still So Many Jobs? The History and Future of Workplace Automation. Journal of Economic Perspectives, 29(3), 3-30.

3. Bakhshi, H., Downing, J., Osborne, M., & Schneider, P. (2017). The Future of Skills: Employment in 2030. Pearson and Nesta.

4. Brynjolfsson, E., & McAfee, A. (2014). The Second Machine Age: Work, Progress, and Prosperity in a Time of Brilliant Technologies. W. W. Norton & Company.

5. Deloitte. (2020). The Future of Work is Now: Accelerated by COVID-19. Deloitte Insights.

6. Eurofound. (2020). Living, Working and COVID-19. Publications Office of the European Union.

7. Frey, C. B., & Osborne, M. A. (2017). The Future of Employment: How Susceptible are Jobs to Computerisation? Technological Forecasting and Social Change, 114, 254-280.

8. Gratton, L., & Scott, A. (2016). The 100-Year Life: Living and Working in an Age of Longevity. Bloomsbury Information.

9. Gray, M. L., & Suri, S. (2019). Ghost Work: How to Stop Silicon Valley from Building a New Global Underclass. Houghton Mifflin Harcourt.

10. International Labour Organization. (2019). Work for a Brighter Future – Global Commission on the Future of Work. ILO.

11. Katz, L. F., & Krueger, A. B. (2019). The Rise and Nature of Alternative Work Arrangements in the United States, 1995–2015. ILR Review, 72(2), 382-416.

12. McKinsey Global Institute. (2017). Jobs Lost, Jobs Gained: Workforce Transitions in a Time of Automation. McKinsey & Company.

13. OECD. (2019). OECD Employment Outlook 2019: The Future of Work. OECD Publishing.

14. Prassl, J. (2018). Humans as a Service: The Promise and Perils of Work in the Gig Economy. Oxford University Press.

15. Schwab, K. (2016). The Fourth Industrial Revolution. World Economic Forum.

16. Standing, G. (2011). The Precariat: The New Dangerous Class. Bloomsbury Academic.

17. Susskind, R., & Susskind, D. (2015). The Future of the Professions: How Technology Will Transform the Work of Human Experts. Oxford University Press.

18. World Economic Forum. (2020). The Future of Jobs Report 2020. World Economic Forum.

19. Zuboff, S. (2019). The Age of Surveillance Capitalism: The Fight for a Human Future at the New Frontier of Power. Public Affairs.

20. Autor, D., Mindell, D., & Reynolds, E. (2020). The Work of the Future: Building Better Jobs in an Age of Intelligent Machines. MIT Work of the Future.

21. Gartner. (2020). 9 Future of Work Trends Post-COVID-19. Gartner, Inc.

22. Manyika, J., et al. (2017). A Future That Works: Automation, Employment, and Productivity. McKinsey Global Institute.

23. World Bank. (2019). World Development Report 2019: The Changing Nature of Work. World Bank Group.

24. Daugherty, P. R., & Wilson, H. J. (2018). Human + Machine: Reimagining Work in the Age of AI. Harvard Business Review Press.

25. Pink, D. H. (2009). Drive: The Surprising Truth About What Motivates Us. Riverhead Books.

Chapter 13 : Global Digital Policies and Regulations

1. Aaronson, S. A., & Leblond, P. (2018). Another Digital Divide: The Rise of Data Realms and its Implications for the WTO. Journal of International Economic Law, 21(2), 245-272.

2. Beaumier, G., & Kalomeni, K. (2020). Governing the digital economy: The evolution of policy preferences in Canada and the United States. Regulation & Governance, 14(3), 497-513.

3. Brynjolfsson, E., & McAfee, A. (2014). The Second Machine Age: Work, Progress, and Prosperity in a Time of Brilliant Technologies. W. W. Norton & Company.

4. Butenko, A., & Larouche, P. (2015). Regulation for innovativeness or regulation of innovation? Law, Innovation and Technology, 7(1), 52-82.

5. Cath, C., & Floridi, L. (2017). The Design of the Internet's Architecture by the Internet Engineering Task Force (IETF) and Human Rights. Science and Engineering Ethics, 23(2), 449-468.

6. Chander, A., & Lê, U. P. (2015). Data Nationalism. Emory Law Journal, 64(3), 677-739.

7. Ciuriak, D., & Ptashkina, M. (2018). The Digital Transformation and the Transformation of International Trade. RTA Exchange. Geneva: International Centre for Trade and Sustainable Development (ICTSD) and Inter-American Development Bank (IDB).

8. DeNardis, L. (2014). The Global War for Internet Governance. Yale University Press.

9. European Commission. (2020). A European strategy for data. COM(2020) 66 final.

10. European Union. (2016). Regulation (EU) 2016/679 of the European Parliament and of the Council of 27 April 2016 on the protection of natural persons with regard to the processing of personal data and on the free movement of such data, and repealing Directive 95/46/EC (General Data Protection Regulation).

11. Fefer, R. F. (2020). Data Flows, Online Privacy, and Trade Policy. Congressional Research Service.

12. Ferracane, M. F., & van der Marel, E. (2021). Regulating Personal Data: Data Models and Digital Services Trade. World Bank Policy Research Working Paper No. 9596.

13. Flyverbom, M., Deibert, R., & Matten, D. (2019). The Governance of Digital Technology, Big Data, and the Internet: New Roles and Responsibilities for Business. Business & Society, 58(1), 3-19.

14. Goldfarb, A., & Trefler, D. (2018). AI and International Trade. National Bureau of Economic Research Working Paper 24254.

15. Goldsmith, J., & Wu, T. (2006). Who Controls the Internet?: Illusions of a Borderless World. Oxford University Press.

16. ITU. (2023). Global Cybersecurity Index. International Telecommunication Union.

17. Kettemann, M. C. (2020). The Normative Order of the Internet: A Theory of Rule and Regulation Online. Oxford University Press.

18. Kostka, G. (2019). China's social credit systems and public opinion: Explaining high levels of approval. New Media & Society, 21(7), 1565-1593.

19. Kuner, C., Cate, F. H., Millard, C., & Svantesson, D. J. B. (2013). PRISM and privacy: Will this change everything? International Data Privacy

Law, 3(4), 217-219.

20. Lessig, L. (2006). Code: Version 2.0. Basic Books.

21. Mueller, M. (2010). Networks and States: The Global Politics of Internet Governance. MIT Press.

22. OECD. (2021). OECD Digital Economy Outlook 2020. OECD Publishing.

23. Pohle, J., & Van Audenhove, L. (2017). Post-Snowden Internet Policy: Between Public Outrage, Resistance and Policy Change. Media and Communication, 5(1), 1-6.

24. Reidenberg, J. R. (2014). The Data Surveillance State in the United States and Europe. Wake Forest Law Review, 49, 583-608.

25. Schneier, B. (2015). Data and Goliath: The Hidden Battles to Collect Your Data and Control Your World. W. W. Norton & Company.

26. Schwab, K. (2016). The Fourth Industrial Revolution. World Economic Forum.

27. Spar, D. L. (2001). Ruling the Waves: Cycles of Discovery, Chaos, and Wealth from the Compass to the Internet. Harcourt.

28. Susskind, J. (2018). Future Politics: Living Together in a World Transformed by Tech. Oxford University Press.

29. United Nations. (2018). United Nations E-Government Survey 2018: Gearing E-Government to Support Transformation Towards Sustainable and Resilient Societies. United Nations Publications.

30. UNCTAD. (2021). Digital Economy Report 2021: Cross-border data flows and development: For whom the data flow. United Nations Conference on Trade and Development.

31. Van Dijck, J. (2014). Datafication, dataism and dataveillance: Big Data between scientific paradigm and ideology. Surveillance & Society, 12(2), 197-208.

32. World Bank. (2016). World Development Report 2016: Digital Dividends. World Bank Group.

33. World Economic Forum. (2023). Global Technology Governance Report 2023: Artificial Intelligence. World Economic Forum.

34. Wu, T. (2010). The Master Switch: The Rise and Fall of Information Empires. Alfred A. Knopf.

35. Zuboff, S. (2019). The Age of Surveillance Capitalism: The Fight for a Human Future at the New Frontier of Power. PublicAffairs.

Chapter 14 : Conclusion: Navigating the Digital

Landscape as a Manager

1. Acemoglu, D., & Restrepo, P. (2019). Automation and New Tasks: How Technology Displaces and Reinstates Labor. Journal of Economic Perspectives, 33(2), 3-30.

2. Agrawal, A., Gans, J., & Goldfarb, A. (2018). Prediction Machines: The Simple Economics of Artificial Intelligence. Harvard Business Review Press.

3. Autor, D. H. (2015). Why Are There Still So Many Jobs? The History and Future of Workplace Automation. Journal of Economic Perspectives, 29(3), 3-30.

4. Bostrom, N. (2014). Superintelligence: Paths, Dangers, Strategies. Oxford University Press.

5. Brynjolfsson, E., & McAfee, A. (2014). The Second Machine Age: Work, Progress, and Prosperity in a Time of Brilliant Technologies. W.W. Norton & Company.

6. Chui, M., Manyika, J., & Miremadi, M. (2018). What AI can and can't do (yet) for your business. McKinsey Quarterly.

7. Davenport, T. H., & Kirby, J. (2016). Only Humans Need Apply: Winners and Losers in the Age of Smart Machines. Harper Business.

8. Diamandis, P. H., & Kotler, S. (2020). The Future Is Faster Than You Think: How Converging Technologies Are Transforming Business, Industries, and Our Lives. Simon & Schuster.

9. Ford, M. (2015). Rise of the Robots: Technology and the Threat of a Jobless Future. Basic Books.

10. Gartner. (2021). Top Strategic Technology Trends for 2022. Gartner, Inc.

11. Harari, Y. N. (2018). 21 Lessons for the 21st Century. Spiegel & Grau.

12. Iansiti, M., & Lakhani, K. R. (2020). Competing in the Age of AI: Strategy and Leadership When Algorithms and Networks Run the World. Harvard Business Review Press.

13. Kelly, K. (2016). The Inevitable: Understanding the 12 Technological Forces That Will Shape Our Future. Viking.

14. Lee, K. F. (2018). AI Superpowers: China, Silicon Valley, and the New World Order. Houghton Mifflin Harcourt.

15. McAfee, A., & Brynjolfsson, E. (2017). Machine, Platform, Crowd: Harnessing Our Digital Future. W.W. Norton & Company.

16. Manyika, J., et al. (2017). A Future That Works: Automation, Employment, and Productivity. McKinsey Global Institute.

17. O'Neil, C. (2016). Weapons of Math Destruction: How Big Data Increases Inequality and Threatens Democracy. Crown.

18. Parker, G. G., Van Alstyne, M. W., & Choudary, S. P. (2016). Platform Revolution: How Networked Markets Are Transforming the Economy and How to Make Them Work for You. W.W. Norton & Company.

19. Schwab, K. (2017). The Fourth Industrial Revolution. Currency.

20. Siegel, E. (2016). Predictive Analytics: The Power to Predict Who Will Click, Buy, Lie, or Die. Wiley.